AMY CARMICHAEL OF BOOKSTORE

AMY CARMICHAEL OF DOHNAVUR

The Story of a Lover and her Beloved

By

FRANK HOUGHTON

Bishop

LONDON

SPCK

First published 1953
Sixth impression 1973
Published in paperback by Hodder & Stoughton 1974
First SPCK paperback edition 1981

SPCK
Holy Trinity Church
Marylebone Road
London NW1 4DU

ISBN 0 281 03828 7

Printed in Great Britain by
Ebenezer Baylis & Son Ltd
The Trinity Press, Worcester, and London

TO AMMA'S CHILDREN
and to all who pray for them

CONTENTS

PART III

The Keeping of the Charge

INTRODUCTION

THE Life of Amy Carmichael of Dohnavur falls naturally into three sections. The first, entitled *Preparation for a Life-work*, covers the years 1867–1901. On March 6th, 1901, the work for the Temple children began, and the years from 1901 to 1931 may be called *The Warfare of the Service*. After the accident of October, 1931, she was as active as ever in mind and spirit, but physically she was confined more and more to her room at Dohnavur, and the heading for the years 1931–1951, when she entered into Life, is *The Keeping of the Charge*. Referring to the need of "younger warriors" in *Though the Mountains Shake* (Chapter 23), she says:

> The Lord ordained (Numbers 8. 24–26, marginal reading) that the Levites were to war the warfare of the service from twenty-five years to fifty. After they were fifty years old they were to keep the charge. So there is a difference between the Warfare of the Service and the Keeping of the Charge. It is impossible to think of ever dropping the Keeping of the Charge. *That* goes on to the end, but the young and strong are needed for the Warfare of the Service. In practice, however, we do not keep the Levites' rule, and naturally this means that some are rather like Gideon and his three hundred when they passed over Jordan, faint, yet pursuing.

To the very end, though faintness increased, she was always pursuing.

For facts concerning her early life I am indebted to her brothers and sisters, to her cousin, Miss Edith Carmichael, and to a number of elderly people, especially in Northern Ireland and at Broughton in Cumberland, who have vivid memories of those far-off days. The Rev. T. Kilpatrick, the Presbyterian minister of Millisle, has accumulated valuable information concerning the Carmichael family, and all this he kindly placed at my disposal. While she shrank from the thought that anyone should write her Life, and only accepted the possibility with reluctance when she was persuaded that a narrative which might glorify God belonged properly to Him and not to her, yet she had yielded some years ago to the entreaties of her Family at Dohnavur, and written some chapters of autobiography. "It is just a mother's story," she says, "written for her dear children ", and therefore with no thought of publication, but I have not hesitated to quote largely from it.

For the later life I have relied mainly on her books, the regular Dohnavur Letters, and much other material gathered by Miss Mary Mills and other members of the Fellowship. Moreover, my wife and I have lived for some months in Dohnavur, and have talked with many of her " children ", both men and women. To them, and indeed to an astonishing number of friends outside—astonishing because she never left India from the time of her arrival there in 1895, and was therefore known to these friends only by her books and correspondence—she was always " Amma " (Tamil for " mother "), and I propose to call her " Amy " in the first section of this book, and " Amma " in the last two sections.

Her books, as all their readers know, are self-revealing only in the sense that they conceal the part which she herself took in most of the events that she describes. They are, indeed, absolutely true to fact, since, whatever great things were accomplished, our Lord Himself was the Doer of them. But her own self-effacement (while we love her for it, and would not for the world that she had yielded to the temptation of self-advertisement) is tantalizing, sometimes even exasperating, to her biographer. She was God's chosen instrument, and the glory is His alone, but she was an instrument amazingly fitted for His purpose, and ready to His Hand. In her generous desire to recognize the undoubted gifts of other members of the Family she often uses plural pronouns where the singular would be more accurate, and interesting details concerning herself are so skilfully tucked away in obscure corners that the work of unearthing them, though a labour of love, has been distinctly arduous.

Personally I was attracted to her first of all because, in contrast to so many authors, she steadily refrained from including a picture of herself in any of her books, even in those which were profusely and beautifully illustrated (e.g. *Gold by Moonlight, Kohila, Gold Cord, Ploughed Under, Figures of the True*). In her lifetime she was so averse to portraits of herself that she even went so far as to scratch out her own head from group photographs of the early days in which she appeared! " Till I awake in His likeness," she wrote in 1948, " I think nothing can be less beautiful than I am, and there are enough *not* beautiful things in the world without my adding to the number."

Amy Carmichael was born in 1867. So also was Mme Curie, the discoverer of radium. They were curiously alike in certain ways, utterly dissimilar in others. They were alike in their intense absorption in the task assigned to them, but whereas Amy Carmichael was interested primarily in introducing persons to a Person, Mme Curie abandoned all belief in God, and when she was interviewed by an American newsman, who hoped for a " human interest " story, she closed the conversation with the crushing remark, " In science we must be interested in things, not persons."

But they were alike in their self-effacement—Amy Carmichael in order that Christ might be revealed, Mme Curie in order that the interests of Science might be furthered. " What fiendish ingenuity she used to find impersonal formulas, what a rage for effacing herself, for remaining in the shadows! The ' I ' was not detestable to Marie; it did not exist." So writes Mme Curie's daughter. With necessary verbal alterations, much the same might be said of Amy Carmichael. Alas for the contrast between the two women as they neared the end. Amma was constantly thinking and talking of those whom she loved, for whom she had poured out her life. Mme Curie, though she was a truly affectionate wife and mother, " did not pronounce the name of any living person. . . . Staring fixedly at a teacup in which she was trying to stir a spoon—no, not a spoon, but a glass rod or some delicate laboratory instrument: ' Was it done with radium or mesotherium? ' She had drawn away from human beings; she had joined those beloved ' things ' to which she had devoted her life, and joined them for ever ".

A brief explanation as to why I have been commissioned to write the Life of Amy Carmichael seems to be essential. Why should I, whose life has been given to China, be chosen to write of one who came to India soon after I was born, and remained there till her death? I am acutely conscious of disqualifications. But my chief qualification is that my wife and I came within the privileged circle of those whom she loved. I had corresponded with her for thirty years, and with growing intimacy. In 1943, 1945 and 1947 we paid short visits to Dohnavur, and had long times of fellowship with her in the very room where these words are written—which will always be called " Amma's room ". With a good deal of hesitation I quote from a letter which she wrote on December 27th, 1947: " We have crowds of friends, thank God, and many who are dear enough to love us for Christ's sake—but very, very few of the innermost inner sort on earth now." She regarded us as belonging to the " innermost inner sort ".

In those words are my credentials. But perhaps it may be added that the links between Dohnavur and the China Inland Mission have always been very strong. Amma knew Hudson Taylor, and the C.I.M. was the first society which she approached. It would have been China's gain, but India's sore loss, if the Mission doctor had not advised against accepting her. The pattern shown to Hudson Taylor was so similar to that shown to Amma that, where Dohnavur is known, the friends of Dohnavur are almost always friends of the C.I.M. Apart from my own personal indebtedness to Amma, there is the fact that for a number of years free copies of all her books were sent by her kindness and at her expense to each of our Mission centres in China. We owe her far more than we can ever repay.

This introduction is written before I attempt to portray her as she was. The portrait will be a success only if it shows how Love—the Love of God—was revealed through her. At Keswick, 1890, when she was twenty-two years of age, and had not yet heard the missionary call, the two words which sum up the blessing which came to her that week were, " Thou hast put gladness in my heart ", and, " Thou wilt perfect that which concerneth me ". And she adds the prayer:

> Lord, let the glow of Thy great love
> Through my whole being shine.

The prayer was answered. In Japan for a brief while, and then for a lifetime in India, the glow of God's great love shone forth through her whole being. Ask her " children ", ask the members of the Fellowship, what most impressed them about Amma, and the reply never varies. " It was her love." " I was thinking this morning ", she wrote to a member of the

Fellowship in 1939, " of what I would say if I had to put what I want each of you seniors to do for the others into two sentences. *Love them dearly. Hold them to the Highest.* I think that is what I would say." And that is what she did. She loved with infinite tenderness, but it was not a love that weakened. No—it held her Family to the highest. I truly believe that in none of His disciples in this century was our Lord's prayer, " that the love wherewith Thou hast loved Me may be in them ", more fully answered than in Amy Carmichael.

Where the authorship of verses is not acknowledged it may usually be assumed that they are taken from Amma's own writings.

PART I
PREPARATION FOR A LIFE-WORK

Just a tiny little child
  Three years old,
And a mother with a heart
  All of gold.
Often did that mother say,
Jesus hears us when we pray,
For He's never far away
  And He always answers.

Now, that tiny little child
  Had brown eyes,
And she wanted blue instead
  Like blue skies.
For her mother's eyes were blue
Like forget-me-nots.   She knew
All her mother said was true,
  Jesus always answered.

So she prayed for two blue eyes,
  Said " Good night ",
Went to sleep in deep content
  And delight.
Woke up early, climbed a chair
By a mirror.   Where, O where
Could the blue eyes be?   Not there;
  Jesus hadn't answered.

Hadn't answered her at all;
  Never more
Could she pray; her eyes were brown
  As before.
Did a little soft wind blow?
Came a whisper soft and low,
" Jesus answered.   He said, No;
  Isn't *No* an answer? "

CHAPTER I

She was born on December 16th, 1867, in the sea-coast village of Millisle, County Down, Northern Ireland, and her name—Amy Beatrice Carmichael—appears in the baptismal register of the Presbyterian Church at Ballycopeland on January 19th, 1868. Like many of us, she would have chosen differently if she could have been consulted about her names. " Amy " is presumably a rather mangled version of " Aimée ", and as for " Beatrice ", while she used it for her very earliest literary efforts, she virtually discarded it long before she went to India, and for a very characteristic reason:

> My second name, Beatrice, from the day when I pored over Dante in the Manchester Free Library and came out into the street afterwards wondering what the people who brushed past me would be like if they had seen his visions, had felt too high for me, and so had tucked itself out of sight.*
>
> In my day [she wrote] Millisle was a little old-world village of whitewashed cottages on the shore of the Irish Sea. From our nursery window we could see the great rock called Ailsa Craig rising like a cloud out of the sea. Blueness of sea that looked happy, greyness of sea that looked anxious, greenness of sea that looked angry—these are my first memories of colour.

The village was dominated by the Carmichael flour-mills, leased by Amy's great-grandfather a hundred years before she was born, and developed and enlarged by her father David and her uncle William. There were two mills: the Upper, half a mile inland, and the Lower, close to the sea. A little stream provided power for both mills, and had been dammed up to form a lake, in the midst of which was an islet with one tree growing in its centre. This islet, according to local tradition, gave Mill-isle its name.

For several generations, at least, the Carmichaels had been

* *From the Forest*, p. 68.

3

godfearing people with a well-deserved reputation for integrity
and for generous consideration of their employees.   The family
came from Ayrshire in Scotland, and were of Covenanting
stock.   The first to settle in Ireland was James Carmichael,
born in 1705, and buried with his sons in Bangor Abbey
churchyard.   Amy's great-grandfather, Robert, was forty
years of age when a Presbyterian church was built right on
the sea-shore at Ballycopeland.* Here the Carmichaels
worshipped, and were among the leading members.   Indeed,
three of its ministers married a Carmichael, and it is said that
a fourth desired to do so, but was rejected.

The minister in Amy's time was the Rev. John Beatty,
appointed in 1860, a true man of God who had seen His
Spirit at work in Belfast during the mighty revival of 1859.
David and William Carmichael gave him warm support, and
in 1866 provided over £500 for the building of a schoolhouse—
the first in the Millisle neighbourhood.   There were evening
classes (intended partly for employees in the mills), as well as a
day-school, and evangelistic services on Sunday nights, frequently conducted by Amy's father when Mr Beatty's health
was impaired by creeping paralysis.   He would often read one
of Spurgeon's sermons.† The school still stands—between
the present manse and the David Carmichael home.

The Carmichaels loved to give, and their generosity expressed
itself, not casually but in carefully contrived kindnesses.   One
cannot mention these characteristics without exclaiming,
"Just like Amma!"—though of course it was she who inherited
them, and sought to transmit them to her spiritual children at
Dohnavur.   For instance, Mr Beatty had been grieving over
his increasing inability to visit his flock.   One evening a hand-
some pony-carriage was driven to the door of the manse, the
gift of the Carmichael brothers and other members of the
congregation.   Amy was often to see him driving round the

---

* The Presbyterians who built the church belonged to a small group
known as the "Anti-Burgher Seceders", who left the Church of Scotland
about 1735 on conscientious grounds connected with purity of doctrine and
patronage rights.   A church was erected soon afterwards at Millisle by
non-seceding Presbyterians.   Eventually—after the Carmichael family
had left Millisle—the two congregations united, and Ballycopeland church
fell into disuse.   Its ruins, almost washed by the waves, may still be seen.

† Spurgeon's sermons were issued weekly in those days.   David Carmichael thought there was nothing better and, either before or after the
Sunday afternoon walks, he would read the weekly sermon to the children.

village and among the scattered homesteads of the district. She and her brothers learnt to play chess from watching Mr Beatty and their father engrossed in the game on winter evenings.

David Carmichael did not marry until he was in his thirty-seventh year, but he made a good choice. His wife's name was Catherine Jane Filson, a doctor's daughter from Portaferry, on Strangford Lough, four hours' car drive (jaunting-car, not motor-car) from Millisle. Her father was the leading doctor in the district, greatly respected. Catherine shared with her husband the inestimable advantage of being brought up in a godly home, and like their minister, Mr Beatty, she had seen something of the revival of 1859. For her it meant release from formalism, an entrance upon a freer life of joy in God. Her Bible shows how she cast her anchor in John 10. 27, 28: " My sheep hear My voice, and I know them, and they follow Me: and I give unto them eternal life; and they shall never perish, neither shall any man pluck them out of My Hand." The words " My sheep ", and " they ", and " them ", repeated several times, are marked in red, and linked by red lines to her own name, " Catherine Jane Carmichael ", in the margin, for she applied each of these precious statements to herself.

Amy was the eldest of seven children. Two brothers followed her, then two sisters, and finally two more brothers. They were a happy family, brought up on the Bible and the Shorter Catechism. A well-tended garden, surrounded by a wall, was the first playground for the children in the grey stone house. After colour Amy especially remembered sounds:

the sough of the wind at night sighing down the nursery chimney, the solemn sound, like the rise and fall of the waves on the shore, of my father's voice reading at family worship. Sometimes the great words were understandable—" Let the sea roar, let the floods clap their hands "—I understood that. Pricking through that wavy sound at least once, I can hear the smothered squeak of a mouse. For I had found a mouse drowning in a pail of water and had fished it out; and as the bell for prayers had rung just then, I had hidden it under my pinafore, hoping it wouldn't talk. And there is the sweet, sweet sound of my mother singing to her children; and the merry sound of laughter and play.

But her very first memory as a tiny child was this: "After the nursery light had been turned low and I was quite alone, I used to smooth a little place on the sheet, and say aloud, but softly, to our Father, ' Please come and sit with me '." Some of her children in Dohnavur have followed the same happy custom.* To these earliest days belongs also the story of her prayer, that God would change the colour of her brown eyes, and give her blue instead. The verses in which she describes this experience are printed opposite the beginning of this chapter.

> But what I can never tell you properly [she writes] is the bewilderment that even now I can remember as if it were yesterday. . . . Without a shadow of doubt that my eyes would be blue in the morning I had gone to sleep, and the minute I woke I pushed a chair to the chest of drawers on which there was a looking-glass and climbed up full of eager expectation and saw—mere brown eyes. I don't remember how the words came, " Isn't *No* an answer? " Perhaps my mother, whose blue eyes had made me so much want to change my brown ones, said something of the sort.

In any case, here is the marvel, that at the age of three she began to learn a lesson which she never forgot: the lesson that even silence is an answer, that our gracious Lord may sometimes say " Wait " or even " No " rather than " Yes ", but that He is never heedless of our prayers.

She got over the disappointment, but blue was her favourite colour, right on to the end. In the " Valley of Vision " †

> . . . the wood was blue
> With blue, blue flowers; carpets of gentian spread
> On mossy open floors, and speedwell grew
> Low in a lupin bed.

There were forget-me-nots, blue Indian pea, bluebells, violets, " Delphinia's tall blue rods ", blue lotus, love-in-the-mist. . . .

> A gaiety of blue was everywhere . . .

> Peace walked that wood; and to my questioning,
> All this that buddeth blue on bough or sod
> Is love of God in blossom: therefore sing,
> O sing for love of God.

When her friend and comrade, Mr Walker, returned to Dohnavur in 1911 after furlough, the children were wearing

---

* *Rose from Brier*, p. 202.   † *Pools and the Valley of Vision*, pp. 39, 40.

gay blue rosettes. "It was all blue sky, blue ribbons, blue garments—all that the happy colour seems to express as no other colour can, filled the day." *

It was not by chance that her books were nearly always bound in blue cloth.

But in India it is a distinct advantage to have brown eyes, for blue eyes are foreign, and therefore to be remarked upon. "I know why God gave Amma brown eyes," said one of her "boys". "When she was discovering the facts about the Temple children, she used to stain her hands and arms with coffee, and visit places to which foreign women would never be admitted. Of course she wore Indian dress, but if her eyes had been blue someone might easily have penetrated the disguise."

Her love for all created things,. and her grief if the smallest of animals was needlessly hurt, are other characteristics which go back to the earliest days and continued to the end.

The first grief I remember [she writes]—it was as much fury as grief—was about a frog. Our mother had told the story of Calvary to me for the first time. I had rushed out into the garden in a vain attempt to forget the thoughts that were too dreadful to be borne, for how *could* anybody hurt another so, specially One Who was so good? And there, on the lawn, stood a boy friend, and he had fastened a frog to a monkey-puzzle tree. It looked like a crucified thing. I hope it wasn't as cruel as it looked. Probably only the web between the frog's toes was pierced, but I was frantic. In a passion of pity I tried to get it off the horrid spikes; but I could not reach up to it. So I tore into the house to call someone, and as I ran, suddenly the thought came, " Now all the frogs will go to heaven!"

There was " a dear old nurse called Bessie ", who " had a cosy nursery voice, a buttered toast and raspberry jam sort of voice, except when we were naughty ". But she and other grown-ups " found it difficult to understand that live creatures were better than toys. I had a dolls' house. It was full of nice furniture and nicely dressed dolls. I turned them all out, and filled the rooms with moss and stones and put beetles and even earwigs to live there. Anything alive was far more interesting than those foolish little dolls." But all these treasures were swept out and thrown away.

* *This One Thing*, p. 208.

Not that animal friends were taboo. There was a favourite yellow cat and a collie, and—for riding on the firm sands of Millisle—there were ponies.

> I am very grateful to my father for teaching me never to give in to a difficulty. . . . Fanny, my pony, did startling things if anything frightened her. I found that to sing softly in her ear soothed her. He taught me . . . how to ride with a light rein, and yet never lose control, and he taught me never to nag. All this came in useful long afterwards, for in some ways people are rather like ponies.*

As the children grew, Amy was the recognized leader in all pranks and adventures. Uncle William had five children, who were brought up a little less strictly, and had some prejudice against their cousins, because Uncle David's children were always pointed to as models of good behaviour. They were not as good as they looked. Near the garden gate that opened on to the village street was a laburnum tree. Amy and her two brothers were swinging on the gate on a certain sunny afternoon when she remembered she had been told that laburnum pods were poisonous. " Let's count how many we can eat before we die," she suggested, and all three set to work with zest. It was not long before they began to feel very uncomfortable. " We stood in a woebegone little group round the tree, and wondered what would happen next. What happened next was—' Gregory '."

Gregory's powder was the punishment that the children dreaded most.

> Punishment was normally swift, simple and direct . . . but if we ate unwholesome things in the garden we came home to this:—a tray set on the dining-room table, with, neatly arranged upon it, a tall jug of hot water, a small jug of cold milk, a tea cup, a teaspoon and a bottle of the odious pink powder. It was useless to say how sorry you were and that you would never do it again. It was not the time for promises. It was the time for " Gregory ". So you stood beside the table, and felt all sorts of feelings while your mother carefully measured the abominable stuff, and mixed

---

* " Do you remember anything about the Carmichael family? " I asked one of the oldest inhabitants of Millisle. His face lit up. " I mind Miss Amy Carmichael," he said, and he told me how as a small boy he saw her riding fearlessly up and down " the lang sand ". He remembered how she was thrown on one occasion, when riding on the main road, and lay stunned by the sea-wall. She was in bed for weeks, but she did not give up riding.

it, and gave you the cup which you had to receive with a
"Thank you, Mother." Then came the misery of drinking
it. It was too much to drink straight off, but it had to be
drained to the last drop.

And yet we got endless fun out of life. If retribution
followed, well, the game was worth the candle. Once we
stood on the sea-wall when the tide was high and the wind
blew the spray right over us. This was simply splendid;
but as we came home drenched, and as there was no way of
getting our things dried except at the nursery fire, I expect
there were less splendid minutes afterwards. Another day
when our parents were out and Bessie busy with the younger
children, my two brothers and I fulfilled a long cherished
desire. We climbed through a skylight which was in the
ceiling above the bath in the bathroom (I can't imagine
how we did it) and so got out on the roof. Round the edge
of the roof was a lead gutter. I had set my heart on walking
on this gutter. My little brothers followed me most loyally.
We walked triumphantly round the roof along the gutter—
and when we came to the front of the house we looked down.
There, on the lawn below us, stood our father and mother,
looking up. And we had to crawl down through that skylight into their waiting arms.

But when the children of Dohnavur were really difficult,
Amma sometimes told them of a day when she sorely grieved
her mother.

I had been very wilful and, as you know, the will of a child
can be like steel. My mother did not know what to do with
me, for I would not give in, and was not at all sorry. So at
last she set me upon a green ottoman which was at the foot of
the bed, and, perhaps to give me time to think, she said, " I
am going out now." Then she put on her bonnet.

And as she tied the ribbons of her bonnet I watched her
hands moving in the dressing-table looking-glass. The table
was across the corner of the room opposite the ottoman, so
that when she stood with her back to me I could see her
reflected in the mirror. And then I found myself looking
not at her hands tying on her bonnet, but at her face.

Suddenly something melted inside me. In one moment
I was in her arms, soft and sorry and wanting to be good.
It was the look on her face, such a grieved look, that was too
much for me.

And often since then I have thought that if when we sin
we could see the face of our Saviour as in a mirror, we should
never have the heart to grieve Him again.

Even when they were quite small Mrs Carmichael used to send the children to the village with soup for the old and poor. It was not easy to walk quickly and not to spill the soup. But " we had our reward when we came to the cottages and saw the old faces crinkle with smiles ". Amy's brothers libellously maintain that she used to know when to visit some of these cottages, for there would be buttered potato cake on the griddles to be eaten on the spot in return for the soup.

The earliest journeys were made to Portaferry. Amy's grandmother had moved to a smaller house close to the Lough when her husband died, and the practice was being carried on by her son. This house was near to the " demesne ", or park, belonging to the Nugent family, who were friends of the Filsons, and here Amy and her brothers and sisters loved to play.

> Every Sunday morning, before church, our grandmother used to go into the garden and pick tiny nosegays of lily of the valley, sweet pea, jessamine or whatever flowers we chose, so that we might have something lovely to look at during the long service; it was never less than two hours long.

David Carmichael had taught the children to swim by fastening a belt round them, one by one, with a rope attached, and then throwing them into the deep water of the dam. But her story of Strangford Lough must belong to a somewhat later period.

> Strangford Lough is not a safe place for children (the tides are said to be the second strongest in the world) but we were allowed to go out rowing within limits. One evening my two brothers and I overpassed those limits and were caught in a swift current which swept towards the bar. I was steering, my brothers were rowing hard, but they were powerless against the current—" Sing ! " they shouted to me, and I sang at the top of my voice the first thing that came into my head,

> > He leadeth me, O blessed thought,
> > O words with heavenly comfort fraught;
> > Whate'er I do, where'er I be,
> > Still 'tis God's hand that leadeth me!

It certainly wasn't God's hand that led us out into forbidden waters, but it was He Who caused the coastguard men to hear that song and row quickly to the rescue; so we weren't swept over the bar.

Naturally most of her Sunday recollections are of Ballycopeland. There was, for instance, the strain of watching the
courageous but partly crippled minister struggling up the aisle
Sunday by Sunday. Uncle William was the precentor, and
the children loved to watch him with his tuning-fork pitching
the note for the psalms. Hymns were taboo on Sundays, but
might be sung at the weekday prayer meeting. At one such
meeting the theme was " our departure from this world ",
and Amy carefully counted the various things which, according
to the hymn, you were supposed to say at that exact moment.
This occupation helped to pass the time, though she was
puzzled to know how a dying person could say so many things
at once. With one of these remarks she had heartily concurred:

> I'll sing while flying through the air,
> Farewell, farewell, sweet hour of prayer.

The " sweet hour " must, of course, mean the Wednesday
evening prayer meeting.

That prayer meeting meant much to a farmer's lad some
years older than Amy, who is still alive and deeply interested
in the Dohnavur work. He tells how after a certain Sunday
morning service the Carmichael family " filled the road "—
Mr and Mrs David with seven children and Mr and Mrs
William with five ! And Mr David spoke to him. " Robert,"
he said, " will you take part in the prayer meeting next Wednesday ? " He has never forgotten the sense of privilege that
Mr David Carmichael should ask *him* to take part in the prayer
meeting.

Robert Brown sat in the pew immediately behind the Carmichael family. Contrary to the suggestion made in *Windows*
(p. 111), he did not eat peppermints in church, but he knows
very well who did !

So Amy grew. Even as a child she was very gentle with sick
people. One of her sisters, who suffered from headaches,
remembers that she had a wonderful touch, and when she was
in pain she would ask for Amy to come and " make it better ".
But she was a very normal child, and not always as considerate
for others as she became later. The Carmichael children did
not go to school in their early years, but had a succession of
governesses. One of them, an unfortunate Englishwoman—
probably very unsuitable for her task—so annoyed the children

that they made her life unbearable.   When she finally departed
they all trooped out to see her off.   " But why did you go to
see her off if you did not like her? " asked the schoolfellow to
whom Amy retailed the story.   " We wanted to be sure she
went."

Very different was their attitude to Eleanor Milne, whom
they all loved, and whom Mrs Carmichael regarded as an elder
daughter.

> She cared very much for all that was lovely and of good
> report.   She thought of those things and taught us to do so.
> Often as we walked among the lanes near our home she
> would repeat some poem to us till we knew it off by heart.
> Even now some of those poems are fast in my memory.
> She hated cruelty with such a bitter hatred that I can recall
> her very look and the flash of anger in her eyes when she
> saw horses driven with a bearing-rein.   She told us martyr
> stories; stories of our Scottish Covenanting fathers and of
> the English martyrs like Ridley and Latimer.   She taught us
> their great words.

And there was one person who told them of India.   The
brother of the Rev. John Beatty was a missionary in India.
On one of his furloughs he came and lived for a year in a house
next door to the manse, and his wife used to gather the children
on Sunday afternoons and tell them stories of India.   It is
reported that Amy would often stay behind and beg to hear
more.

NOTE

The motto of the armigerous branch of the Carmichael
family is " *Toujours prest* ", and their crest is an arm holding a
broken spear.   Someone reminded Amma of this crest when
she quoted, as she loved to do in later years, the words:

> What though I stand with the winners,
>   Or perish with those that fall?
> Only the cowards are sinners,
>   Fighting the fight is all.
> Strong is my foe, who advances,
>   Snapped is my blade, O Lord;
> See their proud banners and lances—
>   But *spare me the stub of a sword.*

Amy's grandmother was Jane Dalzell.   (The name is inter-
changeable with " Dalziel ".)   She used to tell the children
how the name was given.   It is said that King Kenneth II of

Scotland (A.D. 971–995), grieved that a friend and kinsman had been slain and hung on a gibbet, offered a reward to any of his subjects who would venture to remove the body. Then a brave man came forward, and said, " I dare ", which, in the old Scots language, is written " Dal-ziel ". In remembrance of a hazardous enterprise successfully performed he and his family later took " Dalziel " as their surname, and " I dare " as their motto. Whether the story is authentic or not, this is still the motto of the family.

In the seventeenth century a General Dalziel was a friend of Claverhouse, and joined him in persecuting the Covenanters. Amma liked to think that she came of Covenanter stock on her father's side, and Royalist or anti-Covenanter on her mother's. Thus the persecutor and the persecuted became one in her parents' marriage.

INFLUENCE

Place: a boarding-school in Yorkshire.
Flower: a very lovely Madonna lily.
Child: a homesick little girl.

She grew a plant of fair renown
    Where other lilies be;
They saw her white and golden crown,
    And never more was she
Among the lilies of the wood,
For they that plucked her thought it good
That in another kind of room
That lily-flower should bloom.

And to that room one day there came
    A little wild-bird child,
But lately caught, and nowise tame,
    And all unreconciled
To cages and to careful bars
That seemed to ban the very stars;
The lily looked at her and smiled
As though herself a child.

And their eyes met, no word was said
    That man could hear or say,
But thus the child was comforted;
    And after, flown away
To far, far lands, remembering this,
A comfort it were loss to miss,
Would even in this later hour
Sing joy to some dear flower.

O whosoe'er ye be, and where,
    However straitly bound,
Your ministry is as the air
    That sails the whole world round.
Do ye but fill your present room
With sweetness as of heavenly bloom,
Ye know not where it may be found:
Is Christ within you bound?

CHAPTER II

THEY were happy days in Millisle—for others as well as for the Carmichael families. For many years the mills prospered. Steam power was added to water power, and the brothers were the first in Ireland to introduce the roller system for grinding wheat and to install incandescent lighting. Wheat was imported from America, trans-shipped at Liverpool, and landed at the little port of Donaghadee, four miles from Millisle. The Carmichael brothers won and retained the respect and affection of their neighbours. They made friends with the humblest, and received them as guests at their table in order to lift them spiritually. Some of the older girls came to Amy's mother for instruction in cooking and singing. One or two of them were taught to play the piano. When boys grew to the age of fourteen David Carmichael would ask their parents if they had any plans for them, and offer to recommend them to business firms in Belfast. It was well known that a boy recommended by David Carmichael would be truthful and hardworking. From an elderly man in Millisle comes an amusing reminiscence which, rightly understood, shows the happy relationship between the Carmichaels and others in the village. A boy was reproved by his mother for not raising his cap to ladies as they passed him in the street. "There weren't any ladies," he said wonderingly. "There was just Mrs David and Mrs William Carmichael."

It seems to have been competition with American flour which brought about the first great change in Amy's life—a move from Millisle to Belfast. The brothers built a new mill near the Dufferin Dock, and David Carmichael took his family to a tall house in College Gardens where he could more easily superintend the new enterprise.

But before the move to Belfast, Amy had spent three years at a Wesleyan Methodist boarding-school at Harrogate, Yorkshire.* Looking back after more than sixty years, a

---

* In those days it was called Marlborough House, and a Miss Kay was the Principal; but the school has changed hands more than once, and is now the Harrogate Ladies' College.

schoolfellow remembers the "numerous petty rules and re-
strictions" which hedged them round, and she adds, "We
looked upon Amy as a rather wild Irish girl who was often in
trouble with the mistresses, as she was something of a rebel.
But I do remember that she was very kind to, and popular
with, the little girls, as she was with my brothers and sisters
when she stayed with us [in Cheshire]."

Well, it is no wonder that Amy found life difficult in such a
school, after the freedom that she had enjoyed at home.   One
has to admit that this was not the only time in her life when she
shocked the prim and proper by unconventional behaviour.
But in the autobiography prepared for the Dohnavur Family
she felt it best to say little about the three years at Harrogate.
"If I told you much it would not help you, for I was not at
all what I want you to be."

Although her brother was in a boys' school near by and they
could meet occasionally, she was very homesick.

> Three comforters helped me through those first difficult
> days.   The first was a saucer of moss on the dinner-table.
> Our father had once told us a story of an African explorer,
> Mungo Park, I think, who was comforted by seeing a little
> moss and feeling, as he looked at it, that the God Who made
> it would take care of him.   The second was a tall white lily
> which stood in a pot in the bow-window of the same room.
> The beauty of that lily was very consoling, and I used to look
> across from my place at the long table and listen to that lily.
> She seemed almost to speak.   The third was a box of
> chrysanthemums which my mother sent from our little
> greenhouse.
>
> One day a sorrowful postcard came from my father,
> "Carolus mortuus est"—Charlie (my brother's pony) was
> dead.   My father wrote the sad words in Latin, I suppose,
> because he wanted to remind me to work hard at my Latin.
> I wish I had.

For good or ill—for good, probably, oftener than she would
admit—she was a leader amongst the girls, and now at last,
when she was fourteen, she found herself in serious trouble.

> It was the year of the 1882 comet—there is a picture of it
> in *The Story of the Heavens*, by Sir Robert Ball.   The girls in
> my dormitory and I also wanted to see it.   I was always the
> one sent to ask for favours; when the school wanted a
> specially delicious second-course made of golden syrup and

pastry, they used to send me to the kitchen to coax the cook to suggest to the housekeeper that golden syrup pastry would be a suitable thing for her to order. So now I was sent to Miss Kay, the Principal, to ask her to allow us to sit up and see the comet. And she said, " Certainly not ". Well, it was all wrong, but I tied threads to the great toes of the girls and held the ends of the threads, and promised to keep awake and pull those threads when everyone in the house was asleep. So the other five girls went to sleep in peace till, after having kept awake for what seemed a long time, I pulled the threads. Then, without a word spoken, we stole softly, oh so softly, up the stairs to the attic from whose window we knew that comet could be seen. And all the stairs creaked. And when we got there what do you think we saw? We saw the Principal and teachers; they were looking at the comet.

We looked at it too. We had time to see it beautifully before anyone had recovered sufficiently from the shock of our arrival to order us back to bed. That was a woeful night for me. I was sure I would be expelled and that would break my parents' hearts. Happily that did not come to pass. There was a rather solemn hour next morning, for the matter of threads tied round toes showed such purposeful audacity that it could not be passed over. It was taken for granted that I was the ringleader, but in the end I was forgiven, and there wasn't a teacher I didn't love, and one of the new girls became my special friend. (She is my friend today.) So life was livable after all.

But it was in Harrogate, probably in 1883, shortly before she left, that something happened which brought to a head, or made vital, truths that had been familiar since babyhood.

Near the end of my three years at school the C.S.S.M. held a Mission in Harrogate. My mother had often talked to me about the Lord Jesus, and often, as I sat on her knee, with her arms about me while she sang, " Jesus, the very thought of Thee ", and " It passeth knowledge, that dear love of Thine ", I had felt the love of the Lord Jesus, and, as it were, nestled in His love just as I nestled in her arms. But I had not understood that there was something more to do, something that may be called coming to Him, or opening the door to Him, or giving oneself to Him.

I don't remember what the speaker, Mr Edwin Arrowsmith, spoke about, but after his address he told us to sing " Jesus loves me, this I know ", and then to be quiet. During those quiet few minutes, in His great mercy the Good

Shepherd answered the prayers of my mother and father and many other loving ones, and drew me, even me, into His fold.

Afterwards when I began to understand more of what all this meant I found words which satisfied me. I do not know who wrote them:

> Upon a life I did not live,
>   Upon a death I did not die,
> Another's life, Another's death,
>   I stake my whole eternity.

The shadow of financial straitness began to fall across their path about this time. Amy left Harrogate and took lessons in music, singing and painting at a school in Belfast. Her brothers were withdrawn from King William's College, Isle of Man, and they, too, went to school in Belfast. She and her father became closer friends and companions in those days. He was the kind of man who was constantly being invited to preside at meetings, and who always had something worth while to say. Visiting speakers were often entertained at College Gardens. Probably they did not always realize how seven children around the table were noting all that they said and did. (In 1948, for instance, Amma writes to a grand-daughter of Dr Grattan Guinness: " I feel as if I knew you a little, for your grandfather used to stay with us in Ireland— and always chose ' The sands of time are sinking ' for prayers, and sang a note or two behind everybody else, and *yet* in tune !")

But the shadow lengthened. With characteristic generosity David Carmichael had lent some thousands of pounds to a friend who was in serious need. When he might have been expected to repay the debt he found himself quite unable to do so, and Mr Carmichael would not press him, even though his own financial position had been weakened by other losses. The strain may have predisposed him to the infection of a severe chill, which developed into double pneumonia. At first the children had no idea how serious the sickness was. He used to ask Amy to read to him, and she turned to *Samson Agonistes* without realizing the pertinence of the words.

> All is best, though we oft doubt
> What th'unsearchable dispose
> Of Highest Wisdom brings about,
> And ever best found in the close.

The last hymn he asked for was, " My faith looks up to Thee, Thou Lamb of Calvary, Saviour Divine ". He died on April

12th, 1885, just as the church bells were ringing for the Sunday
morning service.   He was only fifty-four years of age.

In His loving-kindness God had prepared Mrs Carmichael
by turning her thoughts on the previous Sunday to the strong
assurance of Nahum 1. 7 : " The Lord is good, a stronghold in the
day of trouble; and He knoweth them that trust in Him."
On this word she now rested, and was comforted in her desolation.   Years later she marked the verse again in her Bible,
and wrote in the margin : " Found true all along the line ever
since."   And Amy passed—suddenly, it seems—out of child-
hood into young womanhood.   Her mother needed her, and
she became her inseparable companion and confidante.   The
rest of the family needed her too, and she became almost a
second mother to the younger children.   " My memories ",
writes the third of the brothers, who was only eleven when his
father died, " are of a wonderfully sincere, downright, unafraid
and sympathetic sister.   Amy had the faculty of placing herself
in the position of the one in trouble."

Her younger sister Ethel writes a little more fully :

> The time when she impinged on my life was during about
> five years after our father died.   She lived an amazingly
> full life in those years, taking classes in painting and other
> subjects, teaching Eva and me during a period when we were
> not well enough to go to school, and starting various " good
> works ". . . . If anybody asked me what were the strongest
> impressions Amy made on me in her youth, I think I would
> say—her enthusiasms.   She would kindle so quickly to
> anything that promised the betterment of the poor or un-
> happy.   She was fired by the hope that socialism presented
> when she first read about it, and I remember her holding
> forth to me by myself (the only available audience at the
> moment, I expect) on the El Dorado it opened up to the
> world. . . . She was always able to see the positive and
> ignore the negative, and once she had an object before her
> which she was convinced was worth working for, no difficulty
> in the way would deter her.

To this year belongs the incident related in *Gold Cord*, which
marked such an important stage in her spiritual growth that
it must be included here.

> It was a dull Sunday morning in a street in Belfast.   My
> brothers and sisters and I were returning with our mother
> from church when we met a poor pathetic old woman who

was carrying a heavy bundle. We had never seen such a thing in Presbyterian Belfast on Sunday, and, moved by sudden pity, my brothers and I turned with her, relieved her of the bundle, took her by her arms as though they had been handles, and helped her along. This meant facing all the respectable people who were, like ourselves, on their way home. It was a horrid moment. We were only two boys and a girl, and not at all exalted Christians. We hated doing it. Crimson all over (at least we felt crimson, soul and body of us) we plodded on, a wet wind blowing us about, and blowing, too, the rags of that poor old woman, till she seemed like a bundle of feathers and we unhappily mixed up with them. But just as we passed a fountain, recently built near the kerbstone, this mighty phrase was suddenly flashed as it were through the grey drizzle:—

" Gold, silver, precious stones, wood, hay, stubble—every man's work shall be made manifest; for the day shall declare it, because it shall be declared by fire; and the fire shall try every man's work of what sort it is. If any man's work abide——"

If any man's work abide—— I turned to see the voice that spoke with me. The fountain, the muddy street, the people with their politely surprised faces, all this I saw, but saw nothing else. The blinding flash had come and gone; the ordinary was all about us. We went on. I said nothing to anyone, but I knew that something had happened that had changed life's values. Nothing could ever matter again but the things that were eternal.

One of her brothers recalls that Amy " shut herself in her room that afternoon, talked to God, and settled once and for all the pattern of her future life ".

Her sister speaks of " various good works ", and truly their number and variety are astonishing. She was only a girl of seventeen, but in this year or the next we find her, on her own initiative, visiting the streets behind College Gardens on Sunday afternoons, gathering children around her, and bringing them back to her own home for a children's meeting. It is recorded that her mother was persuaded to provide them with something to eat before they left. Then she came in touch with Henry Montgomery, of the Belfast City Mission. He used to take her out on Saturday evenings through the streets of Belfast, saying little, but leaving the sights of poverty and evil to make their own impression. One result was that with Dr Montgomery's daughter Eleanor and two other girls she went to a Night School on Monday evenings, and helped to teach a lively group of boys. The classes ended with a " good-night service ". Yet another enterprise—and this was entirely her own conception—was the Morning Watch. A group of boys and girls, including two of her brothers, pledged themselves to spend a certain time each morning in prayer and Bible-reading. Each member of the group received a dainty card (blue, of course, with a gilt edge) on which the pledge was printed, and room was left for the signature. The members met on Saturday mornings. They took the chair in turn, and spoke of anything which had helped them in their reading during the week—or confessed it if they had failed to get up in time. It was a very solemn thing to join the group, and yet (as one member recalls) when new tenants with children came to the house next door Amy's first thought was, " Can we get any of them to join the Morning Watch? " But another member recalls chiefly how very happy the gatherings were. " Amy saw to it that there were no dull moments, and we all loved her." As if this were not enough, she started a weekly schoolgirls' prayer meeting, held first of all in their own homes. Then, when some of the staff and of the girls at Victoria College wished to join, the meeting was held in the College premises. She was often at the Y.W.C.A. in Donegal Square. " She had a merry eye," says one old friend, " and was always full of life. She would come into a room, and without being told she would see what needed doing, and set about doing it, efficiently but quite unobtrusively."

Meanwhile on Sunday mornings she had a class for " shaw-lies "—i.e. mill-girls who wore shawls instead of hats, and therefore shocked the sensibilities of respectable people! Little or nothing was being attempted for them, and Dr Park, the minister at Rosemary Street Presbyterian Church, where the Carmichaels had always attended since they came to Belfast, was regarded as a very bold innovator when he agreed to Amy's request that the " shawlies " should meet each Sunday morning in the Church Hall. Her mother supported her in everything, even when visiting her girls meant venturing into parts of the city that were regarded as dangerous. " I would let no child of mine go down those streets," said the minister's wife. " But [says Amy] perhaps my mother believed in an angel guard."

It was typical of her that, as her brother says, " she was determined to get down to the root of things ", and that included discovering the kind of temptations that the mill-girls might be facing in their home life. So she pressed her brother Ernest, then an apprentice in the Northern Counties Railway shops, to tell her (from his experience amongst men of the same class) " just what kind of conversation they would hear ". She was horrified when he yielded to her coaxing and told her the truth, but at least she knew a little better the environment in which she longed and prayed that her girls might grow up pure and true.

Then surely the Lord saw that if all these " good works " were to be fruitful for eternity, Amy needed to know Him more intimately, and to rest more securely upon the everlasting Arms. She had visited London with her father in 1884. Now in September, 1886, friends invited her to Scotland, and

something happened that changed everything for me. The friends with whom I was staying took me with them to Glasgow, where a convention on Keswick lines was being held. The hall was full of a sort of grey mist, very dull and chilly. I had been longing for months, perhaps years, to know how one could live a holy life, and a life that would help others. I came to that meeting half hoping, half fearing. Would there be anything for me? I don't remember feeling there was anything (my fault) in either of the two addresses. The fog in the hall seemed to soak into me. My soul was in a fog. Then the chairman rose for the last prayer. Perhaps the previous address had been about Peter walking on the water, and perhaps it had closed with the words of Jude 24, for the one who prayed began like this, " *O Lord, we know Thou art able to keep us from falling* ". Those words found me. It was as if they were alight, and they shone for me. In that light I followed my hostess out of the hall.

She took me to a restaurant for lunch. The mutton chop wasn't properly cooked and somebody said so. I remember wondering, " Whatever does it matter about mutton chops? *O Lord, we know Thou art able to keep us from falling.*"

Soon after that shining day I went home to Belfast. The long time of being " in mourning " for our father was over. So my mother took me to a shop to buy coloured things, and among them was to be an evening dress. That meant something exceedingly pretty. It meant that once more I would be going to parties and spending time in all sorts of pleasant ways. Suddenly I felt I couldn't do that. To

my startled mother I said so. The shopman came and unrolled his loveliest materials, his loveliest colours too, and
my mother, looking rather pained, apologized for troubling
him and we left the shop. North of Ireland people are very
reserved. I had told my mother nothing of that meeting
in Glasgow. No wonder she was perplexed. But she
understood a little later.

Love that never faileth,
Love that all prevaileth—
Saviour Christ, O hear me now
And give Thy love to me.

Round me souls are dying,
Deep in darkness lying;
Thou didst love them unto death,
O give Thy love to me.

Grant that I may reach them,
Grant that I may teach them,
Loving them as Thou dost love,
O give Thy love to me.

Love that ever burneth,
Love that ever yearneth—
Saviour Christ, O hear me now
And give Thy love to me.

CHAPTER III

THE story of " The Welcome "—for it was called just that
rather than " The Welcome Hall "—is best told in Amma's
own words to her children.

From this time on, the work for the mill-girls grew and
grew till we needed a hall that would seat 500; just then we
saw an advertisement in *The Christian*. An iron hall could
be put up for £500 and it would seat 500 people.

When I was about ten or eleven I was asked to collect
money for the Birds' Nest, Dublin, and as I happened to be
staying with my grandmother I took the collecting card to
her various friends in Portaferry and asked them to help.
There was one who had just built a new house for himself.
He refused to give anything.

Perhaps it was the repulse of that refusal that set me
thinking: Why not ask God to make those who love Him
want to help the little children whom He loves, instead of
asking for help from those who perhaps don't love Him?

Later on many other thoughts came, and in the end I
settled that it is enough to ask our Father only, for money
for his work. I had no thought then, no faintest dream,
of what He was going to do in answer to prayer like that.

Now as we looked at the advertisement for the iron hall—
there was a picture showing it—we decided to pray for £500.
One day soon after this, my mother asked me to go to " return calls " with her. You know nothing of this tiresome
duty, and it would take longer than it is worth to explain it,
so I will just say that it used time which might have been
more usefully spent, for it meant sitting in drawing-rooms,
taking tea (trying to balance a piece of cake in the saucer
without dropping it, or spilling the tea), and in talk which
could never be of the deepest sort because it could never be
private. I hated going; but I went. Most of the people
on whom we called were out, which was nice, as then we only
had to leave cards; and we went on to see some keen
Christians, friends of my mother's. They had heard of the
overflowing mill-girls' meetings, and that something was
happening which at first had made the church officials
uneasy, but which they had come to believe was a work of

God and should not be stopped. (One of them, I remember, came and stood in the open doorway with his arms folded and his anxious eyes bent upon us as the girls prayed, sometimes two or three together in their earnestness). Our friends told us of one who wanted to do something in memory of a friend who had died. They thought that to build a hall for the mill-girls was the sort of thing she would love to do. They must have written to her, for a few days afterwards she wrote asking me to lunch. She wanted to know about the mill-girls. Miss Kate Mitchell of Olinda was her name. Olinda was a charming old house in a charming old garden; all the servants had been led to the Lord by the mistress of the house, Miss Kate Mitchell. I felt welcomed from the moment the butler opened the hall door and showed me in. As for Miss Kate Mitchell, she was like a white violet flower. She was God's white violet.

How is it that one remembers some things so distinctly, perhaps quite little things, and forgets far bigger things completely? That lunch table set in a sunny room looking out on the garden, I remember as if I had seen it yesterday; white table-cloth, shining silver, I see it all. The White Violet wanted to know about the mill-girls and I answered her questions. A few days afterwards she wrote to say that she wished to give the hall. Land in cities is very valuable; we wanted land enough to set up that hall in the midst of the mill-girls' streets near one of the big mills. How get it? We prayed again, and someone suggested that I should go to the head of the biggest mill in that part of the city, and ask him what he would charge for a slice of his land. So I went. It was shy work facing that great man in his office, but he must have been a friend of God, for he said at once that we might have what we wanted. I forget the rent he named. It was nominal, something like a rupee a year. "When Thou dost favour any action, it runs, it flies. All things concur to give it a perfection." All things concurred then, and in spite of mistakes I made, for I knew nothing of dealing with builders of iron halls, that hall was put up, and our minister, Dr Park, came to dedicate it.

On the day of the dedication of the hall, which we called " The Welcome ", my mother's beloved Quakeress friend * came to lunch with my mother and me at a teashop. Food was the last thing I was thinking of then. I suppose this troubled my mother, for I remember Mrs Bell telling her not to be troubled. " The Lord takes care of that sort of

---

* When Amy was quite small the family left Millisle for a short time and lived at Knock near Belfast, almost next door to a Mr and Mrs Bell, earnest Christians who were members of the Society of Friends.

child ", she said. I heard the words, as one hears words in dreams, and did not understand what she meant. But often since then I have thought that if she is one of the cloud of witnesses round about Dohnavur, she must smile as she sees how truly the Lord did take care of " that sort of child ".

During the Dedication Service I sat in the middle of the hall among the people and read over and over again the words printed by hand in large letters and hung in a long strip just above the low platform: *That in all things He may have the pre-eminence.* Truly, as truly as I knew how, I wanted those words to be fulfilled.

The work of " The Welcome " opened with a mission led by two of Moody's students who happened to be in Belfast then. The hymn you all know so well, " I know not why God's wondrous grace to me hath been made known ", was sung there for the first time in the British Isles. The chorus,

> " But I know whom I have believed,
> And am persuaded that He is able
> To keep that which I've committed
> Unto Him against that day ",

used to ring through the streets about the hall. And for some nights souls were saved every night, and then, suddenly there was nothing, no power in the meeting. It was dead.

Can you imagine how troubled we were and how perplexed? Why had the Power departed? Lord, is it I? And then, as I prayed that prayer, I remembered something, a rollicking hour when we reached home after the meeting and, as usual, it was my fault. There was nothing wrong in the fun, *but it was not the time for it.* I have never forgotten the shock of that discovery. *Grieve not the Spirit,* that was the word then. In His mercy He forgave; and the work went on again.

After this, whenever I needed money for the work of the hall, I prayed for it and it came. Once when I was asking the Lord for money for a meal for the poor girls an old man* came into the meeting and dropped half a sovereign on a table near the door as he went out.

Years afterwards she discovered that he was a sweet manufacturer in Glasgow, and that people called him " Sweetie Buchanan ". He often sent sweets to Dohnavur, and followed the work with love and prayer till he went Home.

---

* In 1945 Amma adds the note that he cannot have been really old at that time (about 1887), " though he seemed so to me, for I was very young ".

The principle of looking to the Lord alone for financial supplies was not the only one which Amy began to follow at this time, and followed without swerving all the rest of her life. As the work of " The Welcome " became known, friends offered to help, and help was sorely needed, for, as a printed card shows, " Welcome " doings were many and various.

Sunday 4.30.	Bible Class.
„ 5.30.	Sunbeam Band Meeting.
Monday 7.30.	Singing Practice.
Tuesday 7.30.	Night School.
Wednesday 7.30.	Girls' Meeting.
Thursday 7.30.	Sewing Club.
Friday 7.30.	Home Evening.

Monday and Friday 1.20.	Dinner-Hour Meeting.
Wednesday 1.20.	Dinner Prayer Meeting.
Thursday 4 p.m.	Mothers' Meeting.

First Wednesday in the month—Gospel Meeting—All welcome.

What was required in one who was to take part in this work? As Amy studied the book of Ezra the question was answered. At that time others besides the Lord's people offered to help in building His house, but their offers were refused. Even though refusal caused offence, and in fact delayed the completion of the work, the Jewish leaders held firmly to the principle that none but the Lord's people could share in the task (Ezra 4).

It is the word of I Corinthians 3. 11–15 again. Do we want to build in substance that will abide the test of fire? Then let us see to it that the builders are those whose hearts are set on building in gold, silver, precious stones. This was what was taught to us then.

You will not find it difficult to see the bearing this has on all that was " before ordained " to be. What I want you to notice specially is the great kindness of our Lord. He led me into this truth at the very beginning, and He has kept it as a settled thing in my heart ever since. Nothing that I have told you made for a superior attitude, as some said it would. It was just the opposite. It had, and it has, a very humbling influence.

And as she waited, refusing to accept kindly offers of help from any who were not utterly one with her in her desire for the salvation of the mill-girls, a band of loyal friends was given, including older Christian women as well as Amy's contemporaries. She was the leader, the organizer, but she had the gift of enthusing others, and of using their special aptitudes to teach what she had neither time nor ability to teach herself. One of her sisters recalls that Amy usually reserved the Gospel service for herself. " Frequently I played the hymns for her, and so heard the Gospel message, clearly given, full of power and the longing of her heart for the conversion of those rough but attractive girls." And she adds that " she was often depressed in the tram afterwards as we returned home, but was cheered by a word of comfort, leaving results with the Lord ". On the other hand, her brother remembers how on returning from " The Welcome " she shocked their mother by retailing the comical way in which the mill-girls had rendered one of the hymns. " My poor mother could not help joining in the hilarity that convulsed us all."

When the Carmichael family left Belfast, Miss Mitchell took charge of " The Welcome ", and left her lovely home every day to work among the girls. After more than sixty years the hall still stands, and though the work has changed its character, in that not only mill-girls but people of all ages are reached with the Gospel, anyone who visits it today will find that the work throbs with spiritual life. Souls are being saved, a number of young people from the hall are in the Mission field, and four more are in training. There is a Sunday School with twenty-one teachers and two hundred children. Hundreds of pounds are given every year—and doubtless at real cost to the donors—for work in other lands.

" Every foot of that place is dear to me," wrote Amma in 1948. " Everything concerning it was prayed over . . . I never, never forget the ' Welcome ' and my beloved girls."

Lord, give me this new year a burning zeal
For souls immortal; make me plead for such
With earnestness intense, love strong as death
And faith God-given.   Will the world cry " mad " ?
I would be mad.   Such madness be my joy.
For thrice it blesses—first my own cold heart,
Then glorifies my God, and straightway plucks
My sin-stained brother from the jaws of death.

CHARLES KINGSLEY.

Amma often quoted these words.   In writing to the Dohnavur
Family she includes them with other verses under the heading,
" Some of the lights I steer by—apart from the great Light."

CHAPTER IV

MANCHESTER AND THE D.O.M.

THE Keswick Convention for the deepening of spiritual life
had been founded in 1875 by Canon Harford-Battersby, Vicar
of St John's, Keswick, and Robert Wilson, a member of the
Society of Friends, who lived at Broughton, near Cockermouth.
As the movement gained in spiritual momentum, conventions
were held in other centres, often with speakers who had taken
part in the meetings at Keswick. Thus Amy had attended the
Glasgow Convention in September, 1886, and now—exactly a
year later—convention meetings were held at the Exhibition
Hall in Belfast. In the margin of his Bible at Zephaniah 3,
under the date September 4th, 1887, Robert Wilson has written,
" Belfast with Hudson Taylor ".

Our grandmother and aunts were staying with us then,
and our aunts came with my mother and me to the meetings.
The chairman was Mr Robert Wilson of Broughton Grange,
Cumberland, a name known and loved by thousands, but
we had not heard it before and it meant nothing to us. At
one of the meetings he asked any who had questions they
wished to ask to write them and send them to him at the
close of the next meeting. My aunts had questions. I got a
nice pink card with gold edges—we wanted to be polite to
the speakers—and wrote a list of questions, the kind of
questions good Presbyterians would ask, doctrinal and
argumentative. This card was passed up to the chairman
with the others.

After the meeting, to our surprise, Mr Wilson found us out,
and asked if he might call. So he came and was welcomed
by my old grandmother—of whom someone said, " A glance
shows you that she is a King's daughter "—and by my
mother and aunts.

Mr Wilson was not much more than sixty years old then,
but he had wavy silver hair. His eyes were as blue and
candid as a child's, and his face was like a child's too in its
fresh colouring; his big frame almost filled our biggest armchair. He made a beautiful picture as he sat in the firelight,
for we had drawn our chairs round the fire, and he smiled
in a peaceful benevolent way as he pulled my pink card out

31

of his pocket. We thought he was going to answer those questions, but no, he only said, "May I read you something?" And he read from the first word to the last of a long joyous hymn written by Frances Ridley Havergal after she came into the life of restful faith:

> Master, how shall I bless Thy name
>   For love so great to me!
> For sweet enablings of Thy grace,
>   So sovereign, yet so free,
> That taught me to obey Thy word,
>   And cast my care on Thee?

Only a few verses are in the Keswick hymn-book now, but his book held the whole poem, and he read it all in his deep rich voice. Then he said, " May we pray together? " and he prayed.

After that he shook hands with us and said good-bye. Not one question on the pink card had he answered and yet all the questions were answered. It was an unforgettable half-hour.

We did not expect to see Mr Wilson again, but somehow we became friends, and when he returned home he wrote to us and we wrote to him. So simply, so without observation, do we turn the corner of the road of life, but as yet we did not know that we had turned the corner.

At the beginning of 1888, however, when Amy was just over twenty years old—of medium height, with dark brown wavy hair matching her brown eyes—a change took place in the circumstances of the happy family at College Gardens. All, or nearly all, the money left by David Carmichael was lost. As soon as Mrs Carmichael heard the news, she called the seven children together, and as they knelt round the dining-room table, she committed the whole matter to Him Who is " Father of the fatherless, and a Judge of the widows ". Once again He proved to be a stronghold in the day of trouble.

But plans for the future required drastic revision, and it was Amy who, as her brother recalls, " came to the fore with the ideas and suggestions which, when put into effect, enabled our mother to keep the family until each member became self-supporting, and could afterwards help to take care of her ".

During the next few years the two older boys went to America, and later the other two to Canada and South Africa. In 1889 Mrs Carmichael and two of the three daughters left Belfast, and crossed to England.

This move was made in response to an invitation from Mr Jacob Wakefield MacGill, of the Manchester City Mission, an old friend of the Carmichaels, and known to the family as Uncle Jacob. (To users of the hymn-books *Consecration and Faith* and the *Keswick Hymn-book* he is remembered as the author of a missionary hymn, " Coming, coming—yes, they are ".) Amy was asked to carry on work for factory girls in Ancoats, Manchester, on the lines of " The Welcome " in Belfast, while Mrs Carmichael became Lady Superintendent of a Rescue Home, which was one of the many activities of Mr Frank Crossley's work at the Star Hall, Ancoats. The family lived for a year or more at Lymm, in Cheshire, since Mrs Carmichael's position was not a residential one, but later they set up house in Halliwell Lane, not far from the Home.

From the beginning, however, Amy rented a room (particularly for use at week-ends) close to the Hall which Mr MacGill had assigned to her for the Manchester " Welcome ". It was ideal for her purpose—except that it was very filthy. " Well I remember that awful room ", writes her sister, and even Amy herself writes of the " most loathly sort of insect " which " used to crawl through the thin walls from our next-door neighbour's house into ours ". But it was here in Manchester that she came to know Mr Crossley's daughter Ella and her friend Mary Hatch, who were to be among the earliest and most faithful supporters of the Dohnavur work. Miss Crossley remembers her eating oranges and tomatoes— presumably too busy to cook for herself—and reading incessantly whenever she had a spare minute. (Even in College Gardens she would bring a book to meals, in order to avoid being pressed to eat.)

> The training in that slum work [she writes] was splendid in every way. Uncle Jacob had no patience with people who weren't ready at a moment's notice to do whatever was required. If you worked with him you had to be ready. You had to learn to use odd minutes to prepare. You had to learn to do without a quiet room for preparation.
>
> My mother had a cottage in the country and sometimes I used to go home by a late train. There were no Boy Scouts in those days, and one night as I set out for the station the hooligans of Ancoats mobbed me. I don't think I then knew what fear was. If I had, I might have prayed the prayer of Psalm 140. 4, " Keep me, O Lord, from the hands

of the wicked; preserve me from the violent man; who have
purposed to overthrow my goings ", for those great lads,
some of them full-grown men, were wicked and violent and
they purposed to overthrow my goings.   As it was I walked
on peacefully thinking of a great-great-uncle who had been
in one of the Irish troubles, and who marched straight
through a crowd who had gathered and filled the streets
between his house in Portaferry and Strangford Lough,
where a boat was waiting for him.   And nobody dared
touch him—so the story said.   He reached the shore un-
molested and sailed off.

But things grew more and more threatening and then,
suddenly, help came.   A woman standing by her open door
saw me in the midst of the mob and ran out and caught my
hand.   Before anyone knew what she meant to do she had
me in her kitchen and had set a clothes-horse between me
and the street.   A white sheet hung on that clothes-horse
and was not much of a protection, you will think; but that
woman must have said something that put fear into the
hearts of those lads, for they slunk off, and as I am here
today you know that I reached the station safely just as my
great-great-uncle reached the boat on Strangford Lough.

Perhaps it is not surprising that illness, due to overwork and
poor living conditions, cut short her work in Manchester.   But
meanwhile God had been planning a very different form of
preparation for her life-work.   Robert Wilson, the Dear Old
Man (" D.O.M.", for short), as the family used to call him,
had become a very great friend.   Amy and her sisters and her
younger brothers visited him from time to time at his home,
Broughton Grange.   At his invitation she attended her first
Keswick in 1888.   " It was an unforgettable time; it meant a
new committal of one's whole life."

As time went on the visits to Broughton lengthened, and
sickness made it inadvisable for Amy to continue her work in
Ancoats.   Moreover, the D.O.M. was very lonely.   His wife
had died in the same year as David Carmichael, and his
only daughter still earlier.   She was about Amy's age when she
died, and it was no wonder that he longed for Amy to fill the
vacant place.

At last in 1890 he asked my mother to let me stay with him
for the greater part of the year and be as his own daughter.
She had a dear daughter with her, and he had nobody.   She
knew how lonely he was and she consented; so, though I was

often with her, it came to be that I was more and more with him. It was just like my dear mother to give to him that asked of her, but I knew afterwards that it had not been easy for her to do, and yet looking back I can see that it fitted into the Plan, it was part of the preparation for something out of sight. For if ever I was to do the things " before prepared " (see Ephesians 2. 10 R.V.), certain great lessons not learned yet had to be learned, and Broughton Grange was the appointed school.

From prayer that asks that I may be
Sheltered from winds that beat on Thee,
From fearing when I should aspire,
From faltering when I should climb higher,
From silken self, O Captain, free
Thy soldier who would follow Thee.

From subtle love of softening things,
From easy choices, weakenings,
Not thus are spirits fortified,
Not this way went the Crucified,
From all that dims Thy Calvary,
O Lamb of God, deliver me

Give me the love that leads the way,
The faith that nothing can dismay,
The hope no disappointments tire,
The passion that will burn like fire,
Let me not sink to be a clod:
Make me Thy fuel, Flame of God.

CHAPTER V

BROUGHTON GRANGE

ROBERT WILSON was born at Kendal, but after his marriage he made his home at Broughton, near Cockermouth, and in 1858, on the rising ground above the river Derwent, and commanding from its terrace a glorious view of the whole Cumbrian Range from Skiddaw to Scafell, he built Broughton Grange. Close by was the Friends' Meeting House, where Quakers had met for worship since 1653, and the Baptist Chapel, a still older building, erected in 1648 by a godly colonel in Cromwell's army, who was quartered with his troops in Broughton during the siege of Cockermouth.

Mr Wilson had been born a Friend, and the family continued to attend the First-Day meeting on Sunday mornings, but from 1860 right on till 1915 either he himself or one of his sons superintended the Baptist Sunday School, and in later years he had two seats at the parish church, and used to take his wife there on Sunday evenings. Later Amy often accompanied him. From his own study of the Scriptures he concluded that baptism and the Lord's Supper " were in our Lord's thought for us ", and therefore, contrary to Quaker usage, he was baptized.

Thus, one of the first lessons that the staunch Presbyterian from Ireland had to learn was (as she says)

> to drop labels, and to think only of the one true invisible Church, to which all who truly love the Lord belong. Suppose He came tomorrow, what would labels matter? I could almost see them dropping off as those who were waiting for their Lord rose in the air to meet Him. They would never think of them then. Why think much of them now? . . . I grew to value the quietness of the Friends' way of worship, and also to care very much for the beauty of the Church of England ways.

It is this part of her heritage which explains the times of vital silence in the half-hour English service in the House of Prayer at Dohnavur, and also the use of parts of the Anglican liturgy.

A Friend who was a child when Amy went to Broughton
Grange remembers her brightness and cheerfulness, and says
that " we children used to enjoy her verbal messages in our
meeting for worship ", so evidently she felt free to obey the
Spirit's promptings and to speak when He gave her a message.
It was Robert Wilson himself who chose the words " All one in
Christ Jesus " as the Keswick motto, and his life was an
illustration of its truth.

From Mr Wilson also she learned the necessity of refraining
from careless talk about others.

> The D.O.M. was not only chairman of the Keswick Con-
> vention [since 1889] but of other conventions also, and this
> brought him into touch with many people of different ways
> of thinking.   He often heard what, if repeated, would have
> done harm, or, at best, would not have helped towards peace.
> As I was with him so much, sharing his letters, sharing his
> thoughts, naturally I was " in the know ", and had to learn
> to be very careful to be silent.

" Learn to be a deep well," she adds—and perhaps it should
be repeated that all these fragments of autobiography were
written for the Dohnavur Family—" a deep well doesn't talk ".

And of course it was a great experience to meet, whether at
Keswick or at Broughton, men of God such as Hudson Taylor,
Theodore Monod, F. B. Meyer, and a host of others.   Perhaps,
after the strenuous activities of Belfast and Manchester, she
needed this privilege of sitting at the feet of others.   From the
D.O.M. she received " new light on the Bible.   All North of
Ireland children revered the Bible, it was the Book of books to
them from their nurseries.   But the D.O.M. read it in a new
way to me."   And he talked of its truths as they walked by the
way, or drove in a gig round the villages.

> " Thee must never say, thee must never even let thyself
> think, ' I have won that soul for Christ.' "   And he pulled
> up the old horse, Charlie, and stopped near a stonebreaker
> who, squatting beside his pile of stones, was hammering
> steadily.   " I will tell thee a story ", the D.O.M. said,
> pointing with his whip to the stonebreaker who tapped
> stolidly on and never looked up.   " There was one who
> asked a stonebreaker at work by the roadside, ' Friend,
> which blow broke the stone? ' And the stonebreaker
> answered, ' *The first one and the last one, and every one between.*' "

The story was new to Amy then, but she never forgot it. Did she learn from the D.O.M. also the power of apt, concrete illustration? Certainly the Lord showed her how to use it in all her work in India. Nearly all her " children " refer to it in their reminiscences of talks with Amma.

He was always courtly as well as affectionate in his attitude towards her. She could never forget his manner of plucking a rose for her as they walked round the garden. No one had known how his heart ached for the only daughter Rachel, and for his wife. Amy filled a great blank in his life.

But it was by no means an easy position for her. Of his four sons, one had died years before, and another was married, and visited the Grange from time to time with his family. But the other two, George and William, had remained bachelors, and were already in their later thirties. They lived at home, assisted their father in the management of his coal-mines, and were active also in Christian work, including the Baptist Sunday School and all the activities of the well-built Mission Hall which their father had erected in the village. ˙ It was natural enough that they should regard Amy as an interloper, a disturber of the quiet routine of their family life. They accepted her presence because they knew that she made their father happy, but she must have been aware that they did not make her welcome. One of the grandchildren was attracted to her, and enjoyed walks with her round the garden. To the child she was " racy and amusing ", but even a child knew that the family generally disapproved of her.

So this, too, was part of God's training for her.

Meanwhile she was not merely a daughter and companion to the D.O.M., for she found plenty of scope for her activities in the village. There are living in Broughton today about a dozen elderly people who have vivid memories of the Scripture Union meetings held in the Mission Hall on Tuesday evenings. They were probably inaugurated by Josiah Spiers, the founder of the C.S.S.M., who was invited by Mr Wilson more than once to conduct a campaign there. Each child was given a sort of album which Mr Spiers called a " portfolio ", and he would stand at the door as the children entered, and say, " Show your portfolios! "—in which, it would seem, texts were pasted at each meeting. When Amy came to Broughton she was happy to accept responsibility for the Tuesday night meetings, though

George and William Wilson still took some part. William was musical and artistic, and his singing is still remembered; but Amy usually gave the address. The hall was always packed, and you could have heard the proverbial pin dropping when she spoke. The children loved to be there whenever she took the meeting.

In addition, a number of girls were invited to the Grange on Saturdays. They sat at a big round table in the library, and played games before the Bible Class. Then they were conducted round the garden to inspect the rabbits and goldfish, and regaled with milk and gingerbread before they left.

It must have been in 1890 that she joined Hannah Govan, of the Faith Mission, in an evangelistic tour among the villages up the Clyde. Fifty years later she wrote of that journey, " I shall never forget the joy of those days." Not very long ago a member of the Dohnavur Fellowship visiting the same area met with several old people who had not forgotten Amy, and could even recall some of the messages that she had given. It was through her friendship with Hannah Govan that she was invited to write articles for *Bright Words*, the organ of the Faith Mission. She felt it was an impossible thing for her to do. It happened that she was on holiday in Ireland when the invitation came, and as she sat on a rock by the Irish Sea she received the promise, " I will hold thy right hand ", and she stretched out her hand before the Lord and gave it to Him for His service. And so, in February, 1891, appeared the first article over the signature " Amy B. Carmichael ".*   It was entitled " Fightin' Sall "—the story of a " shawlie " converted at " The Welcome " in Belfast, and it was followed by a succession of other articles, all of them showing the yearning of her heart for men and women out of Christ.

The D.O.M. was in his sixty-sixth year, much used of God and very happy. It looked as if Amy would make her home with him as long as he needed her. In spite of difficulties she was happy too, and did not her duty lie with him?

---

* The first, except for those which appeared in a private family periodical to which all seven children contributed.   But (says her brother) " Amy was the most valued contributor ".

Many crowd the Saviour's Kingdom,
    Few receive His Cross,
Many seek His consolation,
    Few will suffer loss
For the dear sake of the Master,
    Counting all but dross.

Many sit at Jesus' table,
    Few will fast with Him
When the sorrow-cup of anguish
    Trembles to the brim—
Few watch with Him in the garden
    Who have sung the hymn.

Many will confess His wisdom,
    Few embrace His shame,
Many, should He smile upon them,
    Will His praise proclaim;
Then, if for a while He leave them,
    They desert His Name.

But the souls who love Him truly
    Whether for woe or bliss,
These will count their truest heart's blood
    Not their own, but His;
Saviour, Thou Who thus hast loved me,
    Give me love like this.

Author unknown

The lines are a paraphrase of a page from Thomas à Kempis' *Imitation* (Book 2, Chapter XI). Someone sent them to Amy, printed as a separate leaflet, at the time of her call to the Mission field. In later years she frequently quoted the verses.

CHAPTER VI

THE CALL

HARROGATE, 1883 ("the one watered moment", as Amy calls it, "in an arid three years"), Glasgow on September 23rd, 1886—these had been important spiritual landmarks. At least equally clear, both at the time and in retrospect, was the voice of God that came to her at Broughton Grange on January 13th, 1892.

I had thought that the plan was for me to stay with the D.O.M. till he went to heaven. But crashing through that thought came a word I could not escape and dare not resist. It came on a snowy evening, January 13th, 1892. Do you remember how one who had a name among David's three mighty men slew a lion in the midst of a pit in time of snow? I had to slay a lion in a pit in time of snow when with all his might the devil sought to hold me back from an obedience which was to cost so much. For I was not with the D.O.M. when he went to heaven. No one had the heart to write and tell me of that going [in 1905]. I read of it in a book several years afterwards as I was coming back to Dohnavur after fighting in the Courts to save Kunmunnie. He died all alone sitting in his armchair in the library of Broughton Grange. I saw it as I read it that day in the bullock cart. I see it now, a lonely, lonely death—and he would have given his life to save me from one minute's loneliness. But he is not sorry now. He is not lonely now. He has been comforted.

On that Wednesday evening the word came again and again, "Go ye . . .". As late as the previous evening (Tuesday, January 12th), no impelling call had come to her. "I had a quiet time," she wrote to her mother a few days later, "and thought I would look over my 'Ask and Receive Book'. The thing I had asked for at Keswick, rest from the cry of the heathen, and *gladness* to stay at home and send others, had been only half answered, and that somehow made me think, though the idea that after all He might want me to go, never once crossed my mind."

43

But letters from the three most concerned—Amy, her mother, and the D.O.M.—have been preserved, and for once they must be quoted *in extenso*.

1. *From Amy to her mother, dated January* 14*th*

My PRECIOUS MOTHER,
            Have you given your child unreservedly to the Lord for whatever He wills? . . .
    Oh may He strengthen you to say " Yes " to Him if He asks something which costs.
    Darling Mother, for a long time as you know the thought of those dying in the dark—50,000 of them every day, while we at home live in the midst of blazing light—has been very present with me, and the longing to go to them, and tell them of Jesus, has been strong upon me. Everything, everything seemed to be saying " Go ", through all sounds the cry seemed to rise, " Come over and help us." Every bit of pleasure or work which has come to me, has had underlying it the thought of those people who have never, never heard of Jesus; before my eyes clearer than any lovely view has been the constant picture of those millions who have no chance, and never had one, of hearing of the love which makes our lives so bright.
    But home claims seemed to say " Stay ", and I thought it was His Will; it was perhaps till yesterday. I can't explain it, but lately the need seems to have come closer, and I wrote down a few days ago, just to have it in black and white, *why* I am not going.

        1. Your need of me, my Mother.
        2. The great loneliness it would mean to my dear second Father.
        3. The thought that by staying I might make it easier for the others to go if He called.
        4. My not being strong.

    But in His sight are these four things worth staying from those poor heathen for? You have given me three-quarters up as it is. My dear old Fatherie is the Lord's wholly, he would not let me be kept just for him. The other two things surely I could trust about. Still they seemed to say " Stay ".
    Yesterday suddenly the impulse came to have a good talk with my dear Fatherie—I can't call him " Mr Wilson ", he is too close for that now—at any rate to you, Mother, and after it I went to my own room and just asked the Lord what

it all meant, what did He wish me to do, and, Mother, as clearly as I ever heard you speak, I heard Him say

"GO YE"

I never heard it just so plainly before; I cannot be mistaken, for I know He spoke. He says "*Go*", I cannot stay.

Mother, I feel as if I had been stabbing someone I loved. It is Friday now, I could not finish this yesterday, and through all the keen sharp pain which has come since Wednesday, the certainty that it was His voice I heard has never wavered; though all my heart has shrunk from what it means, though I seem torn in two, and just feel one big ache all over, yet the certainty is there—He said to me "*Go*". Oh, nothing but that sure word, *His* word, could make it possible to do it, for until He spoke, and I answered, "Yes, Lord", I never knew what it would cost.

These are the verses He gave me, when He spoke to me, "If any man will come after Me, let him deny himself, and take up his cross, and follow Me." "For whosoever will save his life shall lose it, and whosoever will lose his life for My sake shall find it." "He that loveth father or mother more than Me is not worthy of Me."

"To obey is better than sacrifice."

Many difficulties have risen in my mind, they seem very great, the "crooked places" seem very crooked, but it seems to me that all He asks is that we should take the one step He shows us, and in simplest, most practical trust leave all results to Him.

Mother, I know that very few of our friends will think I am right. Those who don't know the Shepherd's Voice themselves will be quite sure I am very wrong and mistaken, but He has said, "Walk before *Me*, and be thou perfect." He knows, and He won't let me dishonour Him by making a mistake and following my own fancy instead of Him. *If* it is so, He will show it to me, but if it is His Will, I must do it.

There isn't much of gladness in this letter, I'm afraid, but I don't feel anything except sore at the pain this must bring to my loved ones.

Goodbye, my Mother. May He come very near to you and strengthen and comfort you.

YOUR OWN AMY.

P.S. Some of these things may cross your mind as they have mine.

What about leaving my God-given Father who does seem to need me a little? Cannot I trust Him to care for him?

If He tells me to leave him, He won't let him suffer. Clara Bradshaw met Hudson Taylor once, and he prayed, " Show this child of Thine what blessing she is keeping from her own father "—by staying when He had called her.

If I stayed, might I not keep those dearest to me from God's richest blessing? But this is a very hard bit to think of, I can hardly face it steadily yet.

Then as to " the children ". [And here she discusses the future of the three who were still in England.] God knows what it means, but " The Lord is able to give thee much more than this." He gave Himself for us, is anything too great to give to Him?

" Health " you will think of. He won't let that hinder if He has said " *Go* ". Then as to the money—I don't see clearly, but I believe He will show us about that. If He does not, I will take it that *that* means " stay ", for He could not mean me to let you suffer wrongly. But I think soon the boys will be able to help.

2. *From her mother to Amy, in firm clear handwriting, dated January 16th, and marked on the back in Amy's writing, " First letter received—praise the Lord ! "*

MY OWN PRECIOUS CHILD,

> He Who *hath* led *will* lead
>   All through the wilderness,
> He Who hath fed will surely feed . . .
> He Who hath heard thy cry
>   Will never close His ear,
> He Who hath marked thy faintest sigh
>   Will not forget thy tear.
> He loveth always, faileth never,
> So rest on Him today—for ever.

Yes, dearest Amy, He has lent you to me all these years. He only knows what a strength, comfort and joy you have been to me. In sorrow He made you my staff and solace, in loneliness my more than child companion, and in gladness my bright and merry-hearted sympathizer. So, darling, when He asks you now to go away from within my reach, can I say nay? No, no, Amy, He is yours—you are His— to take you where He pleases and to use you as He pleases. I can trust you to Him, and I do—and I thank Him for letting you hear His voice as you have done. I shall not speak of your dear loving letter or my feelings. How weak we are. But He knows our frame, and remembers. " Go *ye* "— my heart echoes. " O send forth *Thy* light and *Thy* truth, let *them* lead me—let *them* bring me into Thy holy hill and

to Thy tabernacles ", met my eye as I opened my Bible—
do you see what the holy hill and tabernacles meant to me in
this connection? I never saw it before—and then in the
next page comes, " Therefore God hath blessed thee for
ever." All day He has helped me, and my heart unfailingly
says, " *Go ye* ". He only knows what this means and will
mean to me—to you—to us all. I dare not think—but His
grace *is* sufficient, Amy. Let us keep our eye on *Him*—and
then no wave will swamp us—and He will bear us up in His
arms. Oh, isn't it strange we are not more *cheerfully* willing
followers—to think of His wonderful everlasting love to us,
and how little He ever asks in return. Amy, darling, today
I got a moment's glimpse of it all, and how small this life
seemed. When we are dying, how very little will it seem
that He has asked us to give up for Him. So, my precious
Child, I give you back into His loving arms, saying from the
depths of my being, " Take her, dear Lord—Thou wilt take
the most loving care of her, use her in Thy service and for
Thy glory now and where Thou pleasest, for Christ's sake.
Amen."

For dear Mr Wilson I feel so much, perhaps more than for
myself, but God has *his* happiness in *His* keeping. He cannot and will not make a mistake. *All* other points are minor
and must wait—the one thought has been enough today.
One step is all that I am equal to—all else will clear. " The
Lord is my Shepherd, I shall *not* want." " Goodness and
mercy *shall* follow me "—and those who trust—" all the
days of my life ", and we shall all gather from the north,
south, east and west in His Home above, and will cast our
crowns at His feet, saying, " Worthy is the Lamb that was
slain to receive power and riches and wisdom and strength
and honour and glory and blessing." Till then may we
each one be found faithful.

Ever my darling child's loving MOTHER.

For *days*, it seems to me now, the Lord has been preparing
the way, Amy, for your letter.

3. *From the D.O.M. to Mrs Carmichael, dated January* 18th

My DEAR MRS CARMICHAEL

I do not like Amy's letter to go to you without a few
words of sympathy from me, in your giving up of your dear
Child for the Lord's work amongst the heathen. I know
something of what it must cost you, but am sure He Who calls
for this, will more than fill the void caused, by His own love
fiowing in.

It hardly seems a case for anything but bowing the head

in thankful acquiescence, when the Lord speaks thus decidedly to one so dear, and I was thankful to see how much He had sustained you, from your loving letter this morning to your dear Child, who was much comforted thereby.

I need hardly tell you what it is to me to think of, but the Lord will be with us all, and give us as we need.

It has been a solemn subject before my dear Amy, and she has had many thoughts—but all must bow, she feels, before the one loving and strong Call of the Master.

The future seems changed to me, and my only desire is to do the will of my Master in this, and in all arrangements for the comfort of one so dear to me.

She *has been* and *is* more than I can tell you to me, but not too sweet or too loving to present to Him Who gave Himself for us.

I am not much able to write—so excuse. I join with you in thankful praise that this dear one will be very near and very dear to her Lord, and receive from Him untold blessing.

May the Lord bless you and yours.

Ever affectionately yours,

ROBERT WILSON.

For some days Amy wrote daily to her mother, and they discussed in some detail the future of the family generally, especially those who were not financially independent. Amy was eager not to evade any responsibility to her mother and to them, yet she returns over and over again to the certainty that God had called, and that therefore no one who might conceivably be looking to her for help would be allowed to want. Her mother's letters were an immense comfort. " I want to keep them always, so if you have anything to say you don't want to live for ever, write it on a loose sheet! " Amy discovered that at one time her mother had been so moved by China's need that she had longed to go herself with her seven children. " That was after my father's death, at a time when her heart was very tender towards suffering, as indeed it always was. So when this call came to me she gave me up without a hindering word. But again and again through those piercing days it seemed impossible to leave the D.O.M." Amy used to hear him quoting, half to himself, the words : " If any man say unto you, Why do ye this? say ye that the Lord hath need of him."

The news came as a great shock to the Wilson family. They had reconciled themselves with some difficulty to Amy's presence at the Grange, on the ground that Mr Wilson loved her and seemed to need her. And now they were asked to readjust their thinking again. Was it not heartless on her part to talk of leaving him? Was it not even a breach of faith? " It came to me with such a strong feeling yesterday," she writes to her mother, " when I began to see how the relations would judge me, that I had hardly ever borne shame for His Name's sake. Think of being the follower of a Saviour Who was despised and rejected, and yet wanting to escape being misunderstood and misjudged."

Even her mother's sisters did not fully understand.

It is a case of " distance lends enchantment " to them—they think I *want* to go. If they only knew how torn in two I feel today, and how precious the home ties are, they would understand. . . . Oh how *could* I leave you all, my own precious ones, and leave the joy of being of ever so tiny a bit of help to you (*that* is not easy to give up!) unless the hand of the Lord were upon me. . . . Mother, isn't it strange how though we sing so often,

> Not my own, oh not my own!
> Jesus, I belong to Thee,

we live it so little. We are very much our own, we don't live as strangers and pilgrims at all, and when the call comes to one to leave all and follow, it seems strange to us. Oh that we may die, not in mere hymn and prayer, but in deed and in truth, to ourselves, to our self-life and self-love. I never knew what it meant before—*dead* to all one's natural earthly plans and hopes, *dead* to all voices, however dear, which would deafen our ear to His—*alive* unto God. When I think of Christ's life in its utter self-death, and then think of ours, of *mine*, the contrast is too terrible. We Christians have been trying to get as much as ever we could out of this life, we have followed our Saviour, it seems to me, very, very far off

The D.O.M., with his heart breaking, loyally tried to comfort her when his family expressed their indignation. Was it a breach of faith that she should talk of leaving him? " The D.O.M. says it is not so, and will say so most clearly if need be, as he distinctly wrote to you that this was not a binding arrangement."

"It was a wonderful cheer ", she writes in the autobiography, " when one old friend was glad—Mrs Bell, our Quakeress friend. She clapped her hands when she heard of the call which to most seemed a mistake or worse." But it was not only the Wilson family who were critical. " He will be dead before you are through the Mediterranean," was said by leaders in the Keswick Convention movement—" men and women whose names were honoured everywhere. Their words cut like knives."

The call was simply, " Go ye . . ." But where was she to go? The reply to this question is surprisingly vague. On January 18th she writes to her mother, " You will wonder what place I think of. Ceylon seems to be much upon my mind, but of course I cannot tell yet. I *think* He is guiding me to go there, but we are waiting upon Him to be *sure*. China and Africa are somehow not so strong upon my mind as they used to be, and Ceylon, a place I never knew much of, is constantly before me. *He will choose.*"

Yes, but she was fully expecting to sail *somewhere* in the autumn of 1892. The clear-minded men and women whose business it is to advise young people about this solemn question of a missionary call, will smile or even lift their eyebrows at the *insouciance* of it all. During the few weeks following January 13th that are covered by home letters Ceylon is mentioned again with charming vagueness. It was " not all flat ", as one of her sisters had suggested. But to this sister she must bequeath most of her " treasures in the leather line ", for there are rats there which " devour leather in every shape or form, and ugly airtight tin boxes are disagreeable necessities. The rats and insects are among the powers that be, in Ceylon, and occasionally, it may be, feed upon live missionaries when food is scarce. They have been known to attack human hair anyway, in the still hours of night."

It is pleasant to note how her sense of humour was reasserting itself, after the strain of January. Amy and the D.O.M. had discussed plans, from every angle—except, it would seem, that of making a direct approach to any Mission secretary—until neither of them could sleep, and they agreed that the whole subject should be taboo in the evenings. The D.O.M. wrote letters to warm friends in Ireland, and it was suggested that Amy should visit them in February, and meet a missionary " fresh from the field ". (What field? Was it still Ceylon?) There followed a long visit to her mother's home at 47 Halliwell Lane, Cheetham Hill, Manchester.

As time went on, however, for reasons which cannot now be

discovered, Ceylon faded out of Amy's mind, and the call of China—" a million a month dying without God "—became more insistent. At length in May Mr Wilson took her to Bedford to stay with Mrs Stewart, of Fukien. It was almost settled that she would travel to China with the Stewarts in the autumn—presumably under the Church of England Zenana Missionary Society—but in the margin of her *Daily Light* for July 16th, close to the words, " Speak unto the children of Israel *that they go forward* ", she has written as follows : " Letter came from Mrs Stewart of Fukien, saying that she could not go to China this autumn. Was to have gone with her." The Rev. Robert Stewart and his wife and a group of unmarried women missionaries were murdered at Kucheng, Fukien, on August 1st, 1895. Amy never forgot that she too would almost certainly have been martyred but for a change in Mrs Stewart's plans—she and her husband went first to Australia before returning to China.

The end of July found her with the D.O.M. at the Keswick Convention. Since 1888 this had been an annual privilege, and it was in that year (1888) that the Convention officially sponsored a missionary meeting for the first time. For some years Robert Wilson's predecessor in the office of Chairman had refused to allow the tent to be used for a missionary meeting, in spite of the earnest pleadings of Hudson Taylor and Reginald Radcliffe. But the tent was unofficially " lent " in 1886 and 1887, and at the meeting of 1887 thirty young people offered for missionary service. At the missionary meeting of 1888 someone sent a £10 note to the Chairman " as the nucleus of a fund for sending out a Keswick missionary ". This gift " provoked " others, and a Keswick Mission Committee was formed, with Robert Wilson as Chairman, first, to send out Keswick " Missioners "—men who would visit Mission fields as exponents of the Keswick message—and, second, to support Keswick missionaries. The first to be so supported * was Amy Carmichael. At the meeting of the Keswick Mission Committee held on July 26th (as she records in her *Daily Light*) she was " definitely given up for service abroad ", and she notes that one of the verses for that day was, " He shall choose our inheritance for us ".

* Miss Louisa Townsend went to Palestine in 1892 under the auspices of Keswick, but at her own charges.

She was cheered by the understanding of the Rev. C. A. Fox, one of the Keswick speakers, and Miss Sophia Nugent (of the Mission Committee, and a relative of the Nugents at Portaferry), who agreed that she must obey God's call, even though the cost to Robert Wilson was so great. Hudson Taylor was another who understood. " He took the D.O.M.'s hands in his two hands and spoke words of strong consolation."

It was to the China Inland Mission, of which Hudson Taylor was General Director, that Amy at length offered. She notes September 10th as the day when she first left " home " to stay at the C.I.M. premises in London. The D.O.M. accompanied her, and they stayed with Miss Henrietta Soltau, who was for so many years in charge of women candidates for the Mission. As the autobiography records:

> One evening as we sat together by the fireside of Miss Soltau's house, he said in the dear " thee and thou " of Quaker speech, " Thee must sign thy name Carmichael Wilson in the C.I.M. papers. I would not have the world think that thou art not my child any more!" A little later he said, " Thee had better write Wilson Carmichael "; and that is how it came to pass that his name was in my name.*

The D.O.M. returned to Broughton, but the knowledge of his suffering was torture to Amy.

> Miss Soltau, perhaps seeing or feeling my distress, came to me that night in the little bedroom at the old Pyrland Road house. The window had been open and the little white dressing-table cover was powdered with smuts. We stood beside it, and as a tortured heart does always notice trifles, so I noticed those smuts. The words broke from me : " They say that if I leave him he will die—even so am I right to go? " She did not answer for a moment, then said solemnly, " Yes, I think even so, that you are right to go."
> It was a tremendous answer. She must have added something about trusting our Father to deal tenderly with His servant who had truly given me to Him, though his heart still clung to me. But all I remember of the next few minutes is that with her arms around me I entered into peace. Often, through the many years that have passed since that night, I have been helped by the memory of her courage in

* After Mr Wilson's death, she records, " It became a little difficult in some small ways, and as I knew he would not misunderstand and be hurt, I went back to my own name ".

the ways of God, to strengthen a younger soul who was being torn as I was then.*

There was another who longed to help—Geraldine Guinness, afterwards Mrs Howard Taylor. To the end of her life Amy preserved a folded half-sheet of paper given to her by Geraldine on September 27th. Outside she had written, " Love and deepest sympathy, my dear Amy, and *many* thanks for your precious helpful words yesterday ", and inside were these words :

Can ye ?	*Can God ?*
(Mark 10. 28)	(Psalm 78. 19)

Can ye drink of the cup that I drink of—and be baptized with the baptism that I am baptized with ?

Ye shall, indeed. . . . For *with God* all things are possible.

Now is my soul troubled—and what shall I say?
Father, save Me. . . . Father, *glorify Thy Name.* For this cause came I unto this hour. (John 12. 24—28.)

"I don't think an older girl could have helped a younger girl more," wrote Amma in 1948. " There was no weakening, that was what helped so much. There was just the steadfast look towards Gethsemane and Calvary."

So Miss Soltau took her to buy her outfit, and it was packed into the two airtight boxes. And then—the C.I.M. doctor refused to pass Amy for China! " He has given me back my Isaac. Praise Him! " So said the D.O.M. Did not the doctor's verdict mean that Isaac might now get down from the altar?

But as I rode about in the lanes round Broughton, for the D.O.M. had given me a pony, or met the adoring eyes of my black-and-tan terrier, Scamp, another of his gifts, and as I helped him with his Convention writing and took Convention women's meetings, always the thought was with me, " This is not your rest ". I knew that I must go, but where?

* *A Woman Who Laughed.* Biography of Henrietta Soltau. By Mildred Cable and Francesca French. pp. 154, 155.

Then with a rush the intolerable craving
   Shivers throughout me like a trumpet call—
Oh to save these! to perish for their saving!
   Die for their life, be offered for them all! . . . .
Therefore, O Lord, I will not fail nor falter,
   Nay but I ask it, nay but I desire,
Lay on my lips Thine embers of the altar,
   Seal with the sting, and furnish with the fire.
Give me a voice, a cry, and a complaining—
   Oh let my sound be stormy in their ears!
Throat that would shout, but cannot stay for straining,
   Eyes that would weep, but cannot wait for tears.
Quick in a moment, infinite for ever,
   Send an arousal better than I pray,
Give me a grace upon the faint endeavour,
   Souls for my hire and Pentecost today.

                    —From *St Paul*, by F. W. H. Myers.

CHAPTER VII

TO JAPAN

It was January 13th, 1893—the first anniversary of God's call to the Mission field. For a whole year Amy had been pushing doors that seemed to be ajar, and not one had opened to her. As the word "Go ye . . ." was repeated, somehow the thought of Japan as a field of work came before her mind. As usual, she confided in the D.O.M., and, again as usual, he wondered how he could help, and offered to write to the Rev. Barclay F. Buxton, who had been working at Matsuye, on the west coast of Japan, since 1891.

Though himself a C.M.S. missionary, he was the leader, by special arrangement, of a group of young missionaries not necessarily associated with the C.M.S. The D.O.M. knew Mr Buxton, and doubtless spoke very highly of Amy in asking whether she might join the party. With impetuosity which may have been born of true faith and not of impatience— certainly she was assured that it was right to take the step—she felt she should set out without waiting for time to receive Mr Buxton's reply. So there was correspondence with the China Inland Mission, and it was agreed that she should sail on the P. & O. *S.S. Valetta* on March 3rd, together with three women missionaries of the C.I.M., and wait in Shanghai for Mr Buxton's reply.

The double parting—first, from her mother in Manchester, and then from the D.O.M. as the vessel left Tilbury—was painful in the extreme. "Never, I think, not even in Heaven shall I forget that parting. It was such a rending thing that I never wanted to repeat it. . . . Even now [1945] my heart winces at the thought of it." " I never knew how tears could scald ", she wrote to her mother, " till the last wave of your handkerchief disappeared today." In London there was a farewell meeting, at which Hudson Taylor, F. B. Meyer and C. A. Fox were present. Mr Fox wrote a farewell letter too, quoting II Corinthians 9. 8—" a Divine portmanteau already packed with all essentials ". At Tilbury the parting was cruelly protracted.

For an hour or so we were within a stone's throw. We sang " Crown Him " and " Like a river glorious ", and then " Crown Him " again and again. The D.O.M. and Mrs Campbell walked half a mile down the docks, and once again we were close to each other as we rounded the last corner—so close that we could give each other parting texts. [She quotes a sentence from an address at the farewell meeting.] " Jesus has two nail-pierced Hands. He lays one upon each and parts us so—*He* does the parting."

In those days the journey to Shanghai was in two stages, and it was necessary to change at Colombo. Second class on the *Valetta* was reasonably comfortable, and Amy seems to have been a good sailor—she truly enjoyed her first experience of a storm at sea. " Life on board is very rich in opportunities for quiet talks with one and another ", she writes from the Mediterranean. On the first Sunday a service was held in the second saloon, but the congregation dwindled as the weather deteriorated, and a gentleman from the first class rose and suggested that the Salvation Army ladies should address what Amy calls the " survivors ". " Finding *we* were indicated, two of us responded briefly, glad of an opportunity to witness for our Master." As time went on, she and one of the C.I.M. ladies had daily Bible Classes with a rather mixed group—an aristocratic but seemingly unconverted " Christian " Indian, a Chinese Christian from Swatow, a poor deck passenger from northern India who " had been decoyed away to the sugar plantations of the West Indies ", and an *ayah*. It was the deck passenger whose need moved Amy most, and he seems to have responded to the love of God in Christ.

They met many friends in Colombo, including the Lieschings, of whom she already knew a good deal. They " had hoped that I might join their circle ". But Amy was sure that no mistake had been made.

When they boarded the *Sutlej*, Amy found that their cabin was very tiny, and infested with rats, cockroaches and other insects. But it was possible to sleep on deck, and Amy painted a text for the cabin, " In everything give thanks ", with the initial letters of the various " plagues " in the corners of it.

Perhaps the chief joy on this boat was the Captain's conversion. " I am so happy about the Captain," says Amy in a home letter. " He told me it was seeing the reality Christ was to me, which drew him. My heart just sings every time I think of him."

It was an immense relief to find letters from Mr and Mrs Buxton awaiting her when she reached the C.I.M. Home in Shanghai. They offered her a warm welcome to Japan. "Everything has been planned by Him," she writes on April 14th. "They are losing three of their workers, a new province has been given to them, 1100 towns and villages, unreached, surround them. . . . This leap in the dark is a leap into sunshine after all." Mr Buxton wrote that he cared little for denominational differences, and stressed the Keswick motto, "All one in Christ Jesus". "As I am as much Church of England as anything else," Amy comments, "I don't fancy that will be a difficulty!"

She addressed several meetings of missionaries and others in Shanghai. "Many of the missionaries were stirred, and began to pray for the filling of the Holy Spirit—a personal Pentecost for service."

On April 25th she arrived at Shimonoseki, in the midst of a raging storm. She landed from the steamer in a small tug, and found that there was no one to meet her. The missionary assigned to this task by Mr Buxton was delayed elsewhere by the storm. "Of all funny experiences", she writes that evening, "this morning's was the funniest." One wonders if many other new missionaries would have seen the humour of it. She and her baggage were surrounded by Japanese, whose words sounded like gibberish. The rain pelted down, and she had no idea what to do, but she goes on, "I laughed till I was positively aching at the absurdity of the whole affair." She took shelter in a dark room, and for a whole hour tried to explain her predicament to the friendly but helpless crowd. Then an American "happened" to pass by, and sent her in a rickshaw to the American missionaries with whom she and her escort were to stay. It was an experience which partly explains the meticulous care that she took in arranging for new arrivals at Dohnavur to be properly met.

She made light of these circumstances, but she never forgot a talk with a fellow-missionary on the beach at Shimonoseki before she went on to Matsuye. "Grey sea and grey talk," she wrote in her *Daily Light* for April 28th, and in private memoranda prepared long years afterwards for the

Dohnavur Family she explains a little of the shock that came to her.

As we walked along the sea-shore she mentioned casually something which led to an astonished question from me. And then she said—and the words chilled my very heart— " You don't mean to say you think that all missionaries love one another? " Of course I had thought they did. I had never dreamed they didn't. . . . No faintest foreshadowing of the purposes of God was mine that morning . . . but I remember the thoughts that rushed through me then. What of " See that ye love one another with a pure heart fervently? " Was such a life of love lived *nowhere*? And I did earnestly ask for the love about which our Lord spoke on the evening before He suffered. That evening so long ago in Jerusalem, and yet so present with us now, and that morning fifty-six years ago by the shore of Japan, are for ever linked together in my mind.

She reached Matsuye on May 1st. Nothing was lacking in the welcome of her fellow-missionaries. She always spoke of Mr Buxton with an affection akin to reverence. " Barclay F. Buxton," she writes,* " a name that for me and many others wears a little crown of light."

From her home letters and the book, *From Sunrise Land*, published in 1895, and long since out of print, a few incidents must be selected which have significance from the point of view of her preparation for a life-work in a very different land from Japan.

How little she guessed that in less than fifteen months she would have left Japan, never to return. But God knew it, and surely that is why He permitted her to plunge so boldly and hastily into the work. For the fact that strikes one about the brief period in Japan is the work for eternity which was actually accomplished in those few months. It was indeed a time of training for her, but her Master sent her to reap as well as to sow. Yet both sowing and reaping were by interpretation. She was touring in the villages with Misaki San, a young Japanese woman who proved to be a true helpmeet, within a few weeks of her arrival at Matsuye, and language study was fitted in between itinerations. It was not a method that she approved for others who joined her in Dohnavur in later years, nor did she follow it herself when God brought her to India. Even in

* *Though the Mountains Shake*, p. 201.

Japan she and her friends noted rather wistfully the marginal reading of Genesis 42. 23: " They knew not that Joseph understood them, for *an interpreter was between them.*" Yet in spite of a strong bias against the principle of a recruit spending the first year or two in anything but the hard grind of language study, the chronicler of these pages believes that he will carry his readers with him in suggesting that Amy was a unique person who could not always be judged by ordinary standards. And writing to her mother from Matsuye a few months later, she expresses herself strongly against any other member of the family coming out to Japan unlinked with a recognized missionary society. " Unless God guides definitely to an unlinked coming out, such as ——'s and mine, I never would advise it. In more ways than one it is trying." Rules based on experience in many fields are not to be lightly disregarded, but Amy was a shining example of the rare exception that justifies itself—or, rather, that God justifies.

For God set His seal upon her ardent ministry, and if the method of soul-winning by interpretation raises doubts in our minds, we have none at all concerning her identification with the people. If her words were halting they knew that she loved them. One evidence of it was the wearing of Japanese dress. It was the custom for women missionaries to wear the *kimono* on Sundays, but there came a day when Amy was visiting with Misaki San.

> We went to see an old lady who was very ill. She had not heard the Gospel before, but was willing and eager to listen. So I spoke and Misaki San translated, and our hearts prayed most earnestly. " Lord Jesus, help her. O help her to understand and open her heart to Thee now."
> She seemed to be just about to turn to Him in faith when she suddenly noticed my hands. It was cold weather and I had on fur gloves. " What are these? " she asked, stretching out her hand and touching mine.
> She was old and ill and easily distracted. I cannot remember whether or not we were able to recall her to what mattered so much more than gloves. But this I do remember. I went home, took off my English clothes, put on my Japanese *kimono*, and never again, I trust, risked so very much for the sake of so very little.

It was through this incident that the wearing of Indian dress became part of the Pattern for the Dohnavur Fellowship.

Nothing was further from my mind than to influence others in this direction. But does it not look as if even this tiny incident had been planned by One to Whom nothing is small? The touch of that old lady on my fur gloves set free, though I never imagined it, thousands of hours of time; for the saving of time is great when a company of people live for many years without having to spend any time in giving thought to their clothes. And it set free hundreds of pounds; for the saving of money is also great, when at a stroke all the extras of dress are cut off, and nothing need be spent on them. And all this time and money saved has meant just so much the more to give to Him Who gave us all. But more than that, as I believe, it led to the opening of doors never opened before. It would have been impossible for one in foreign dress to go to the places to which I had to go if I were ever to discover the truth about things in India. And more, far more than that, it opened doors to hearts. If any question that, I can fall back on this: it made it just a little less easy for the great enemy to distract a soul who was drawing near to its Saviour.

Another strand in the Pattern is the avoidance of the use of pictures of our Lord. In Japan, as in India, they were in constant use.

One day, I heard a little girl talking about magic-lantern pictures which were to be shown that night. " They will show their God ", she said. I had just enough Japanese to understand those words and they startled me.

Soon afterwards I was staying with Japanese friends in a village when my mail forwarded from Matsuye came in. Among the magazines was *The Christian*. There was an article in it by Professor Wallace of Dublin. It was about the pictures of our Lord. He felt that, as the Divine could never be painted, such pictures were untrue. Soon after I had read this my host came into the room. He pointed to a picture—it was a copy of a famous one of the Head crowned with thorns which someone had given him, and he said that he was feeling that " to the Father, pictures of His Son are not good ".

For a while I pondered this. I remembered how a very beautiful picture of our Lord, hung alone in a room curtained with crimson velvet and treated with great reverence, had impressed me as a child. I remembered the story of Zinzendorf and the picture of the Crucifixion.

This have I done for thee,
What hast thou done for Me?

And yet here, in this pagan land, where a child could say,
" They will show their God tonight "—was this the place to
use such pictures? And my heart answered, No, I cannot
use them.

Some of you will know how strange this thought appeared
to fellow-missionaries in India, where the use of pictures is
almost universal. I never tried to influence anyone in this
matter, only I did not use them myself. But soon several
others began to feel the same, and among them was Walker
Iyer. And when converts were given, we found that unless
they were taught to do so, they did not want pictures of the
Lord Jesus Christ. And you, who have been brought up
without them, know when you do happen to see them how
much less beautiful such pictures are than the one the Holy
Spirit had shown you. I shall never forget the disappointment of one of you when someone sent you a lovely little
picture of our Lord as a Child in the Temple. I remember
the tears of disappointment when the string was untied, and
the wrappings taken off, and the picture taken out of its
box—" I thought He was far more beautiful than that! "
We may safely leave the blessed Spirit to show to the people
to whom we speak, something " far more beautiful than that."

You will see, I think, how much more this casts us upon the
Lord, the Spirit, when, for example, we are telling of the
Crucifixion. A picture would greatly help to make it clear.
But I know as we trust the Spirit He does not fail us. I have
told that awful story to many a woman and to many a child
who have never heard it before. And I have seen what He
can do, and what He does. O blessed Holy Spirit, forgive
us if we have ever doubted Thy power to take of the things of
our Lord Jesus Christ and shew them unto us, and unto all.

In August the Matsuye Band were at Arima, one of Japan's
sacred mountains, attending a Missionary Conference. " I
never knew ", Amy writes to her mother, " that such need for
real consecration meetings could exist on the Mission field.
But we are here just what we are at home—not one bit better—
and the devil is awfully busy. . . . There are missionary ship-
wrecks of once fair vessels."

It was at Arima that she faced a personal question. Was it
perhaps that someone had begun to show that he cared for her,
and that, while others might be led differently, she had begun
to discern already that marriage was not in the Lord's will for
her? On August 20th, more than forty years later, she wrote
a very private word to one of her " children " in Dohnavur.

On this day many years ago I went away alone to a cave in a mountain called Arima. I had feelings of fear about the future. That was why I went there—to be alone with God. The devil kept on whispering, " It's all right now, but what about afterwards? You are going to be very lonely." And he painted pictures of loneliness—I can see them still. And I turned to my God in a kind of desperation and said, " Lord, what can I do? How can I go on to the end? " And He said, " None of them that trust in Me shall be desolate." That word has been with me ever since. It has been fulfilled to me. It will be fulfilled to you.

She gives an evasive answer to a question in one of her mother's letters, whether she loved " anybody very much ". But more and more her heart was satisfied as she shared with the people not the Gospel of God only but her very life, because they were dear to her.

O for a passionate passion for souls,
   O for a pity that yearns!
O for the love that loves unto death,
   O for the fire that burns!
O for the pure prayer-power that prevails,
   That pours itself out for the lost!
Victorious prayer in the Conqueror's Name,
   O for a *Pentecost*!

Written in Japan, January 1894.

CHAPTER VIII

IN AND AROUND MATSUYE

In the margin of Amma's *Daily Light* for July 14th are the words,
" God's power in casting out the Fox spirit, Matsuye, 1893 ".
This is how she tells the story in her autobiography:

After a while spent very happily with the Buxtons I lived
with two others of our party who had a house at the further
end of the town, and soon after I went there we heard of an
old man who was possessed by an evil demon. As in India,
so in Japan, people might live in the country for years and
never once even hear of, much less come across, this kind of
thing. It was in the purpose of God that it should come my
way, therefore it was so. The man who, as the people believed, was possessed by the Fox spirit lived in a street near
our house. He was in a very desperate condition. When we
were told of this, words I had read often came to me as if
they were new: " All power is given unto Me. . . . These
signs shall follow them that believe; in My Name shall they
cast out devils."

Misaki San and I read these words together and we prayed,
and waited upon the Lord. Then, full of confidence that the
power of the Lord would cast out the Fox spirit, we asked if
we might see the man. We were taken to an upstairs room
where he was confined. He was strapped and bound to two
heavy beams laid crosswise on the floor. His arms were
stretched out as if for crucifixion. His body was covered
with burns. Little cones of powdered medicine had been
set on his skin and lighted. They burned slowly with a red
glow. That alone, one would have thought, was enough to
make him mad; but it had not been done till all other means
known by his people had been tried in vain. The idea was
that the fire would drive out the Fox spirit. We had been
told that he was possessed by six Fox spirits; but that was
nothing to what the man had who said, " My name is
Legion, for we are many."

With confidence, then, we told the old man's wife and the
relations who crowded round, that our mighty Lord Jesus
could cast out the six Fox spirits. But the moment we named
our Saviour it was as if a paroxysm of rage filled the poor
man, he raved and cursed and struggled to get at us. The

men in charge of him held him down and covered his face with a cloth. We were hurried out of the room.

The poor wife followed us to the door. She spoke not one word of reproach, but she must have felt reproachful. As for me I was utterly bewildered and ashamed. It was as if the Name that is above every name had been shamed. What should we have done—stayed and said, " I command thee in the Name of Jesus Christ to come out of him " ?   As we turned to go a sudden quickening of faith was given, and, my Japanese sister interpreting for me, I asked the wife to let us know when her husband was delivered from the power of the Fox spirit, " for our God will conquer, and we shall go home and pray till we hear that He has ".

Within an hour a messenger came to say that the foxes were gone, the cords were off. He was asleep.

Next day he asked to see us. He was sitting quietly with his wife, a well man. Except for the unhealed burns there was nothing to show what had been. He sent for flowers and someone brought a branch of pomegranate in flower. He gave it to me, and I don't think I ever see a pomegranate flower without seeing that old man's face, so courteous and so calm.

Most of our Matsuye workers had by this time gone to a cooler place among the hills of Japan and we had been told to follow; but we knew we might wait to teach that old man, and we did so. His family were strict Buddhists, but they were so grateful that they did not prevent us doing this. (They sent privately to ask our servants if there was any special food we foreigners liked. They wanted to send us something nice.) It was some time before they understood that it was not we who had cast out the foxes, but the Lord Jesus Christ, Whose very Name had been so abhorrent to that old man, or to those spirits who made him their home, on that first dreadful day.   In the end he at least understood it, and he did, we believe, come to that mighty Saviour in faith, and trust himself to Him.

This happened in mid-July. Towards the end of September when we were in the ancient royal city of Kyoto, more than a hundred miles away, we heard that the old man had died of malarial fever. His wife told us afterwards how he died. He had been very peaceful. He died with his New Testament clasped in his hands.

Those of you who remember Chelliyer of Chettimedu,* and especially those of you who went to the village with me at night and saw him bound with a thick rope and thrashed

---

* Sometimes called the Village of the Merchant, close to Dohnavur.

with a heavy stick to drive out the Pig spirit, know that the power of the Lord is as present to heal in India as in Japan. Do you remember how Chelliyer brought the great stick and the coil of rope and laid them on the table in the Praise Hall where we had prayers? * But I think I was taken to that upper room in Japan to learn in such a way that I could never forget, that nothing was impossible to the God of the Impossible, no, not even the salvation of children from the central citadel of Satan. And also this: that when deliverance was wrought and a child was saved from the strong man's house, by a Stronger than he, my heart's word would always be Joseph's to Pharaoh, " *It is not of me.*"

The story of Hirose is also told best by herself:

The first place in Japan which I really loved was Hirose, a large, almost purely Buddhist village. The eight or nine Christians there, fruit given to Matsuye workers, were scattered in that dark village like stars in the night. Before going for the first time I spent a day alone with God. The thought had come, if only I could be sure of what He wanted me to ask for, then I should have no doubt in asking for it. So I wanted to take time to know His mind.

At last I seemed pressed in spirit to ask for a soul, one soul. Next day Misaki San and I set forth together. One young silk weaver gave up a day's weaving that she might have time to listen and understand. She crossed the line that evening. That joy is alive in me now.

A month passed and we went to Hirose again. This time it was laid on my heart to ask for two souls. Three others joined in this prayer. When we reached the village the young silk weaver, saved in November, brought another. She had just found peace when we were called to go to an old woman who wanted to hear. She also turned to the Lord. These we left in loving hands, for there was a dear old Christian there who was a true under-shepherd, and in Japan, unlike India, no one was turned out of the house because of being a Christian.

A fortnight later we went again. *Four souls* had been laid on our hearts. By this time our fellow-workers in Matsuye were much with us in prayer. The rickshaw ride was through deep snow, and we arrived cold and tired. Very few came to the meeting. The Christians felt four too many to ask for. And where were they? We did not know.

Next day we were out visiting most of the day. We found

* It is remarkable that Mr Gurney Barclay, a missionary from Japan, and a nephew of Barclay Buxton, was visiting Dohnavur when this took place and remembers the man coming in during the prayer meeting.

no one the least interested. One could almost see the devil, one could almost hear him laugh. And then came thoughts, the wiles which cling, and twist, and entwine one. " So much for being sure of the Shepherd's Voice. Next time better wait and see, before telling everybody. You can't expect conversions every time you come. It's quite presumptuous. Fancy going back to Matsuye empty-handed! What a pity you told them about the four." But worst of all was the fear that I had missed His will after all. It looked very like it.

The afternoon, upon which I had unconsciously counted so much, was gone; I was at the very end of my resources. Prayers and pleadings alike seemed to rebound like balls hitting a stone wall. The listeners sat and gazed and smiled, and felt nothing. With a sort of blind longing to rush away into the darkness and lose oneself in the snow, and forget, I was rising to bow myself out of what seemed like a prison of mocking spirits, when there was a sudden sense of a presence *gone*, of a Presence *come*. We sat down again, and a hush rested upon us. Then almost without preface one of the women, who had been listening carelessly before, said quietly, " I want to believe." While we were talking to her, a young man, her son, came in and knelt down. Within half-an-hour, mother and son were both Christ's.

Then we came away, and as we passed one of the Christians' homes, we went in to tell them. They said they had one more waiting for us at the preaching room : would we go to see her at our honourable convenience? She was another brought by our first, and she, too, trusted the Lord Jesus, and was saved.

By this time all the Christians had assembled. We told them we knew God's fourth must be somewhere, and one man exclaimed, " Why, it must be my wife. She wants to be a Jesus-person, but she is away at her own village." Next morning early a message came to say the wife had unexpectedly returned. We went to see her. Before her family and relations she confessed her desire to be a Christian, and there and then she too " was illuminated ". And they all, with one consent, praised the Lord.

These four were the first birthday gifts I ever had from heathendom. That day was December 16th, 1893.

Towards the end of January, 1894, we went to Hirose again. For a fortnight the pressure that I could not resist, had been on me to ask and receive according to 1 John 5. 14, 15 eight souls from among the Buddhists of Hirose—that was the petition then. And once again Matsuye stood behind us in prayer.

We found the Christians very happy about the one, two, and the four, but they were not prepared for this. To pray for things and not receive them " would be a very bad happening; better just pray for a blessing, then there would be no disappointment ". We offered to stay longer so as to give God more time to find the eight, but they said they could not arrange for more meetings. No, better be content with a blessing. But

> Whoso hath felt the Spirit of the Highest,
> Cannot confound, nor doubt Him, nor deny.

So we read the great prayer promises with the group of Christians, and the dear old under-shepherd said slowly, " You are a Jesus-walking one; if His voice speaks to you, though it speaks not to us, we will believe." And then, opening their Bibles at Jeremiah 32. 27 and 17, they kept them open there, and prayed. Before they left the room we were all of one mind.

It would take too long to tell how the eight were given. It was like watching an invisible Hand at work. The last was a proud old grandfather who for fifty years had been a slave to sin. Kneeling before all he prayed, " Honourable God, deign to forgive me, deign to wash." It was nearly midnight (meetings are late in Japan), but it felt like the dawn of the morning, so happy and fresh of heart were we.

And afterwards? I wonder if you feel the almost breathless feeling that was mine as I prepared to go to Hirose in February. Would sixteen be the number laid on me to ask? No, there was no number at all laid on my heart. I think the Christians were surprised. They had been so keyed up with the joy of the eight that they were ready for anything; but instead of that we were led to have a time of prayer with them all, Christians and any Buddhist friends who had come with them. At the end they separated into two groups. The Christians drew together into a corner and prayed, and the Lord hearkened. I do not know how many turned to Him for the first time that night. I only know that the Christians were too full of joy for speech, and we parted in a sort of singing silence.

Often in India I thought of Hirose and longed with a great longing to have an Indian Hirose. But it was never given. Perhaps it is that the Lord does not repeat Himself. Does He ever repeat the creation of a single blade of grass? He had other plans for me here. I have told you of that glowing time because it was part of the preparation for something that asked for far more faith than did the one, two, four, or the eight. And yet these fifteen were not without travail. But

I do not think that is a thing to talk about. And at most,
what did I know then, what do I know now, of what St Paul
meant when he said, " My little children, of whom I travail
in birth again until Christ be formed in you " ? There are
some words in the Bible that make one ashamed.

And here is a postscript. When Mr Gurney Barclay joined
his uncle, Barclay Buxton, at Matsuye fourteen years after Amy
had left Japan, he frequently visited Hirose. " I was able ",
he says, " to realize how firmly the converts of her time had
stood by their faith."

Two other incidents cannot be omitted. In *From Sunrise
Land* (pp. 142, 143) she describes a visit of " three thoughtful
well-educated lads ". They talked for an hour—they in broken
English, she in broken Japanese. Then she gave to each of
them an English New Testament, and as she wrote their names
in the fly-leaf, one of them said, " *It will be a seed*." And Amy
adds : " Will you not stop even now as you read this, and pray
an earnest ' Amen ' ? " An Oxford graduate named Paget
Wilkes, recovering from 'flu, read *From Sunrise Land*, and did
as the author begged. He stopped and prayed " five minutes
for these three souls ". Two years later he sailed for Japan,
as a member of Barclay Buxton's band, and three weeks after
landing in the country he met a young man named Kano and
led him to Christ. It was he who had said the words, " It will
be a seed." " How little did I guess ", writes Paget Wilkes,*
" that I should be the one to answer my own prayer ! "

And, finally, there is a section in the autobiography which
links Japan and India.

One evening when my Japanese fellow-workers and I
were visiting in the streets of Matsuye we found an entrance
to a house where three devout Buddhist men were preparing
for the evening worship. One, a thoughtful-looking man,
was arranging lilies before the family shrine. A lamp hung
before an idol which was smothered in chrysanthemums.
We had earnestly asked to be led to prepared hearts that
evening. The man who was laying the lilies round the
shrine seemed to have the heart prepared. Soon we were
reading to him from Romans 5. 10. " For if, when we were
enemies, we were reconciled to God by the death of His Son,
much more, being reconciled, we shall be saved by His life."
This is what he said : " True, true, it must be true. Buddha

---

* *Ablaze for God.* The life-story of Paget Wilkes, pp. 48, 49.

died; we know it. How can he help us, who live today? He may say, Be good; the power to obey he cannot give "— and he pondered the words, "saved by His life". Then looking deep into my eyes he said, "If this be so, you are as an angel from heaven to us; but if it be so we want to see it lived; *can you show it to us?*"

The question was asked almost under his breath, but my Japanese sister caught it. Was I sent to Japan partly that I might hear it? Some of you know how, when this Fellowship was being shaped, an old man in the village of S—— asked me that same question and in almost the same words. "We have heard much preaching", he said, "*can you shew us the life of your Lord Jesus?*" And you know how that question has held a light to Peter's summing up of our Master's life on earth: "God hath anointed Jesus of Nazareth with the Holy Ghost and with power: Who went about doing good and healing all that were oppressed of the devil; for God was with Him. And we are witnesses of all things which He did." And you know, too, how we have been led as a Fellowship and Family to lay special emphasis upon what both Japanese and Indian called *shewing* the life of our Lord Jesus.

That twice-asked question comes home to me as I write it. How am I answering it?

Will not the End explain
The crossed endeavour, earnest purpose foiled,
The strange bewilderment of good work spoiled,
The clinging weariness, the inward strain,
     Will not the End explain?

     Meanwhile He comforteth
Them that are losing patience; 'tis His way.
But none can write the words they hear Him say,
For men to read; only they know He saith
     Kind words, and comforteth.

     Not that He doth explain
The mystery that baffleth; but a sense
Husheth the quiet heart, that far, far hence
Lieth a field set thick with golden grain,
Wetted in seedling days by many a rain.
     The End, it will explain.

CHAPTER IX

CEYLON—AND ENGLAND

JANUARY 13th, 1894, was kept as a day of fasting and prayer, with memories of the general call given on that day in 1892, and the call to Japan in 1893. How little did Amy imagine that she would be at Broughton Grange again on January 13th, 1895! But there are hints in her home letters which must have greatly concerned her mother. "I had a day of bad neuralgia, could neither think nor read, was just lying still waiting for it to go." And a little later at Hirose, when the eight were led to the Lord, "I could hardly think, with acute neuralgia." But she saw the Lord working, the eight were given, and then for a whole week she was unfit for work of any kind.

At length on May 4th she writes to her mother:

Perhaps you had better address my letters c/o the C.I.M., Shanghai, as the doctor wants me to go to China for a complete change this summer. . . . Don't imagine I am ill because I am ordered off. It is only that change of thought is a good thing sometimes, and one dare not risk head trouble here. The climate is dreadful upon brain and eyes especially.

"Japanese head" is a well-known and very painful malady. It was not improved by a touch of the sun, when Amy was travelling on a small steamer, and a gust of wind blew her umbrella overboard. She arrived at Imaichi, her destination, but

suddenly comes a collapse on my part, and I find myself environed by wet towels, doleful faces, and a general sense of blurs. Therefrom emerging I asked them to pray—the meeting must not be missed tonight! You know the word in Isaiah, "They shall walk and not faint"? [she writes to the children much later] I took this literally, putting into it the meaning I wanted it to have—this is something no one should do, as I learned later—and I took that meeting. It did not end till very late. . . . This Imaichi work ended Japan for me.

But she did not know it. The parting from friends in Matsuye, and especially in Hirose, was a sad one. "One might be

going away for six years ", she says, " instead of six weeks."
Early in July she left Japan.

When she reached Shanghai she was obviously ill. " The
C.I.M. must have thought me a very bad penny to turn up like
that, but they were as kind as ever." Chefoo, on the north
China coast, had been suggested as a suitable place for a holiday,
but there seemed to be no accommodation, and in any case
was it likely that in a crowded hotel she would get the rest that
she needed? She had her return ticket to Japan, though even
at the moment of buying it something had seemed to whisper,
" Get a single." Some of her friends in Matsuye had advised
her to go straight home to England, but, naturally enough, she
shrank from such a decisive step after so brief a period of service
in Japan. Altogether it was a dark time for one who had left
Shanghai with such high hopes fifteen months earlier.

But she was not forsaken. As she explains in a long letter,
written jointly to her mother and the D.O.M., it was laid upon
her, on July 18th, that God had work prepared for her in—
Ceylon! Not that Ceylon was necessarily to be her field from
henceforth, but that this was to be the next step. " I was to
gather that all would come straight and plain bit by bit, as I
obeyed in blind faith." Well, all did come straight, but at first
the thought startled her. " I was very much afraid of deception
and prayed much against it." Very wisely she spoke to Mr
William Cooper,* " an oldish man and fatherly ", who was
Deputy Director in the absence of Hudson Taylor and Mr
Stevenson, and she was encouraged as he and another friend
prayed with her " very earnestly and sympathetically ".

And yet—oh the many, many " Buts "—what will people
say? How strange it will look! Nobody will understand.
And then home thoughts that I cannot write down—fears
as to unsettlement of all your minds. Then like a swarm of
mosquitoes the unkind misjudging remarks that many would
make, and then, hardest of all, again and again fears about
those nearest and dearest. Through them all came calmingly
the assurance that, as to what hurt most, He would take care
of that, and as to others, one must be content to be misjudged.
He was. Then it was time to go to the Policemen—a meeting
I had been asked to speak at, and for some hours there was
total change of thought and a great rest—He had known and
so planned it.

* He was amongst the martyrs in the Boxer Year, 1900.

There were various small confirmations. She found she had brought sufficient clothing with her, even though the guidance to bring so much had seemed strange at the time—the cost of the passage to Ceylon was only £10, considerably less than the cost of the journey to Chefoo plus hotel charges there—several people felt that a sea voyage might be the best thing for her tired brain—she remembered that on her way through Colombo friends had said, " Perhaps the Lord will send you back again soon."

Even while she was writing this long letter, a friend who knew nothing at all of her exercise of mind came in and told her that Chefoo was a trying place for head trouble. Then she looked straight at Amy, and said, " I have been feeling lately that the Lord's leadings are often strange to our eyes. He thinks no more of sending us from country to country, than we should of sending a servant from London to Liverpool. It may involve leaving work that we had meant to finish, but that does not matter if He is sending us."

So she begs her dear ones not to be anxious.

Let us give Him the satisfaction of finding that He has some children who can trust their Father. As to not " seeing " the way, did we " see " when I started last time, simply following on? Everything came right, and so we are apt to forget that many a fear was raised, many a doubt expressed.

She quotes from Whittier:

> Nothing before, nothing behind—
>   The steps of faith
> Fall on the seeming void, and find
>   The Rock beneath.

Once have we proved it, twice we shall prove it. And as all life's training is just exactly what is needed for the true Life-work, still out of view but far away from none of us— *don't grudge me the learning of a new lesson.* I shall need it up There.

The next day she discovered that there were five Singhalese in Shanghai, and she went to see them, and borrowed a Singhalese language primer.

Then I asked my great Teacher to give me quickness to learn easily, and in a few minutes, without any effort as to struggling with a " won't-learn " brain, the queer characters had put themselves in.

(If the reader is wise, I think he will echo the words of Mrs Bell the Quakeress, " The Lord takes care of that sort of child.")

She sailed on July 28th, escorted by a kind C.M.S. missionary who was leaving China for Palestine because the doctor would not pass his fiancée for China.   He left her alone to rest, but seemed to be always at hand to move her chair out of the sun, from one side of the deck to the other.   In the margin of her *Daily Light* for August 2nd she wrote, " Very ill—fever—alone— kept—comforted ".   On the 8th she writes cheerfully to her mother.   She wonders if God would have sent her to Ceylon in 1892, if she had been quite ready.   " But I needed to learn some lessons first, so He sent me for training to Japan."

Before leaving Shanghai she had written to a member of a small group in Ceylon—the Heneratgoda Village Mission; but of course no reply had reached her, and it was a comfort to find when she landed in Colombo that she was expected.   In the margin of *Daily Light* for August 17th there is this comment on the words of James 5. 11, " The effectual fervent prayer of a righteous man availeth much " :   " On July 14th they prayed for someone to be sent to help them.   On July 18th He told me to go.   Came out here today, Friday."

The friend to whom Amy had written from Shanghai was the eldest of a band of young women working with a Mr and Mrs Liesching, friends of the Carmichael family.   Both husband and wife had died of fever within a few days of each other. " Those brave girls had never thought of giving up, but they had longed for a leader ", and Amy's coming was a wonderful answer to their prayers.

I went out to their village home, meaning to stay with them till the next step was made plain.   I truly wanted to be led step by step, but this step to Ceylon was still a little puzzling, for life in a cottage in a malarious jungle village did not seem to be likely to send me back to Japan strong and ready for the battle there.

You have seen the blue patch of feldspar in the middle of a piece of grey granite which was found in our Forest.   You know that you do not see the kingfisher blue shining in that grey stone unless you turn the stone in a certain way.   The time I spent in that village is like that blue patch of feldspar. Looked at in one way, you see nothing; looked at in another way, you see the lovely blue of love.

For the time was full of love. If love could have kept me there I should be there today. The workers were Burghers, descendants of the Dutch who had once possessed Ceylon and had intermarried with the Singhalese. They had the language perfectly and they were soul-winners, fearless in their witness. Once when a Buddhist woman was converted an angry man came to the cottage brandishing a knife. It was like an immense carving knife. A defenceless woman in a village near us had been stabbed to death by an angry man a little while before, and Jessie and Alice, the two eldest of the Mission family, were much afraid. But they knelt down on the floor, and I, of course, knelt with them and they prayed. I remember how hard it was to keep my eyes shut. I wanted to watch to see what that man was doing while Jessie and Alice prayed long prayers. When I at last opened my eyes I saw the man flourishing his knife over our heads, but as we looked up at him he changed his mind and went away.

It was not easy to read the letters that reached her from Japan. "Misaki San was piteously loving." But a cable from the D.O.M. advising against "joining" any Mission in Ceylon made her wonder if she had done wrong, and, a little later, a letter showed that he was seriously concerned, and she writes to her mother,

Something told me you would rejoice in my being here . . . but oh my heart aches and aches for the D.O.M. . . . Oh mother, this *was* of Him. How could I wait and hesitate when He said, "Go forward"? But I should have waited in letting it be known, until all was clear at the home end. I so trusted He would show it there as here—but it has not been so, and I see my wrongness and cannot be sorry enough.

One can appreciate the D.O.M.'s point of view. After all, Amy was a Keswick missionary, and he was responsible to the Keswick Mission Committee. What would they think of a missionary, supported from Keswick funds, leaving her chosen field and proceeding to another without waiting even for news of the proposed move to reach them, still less for approval of the move? No doubt he found it hard to reprove one whom he loved so dearly, but he tried to do it, and suggested the exact form of the explanation of her hasty action which should be given to enquirers. With her usual forthrightness she objected, and did not see that he was trying to shield her from misunderstanding. In October she wrote to her mother.

I think there will be puzzling muddles if anything but the real truth is said at home, as everybody here knows it, and before I heard what was " to be said " I had both said and written naturally and not forcedly or half-truthfully.   I simply say that I left Japan for rest and change, that when at Shanghai I believed the Lord told me to follow Him down to Ceylon, and so I came.

But she had made it perfectly clear that she must not be regarded as a permanent member of the Village Mission.

It may be He has only sent me here as a stopgap.   Part of a soldier's duty is to fill gaps, you know.   One must as willingly be nothing, as something.

Meanwhile there was a marked, though only temporary, improvement in her health, and she emphatically rejected her mother's suggestion that she should come home.

Talk of coming home !   Did ever a soldier, worth calling one, run away at the first shot !   Praise Him—the pain is over now, and I am strong for the battle again.

With reference to her sister Eva, who was in training for South Africa,* she writes :

God knows what He is preparing her for in darkest Africa, so He knows how to do the preparing work.   The great lesson we can't learn too well is that of adaptability—the faculty of fitting oneself quite happily into one's circum- stances, be they ever so uncomfortable and changeable. . . . I would advise missionary candidates to practise balancing themselves on pinpoints—it will all come in useful !

She began to talk of the rest of her luggage arriving from Japan " in a year or so ", and meanwhile the D.O.M. was filling a box with clothing and other necessities.   But when she saw a doctor he was not so satisfied with her condition as she herself had been.   He talked of brain exhaustion, and advised complete rest.   Miss Gollock, of the C.M.S., who was then in Ceylon, a friend of the D.O.M., urged her to go home for six months at least, and after a struggle Amy expressed her willingness to go—if the Lord so led !   " However, I don't think He is going to lead that way."   In November she saw the doctor again.   He said she must not return to Japan, but

---

* She joined the South Africa General Mission in 1896, and served there for many years.

that she might stay and work in Ceylon. A return to England was not advisable at present, owing to " the extreme excitement that it would involve ". " Now all is settled," she writes on November 14th.

Mr and Mrs Barclay Buxton had been on furlough when Amy left Japan, and her letter of July 15th did not reach him till October 1st. He wrote at once to say that he could not question the Lord's leading.

> But what a blank for us! . . . I do thank God for His precious gift to us of having you with us for one year, and for all you have been in the work, and as an influence of love and union in our party. You have been, to us all, more than I should like to tell you. . . . Now you can look at our work at Matsuye from a distance. If you have any word from the Lord about it for me, do not be afraid to tell it plainly. I only want that we should be in the line of the work of the Holy Ghost.

Then suddenly, on November 27th, came a home letter reporting that the D.O.M. had had a stroke and was very ill. Amy set out for Colombo within an hour of the letter's arrival, borrowed some warm clothing from an old friend (Mrs Besant), and with the help of Mr Besant, who held an important position on the Ceylon Railways, she secured a passage to London, and sailed next day.

The journey was one long nightmare, but *Daily Light* was still her comfort. " There shall be a tabernacle for a shadow in the daytime from the heat, and for a place of refuge ", is one of the verses for December 1st, and she has written in the margin, " Indian Ocean, on the way home. In much fear, ill, and alone "; but on December 3rd there are the words, " Is anything too hard for the Lord? ", and the marginal note reads, " Realizing this ". She travelled overland from Brindisi to save time.

> I remember the kind angel in the form of a station official, who routed me out of the train in Rome, and put me into the train for Paris. I blessed that Roman angel. By this time I must have been ill, for there are long blank spaces. I came out of one of these to see an old Frenchman looking at me curiously. When he found I was going to Paris he offered to pilot me across the city, where we changed trains for Calais. And he did so. I thought of him as another angel— a French one. When my people at home heard of him they

said he might have been something quite different; but that thought had never come to me.

She had a rough crossing from Calais, but her mother met her in London on December 15th—the day before her 27th birthday.

> Again there are blank days. I see the loving faces of Keswick friends, to whose house I was taken; and a doctor's face; and the feel of, " I must be well, for I must go to Broughton Grange ". So somehow I got my way and was at last with the D.O.M. again.

She arrived in time for Christmas, 1894.

His earnest love, His infinite desires,
His living, endless, and devouring fires,
Do rage in thirst, and fervently require
    A love 'tis strange it should desire.

We cold and careless are, and scarcely think
Upon the glorious spring whereat we drink,
Did He not love us we could be content:
    We wretches are indifferent.

'Tis death, my soul, to be indifferent;
Set forth thyself unto thy whole extent,
And all the glory of His passion prize,
    Who for thee lives, Who for thee dies.

TRAHERNE (17th Century).

Amma frequently quoted these words.

CHAPTER X

TO BANGALORE

CONCERNING the first nine months of 1895 there is strangely little information. Amy spent the major part of it at Broughton Grange. " Friends were very forbearing and forgiving," she writes. " The D.O.M. recovered, and when he knew it must be so, gave me up again. But no doctor would pass me for any tropical land."

The letters from Japan were collected and prepared for publication, and Amy's first book, *From Sunrise Land* —the first of a very long series—appeared, and ran into a second edition that same year. It was illustrated from some of her own sketches, and the D.O.M.'s son, William, contributed others. There is no doubt that its main purpose—the stimulating of vital prayer for Japan—was fulfilled, but in later years Amy did not feel happy about it—as a book. This was her comment in one copy: " Bad rhymes in parts, bad writing all through " !

In the spring there came a letter from a friend * in Bangalore, South India.

> She said the climate was healthy, delightful in fact; it might be possible to live there even if China and Japan and the tropics were taboo. This appealed to my people, though not to me; it sounded much too easy. But I wanted to do whatever would lighten things for those who found it hard to see that I should go anywhere; and in the end it was settled that if the C.E.Z. would take me in spite of the breakdown in Japan I should go to Bangalore. They had a mission station there and a hospital.

So in May she went up to London for interviews with the leaders of the Church of England Zenana Missionary Society, and ultimately she was accepted by the Society at an informal committee meeting held at Keswick on July 26th. Doubtless she was warmly recommended by some of the Keswick leaders, who were Anglican clergy, and of course it was understood that

---

* This friend was sister-in-charge of the C.E.Z. Hospital. Later she married the Rev. E. S. Carr of Palamcottah.

her support would be found by the Keswick Mission Committee, but none the less it argues a refreshing breadth of
sympathy in the members of the C.E.Z. committee that they
accepted a non-Anglican for a purely Anglican society.

Amy spoke at the missionary meeting held in the big tent
on the following day, July 27th. In *Keswick from Within* the
Rev. J. B. Figgis refers to this gathering. " Who can forget
Miss Amy Wilson Carmichael's farewell address, ere she left
for her life of sacrifice in India, as she unrolled a ' ribband of
blue ' with the golden words, ' Nothing too precious for
Jesus ' ? "

The D.O.M. had the joy of her presence with him on August
9th, his seventieth birthday. Then all too soon came what she
calls " the blistering days " before sailing—the parting from
her mother and sisters on September 30th, and (after a few
days in London) from the D.O.M. on October 11th.

The writer of this life of Amy Carmichael prefers to be a
chronicler rather than a commentator, but did ever a prolonged period of missionary service begin so quietly, almost
casually? The call to service had been clamant, overwhelming, but there was apparently no very distinct call to India.
If either the land or the people drew her there, the fact is not
recorded. Yet she remained in India from the day of her
arrival, November 9th, 1895, until the Lord called her to
Himself more than fifty-five years later—on January 18th,
1951, and she loved India as few have loved it.

Amy was detained in Madras for three weeks. The C.M.S.
Secretary, a Mr Arden, asked her to stay with his elder daughter
Mary, while he and his younger daughter Maud went to
Ootacamund (a hill resort in the Nilgiris, called " Ooty " for
short).

> Mary, Maud, and I had some time together before Mr
> Arden left and one day towards the end of the first week
> one of them said, " You have been here for a week and you
> haven't said one word about the Lord Jesus Christ." I shall
> never forget the reproach in her voice, or how deeply I felt
> the rebuke. It was true that I had not said one word. The
> girls were like butterflies, pretty and dressy, and I had
> been shy of them both. I had no idea they cared for the
> things of Christ, and had thought I should wait till I knew
> them better before speaking of these things. But they told
> me now that they had been converted a little while ago and

were hungry. The friend who had led them to Christ had said I would be coming by the next boat and that I would help them. So all the time that I had been thinking of them as pretty butterflies they were really hungry lambs. I have never forgotten the shame of that hour. But we have a forgiving Lord. He gave us a wonderful time together. We rode together, read together, prayed together. We became fast friends. One day Maud and I went into Mary's room and found a great heap of finery on the floor. " I don't want it any more ", she said. We had never once touched on the world and its ways in our talks. We had not read 1 John with its straight teaching about such matters. We had spent most of our reading time in the Song of Songs, a book the D.O.M. used to read every Sunday evening. Mr Buxton had loved it too, and I learned to love it. " How great is His goodness and how great is His beauty " is the sum of that Song. And Mary had seen His goodness and His beauty.

She was soon to see Him face to face. Just before the Gates opened to her, Maud bending over her heard her say, " Glory, all glory ! " So she passed on.

Maud, the younger sister, became one of the dearest of the many dear friends who gathered round this work in its earliest days and prayed for you. " Give me the naughtiest ones ", she used to say; and I gave her the naughtiest. They are not naughty now but valiant in love and service. One of her last joys on earth was hearing about them. A little while ago she too passed on. What a lovely company is There—all loving, all beloved.

One other memory of those first weeks was the question of a young fellow-missionary, who had been writing a story of a Muslim girl. The girl wanted to be a Christian, but the parents forbade her. When the story was sent home, emphasizing the power of Islam, and leaving the girl still bound by it, those responsible in England wrote and told her that it would be too discouraging to home supporters if the story ended thus. So the question was, " Is it right to invent a happy ending? " The daughter of David and Catherine Carmichael had no difficulty in answering this question, but she was horrified that it could ever be put, " that any one could feel it right to play with truth, or paint it to make it more interesting. And that night I resolved that if I ever had to write a story I would not change one word to please anybody. God helping me, I would be very careful about truth."

Amy arrived in Bangalore on December 4th, in the throes of dengue fever. The friend who had written the letter met her at the station, and said, " You look as fresh as a daisy ! " But when it was discovered that she had a temperature of 105° she was, of course, sent to bed and cared for most efficiently. Dengue often leaves a long aftermath of depression.

> For the first time in my life I knew what it was to wake up depressed, and all day long to feel low and grovelly and wormy, not in the least a soldier. The first birthday in India [December 16th] was one of these wormy days. No one, of course, knew it was my birthday, but in the evening somebody who had been given a garland tossed it through the open window to me, as I lay in a long chair. And suddenly, like waves, thoughts swept over me—birthdays at home; the first birthday in Japan; the letter that had come from one of the Matsuye workers—for I was in Hirose on that day —" I am asking for a marked blessing for you for your birthday gift ", and that " marked blessing " was the coming of the Four out of darkness into light. Oh, how different that had been from this that was today !

But God delivered her from self-pity—" of all things on earth the most insidious and pernicious ".

Looking back after fifty years, she felt that the other missionaries in Bangalore had been very considerate to the new arrival. But she was not altogether happy. For instance, one of the group was

> unfair and curiously dominating in certain ways and words. One day I felt the " I " in me rising hotly, and quite clearly —so clearly that I could show you the place on the floor of the room where I was standing when I heard it—the word came, " See in it a chance to die." To this day that word is life and release to me, and it has been to many others. See in this which seems to stir up all you most wish were *not* stirred up—see in it a chance to die to self in every form. Accept it as just that—a chance to die.

In various ways that first difficult year was a valuable time of training. She wrote in the margin of 1 Corinthians 13 an extract from a letter written by the friend who had invited her to Bangalore, and who sensed that the situation was not easy.

> The hardest thing is to keep cheerful (and loving) under little things that come from uncongenial surroundings, the very insignificance of which adds to their power to annoy,

because they must be wrestled with, and overcome, as in the
case of larger hurts. Some disagreeable habit in one to
whom we may owe respect and duty, and which is a constant irritation to our sense of the fitness of things, may
demand of us a greater moral force to keep the spirit serene
than an absolute wrong committed against us.

One must admit that Amy was a rather unusual junior
missionary.

Madcap was one of my names. I had a pony and used
to race the Residency carriage round the race course and
up the long hill that led to the cantonments near where we
lived.

The Resident in Mysore was the Queen's representative, and
it was considered most improper to race his carriage. It is
not recorded whether he saw the humour of it. " Dozens of
similar mad things I did ", she writes to the children. " So
don't imagine me the least good and sober-minded, for I
wasn't. I felt exactly as you feel sometimes, only more so."
The monthly " social evenings " arranged for the missionary
community would not have appealed to her in any case, but
there was one occasion that she could never forget. The
women missionaries were doing fancy work, while one of the
men read a paper on some missionary subject. During the
subsequent discussion the question was asked: Does any one
know of an Indian worker who would work if he were not
paid?

There was dead silence. The lady near me was busy
matching her silks. All the others went on with what they
were doing. Not one, so far as I could see, was astonished
or shocked by such a question. At last one of the men said,
" I must confess I don't ".
But I felt as if a thunderbolt had fallen in the midst of that
pleasant company. It wasn't that I thought the question
referred to those who could not work unless their expenses
were paid. To have one's expenses paid if one had not
money of one's own is apostolic. No, it was not that; it
was that no one in that room knew of any who (whether
they had pay or not) were working purely for love of their
Lord, who loved Him enough to work for love's sake only.
I remember nothing more of that evening, but I never
forgot that question and that answer, and above all the
general acceptance of that answer and what seemed to me

the general indifference. I had half expected that in the moment's silence that followed we would be on our knees in shame and contrition before our God. For if such things were true whose fault was it? But no, the discussion passed on to something else and there was a buzz of conversation, that was all. But I went to bed that night in much perplexity of spirit.

Another perplexity was the complete absence of converts among the Muslims of Bangalore, and what seemed to be a complete absence of expectation that a harvest would ever be reaped. Amy confessed her ignorance of the tremendous power of Islam—and of caste among the Hindus—but was not the power of God greater than the powers of darkness, even in India?

Some of the older missionaries asked her " to pray to be shown what prevented conversions—if anything did ". One obstacle (she felt most clearly) was that, since no Urdu-speaking Christian teachers could be found, Muslim teachers were employed in the Mission schools.

> For days I pondered this. I soon began to understand that, in many schools and colleges in India, Muslims and Hindus, and unconverted Christians, were used as teachers. This became a heavy burden to me, but how could I, so young to India and so much younger than the missionaries in charge, say anything about it? Gradually I knew I must say something. It was then that words which I should never have found for myself, took life for me: " Cease ye from man, whose breath is in his nostrils: for wherein is he to be accounted of? " These who were so much my seniors in goodness as in years, even they were not to be accounted of in comparison with Him Who had long ago spoken so solemnly through the book of Ezra about the kind of builders who alone could build His temple. He could not possibly have one rule for Ireland and another rule for India. In Japan the question had never arisen. No one would have dreamed of asking a Buddhist, of paying a Buddhist, to build the house of the Lord. Nor would a nominal Christian knowingly have been taken into the company of builders. " Gold, silver, precious stones . . . wood, hay, stubble "— surely the truth was inescapable? It was truly inescapable. At last I took courage and spoke.

Here surely is a principle which is basic if education is to be truly Christian. But even today there are few Mission fields where it is accepted. Rather is it regarded as an ideal impossible of attainment.

After this one is not surprised that "the beautiful air of Bangalore, with its many English people, 'delightful amenities', as they were called, and all else that made red-hot evangelism seem a thousand miles away", was alien to her spirit.

> I began to feel like a fish out of water, and such a fish is a discouraged creature. One day, when this feeling was upon me, a letter came from a Keswick friend at home. She wrote of the prayers that were round me, of the sure and certain faith she had that the Lord Jesus Christ had a special purpose in sending me to India. "Do not cool. Look to Him to keep you burning and shining." That letter was like a drink of cold water on a hot day. I can never be grateful enough for the tender mercy that brought it then.

For she was lonely in Bangalore. The other missionaries were kindly enough, but they were very busy and had their own interests. Her mail, so full of things that were vital to her, held no particular interest for them. Many years later she comforted a member of the Dohnavur Family, who saw her surrounded by the love of the Fellowship, by telling her the story of her acute loneliness in her first years in India. One day, she said, it became almost intolerable, and when her mail arrived she ran to her bedroom, locked the door, knelt by the bed, and—read the letters aloud, one by one, to her heavenly Father. And this sharing of all experiences with Him expelled the sense of loneliness. "Treat Him like that", she said to the younger D. F.* "Make Him your chief Love and Friend." That D. F. has been learning to do so ever since, with increasing joy and utter content.

But Amy gave herself very seriously to language study. She made a beginning with Urdu, but then, since no one else in the Zenana Hospital spoke Tamil, it was decided that Amy should begin to learn it—in order to be the Hospital evangelist! In April, 1896, she explains her failure to write as many letters as her family would have liked by the fact that she must give at least six hours a day to the study of Tamil—"a classic language, highly developed, which has three words, each

* The letters "D. F." stand not only for the Dohnavur Fellowship, but also for any individual member of the Fellowship.

expressing a different shade of meaning, for every one in Canarese " (the language of Mysore).

Miss Ella Crossley, who visited Bangalore with her parents quite early in 1896, remembers her room in the hospital, the texts on the walls and the motto, " Nothing too precious for Jesus ". Amy seemed to be surprisingly fluent in her use of Tamil even then.

Language study continued when she went to the hills— first to Kotagiri and then to Ooty. Her health was a frequent source of anxiety to her fellow-workers, and there were those who prophesied that she would not last more than six months in India. But it was at Ooty that she first met Walker of Tinnevelly. He was eight years her senior, and he had been in India for more than ten years. Even at Madras she had noted that " the mention of the proposed resignation of ' Walker of Tinnevelly ' always created a sensation ".* He was quoted everywhere, and she formed a mental picture of a " curious, extreme, a bit narrow-minded but scholarly parson ". When she heard that he was speaking at a convention meeting in Ooty, she took her Tamil grammar along, intending to study if the address proved dull. The grammar remained unopened, but when she was introduced to him after the meeting, and tried to explain that she would like to live in a mud hut among the people, and so learn Tamil properly, rather than enjoy the comfort of a bungalow, he told her she could not stand it for long and " there was not a glimmer of a smile " as he demolished her suggestion. She decided she did not like him at all—but she liked his wife, and when he urged that Tinnevelly was a better place for learning good Tamil than Bangalore, and offered to be her teacher, she asked to be allowed to move there in December.

This was the man who was to be her trusty friend and comrade, her Tamil teacher, her guide and adviser, until the Lord called him Home in August, 1912—and the Tinnevelly District was to be home for her until she too was called Home in 1951.

God used her at Ooty. At an afternoon meeting for young people an impression was left which more than fifty years have not obliterated. " We were all rather nervous as she asked some very searching questions ", but the questions went home.

* *Walker of Tinnevelly*, p. 172.

It was at Ooty, too, that God spoke to her through the ancient word of Genesis 4. 10: " The voice of thy brother's blood crieth unto Me from the ground." (The story is told in *Windows*, pp. 236, 237.) She was sitting under a wide-spreading tree with Tamil grammar and dictionary when she became conscious of the " unfolding sense of a Presence, a Listener. . . . And He looked for some to listen with Him " —to listen to the voice of our brother's blood crying unto Him from the ground. " Time ceased for the girl under the tree." All day long she sat, and " that day on the hillside coloured the years that were to follow and gave depth to them all ".

Writing on November 29th, on the eve of leaving Bangalore for Tinnevelly, she asks prayer supporters in Britain to give thanks for a girl who attended a Bible Class in English, and heard the call to village evangelistic work. Now, it so " happened " that Amy had felt led to pray that at this ordinary Bible Class God would touch and call someone for this very work. The girl was the daughter of Christians, and they consented to her proposal, impressed by the evidence that God's Hand was in it. This answer to prayer (reminiscent of Hirose days) stirred Amy to ask her friends to pray

that He may fit and choose out some Indian Sisters to work with us . . . only those who know something or are willing to learn something of definite trust in God for daily needs. Here it is most sorrowfully true that " What pay shall I get? " is almost always asked when Mission work is mentioned. Many say it will be impossible to get any on any other than the old lines. But it would roll away a great stone of stumbling if we could all answer . . . the invariable question, " How much do you get for coming to talk to us? " by saying, " We don't get pay. God supplies our needs through His servants . . . but we come for love of God and you." So do pray. Pray for the burning love— the life-consuming love—of the Master. Pray that Jesus' love—His own dear love—may shine and burn through the awful darkness of heathendom.

But her own service in India might easily have ended that very evening.

I was out driving with a friend in the moonlight, and she all but drove straight into a deep ditch. I saw the shadow of the deepness first, and pulled the rein sharply from her hand. The horse turned and we were saved—we should almost certainly have been badly hurt, perhaps killed, if it had not been for that.

This and another " almost-accident " a short time before made Amy feel

that a Force—powerful but not all-powerful—was resisting my going south. So you will know how the words in *Daily Light* for the morning I left Bangalore (November 30th, 1896), spoke to me: " My Presence shall go with thee, and I will give thee rest."

Lord Jesus, for me crucified,
Let not my footsteps from Thee slide.
For I would tread where Thou hast trod,
My spirit tender of the glory of God.

That glory which meant all to Thee,
Let it mean all, my Lord, to me.
So would I tread where Thou hast trod,
My spirit tender of the glory of God.

CHAPTER XI

PALAMCOTTAH AND PANNAIVILAI

WE have almost reached the point where place names can no longer serve as chapter headings. From Millisle to Bangalore we have followed Amy to place after place. The scene has shifted continually, and yet it has always been because the pillar of cloud was taken up that she was compelled to move. Even now, spending her twenty-ninth birthday in Palamcottah,* she could not know that her wanderings had ceased, and that she was soon to discover her life-work. For from December, 1896, she lived always in Tinnevelly District. The next few years were, indeed, full of strenuous preparation for that life-work, as she fought and won her battle for mastery of the language, and as she came to know and to love, and be loved by, the people; but at least there was no change of sphere. On the other hand, the chronicler's task is more difficult, partly because there is a wealth of material, from which careful selection must be made, and partly because he is writing for two classes of people—those to whom Amy Carmichael of Dohnavur is only a name, and those who already hold her in the highest esteem because they are readers of her books. Obviously the aim should be to avoid retailing stories which have already been better told in the great series of books from *Things as They Are* to *Though the Mountains Shake*, but to show that which the books so often conceal—the person who took root downward, deeper and deeper into God, and who bore fruit upward, to the praise of His glory.

Mr Walker kept his promise to coach her in Tamil, and he was an ideal teacher, clear and patient. In fact, it was over Tamil that they broke through the reserve which (though few

* Palamcottah has been for many years the centre of Protestant Christian work in the Tinnevelly District. It is across the river from Tinnevelly Town. We have retained the spelling " Palamcottah " and " Tinnevelly ", because these names are familiar to all who have followed the progress of the Gospel in South India. But both are mangled foreign versions of the Indian names (Palaiyam-Kottai and Tirunelveli), and the Post Office now uses the correct forms.

realized it) was a characteristic of both. At breakfast one morning she recounted a dream of an angel who had asked her, " How much do you want of the language? " " Enough to win souls ", she had replied, " and a little over." Walker's grave eyes could be merry at times, and the story appealed to him. " You *shall* have a little over," he said. On January 23rd, 1897, she marked the words " Take no thought . . ." in her *Daily Light*, and wrote in the margin, " Trusted about Tamil exam ". She sat for the examination about a fortnight later. Those who marvelled at her fluency and her wide vocabulary in later years find it difficult to believe that the language did not come easily to her. Half whimsically, but half seriously too, she used to relate how the words of Numbers 22. 28 brought comfort to her: " The Lord opened the mouth of the ass." " They shall speak with new tongues " was a promise which meant much to her when its fulfilment, as far as she was concerned, seemed painfully distant.

Meanwhile the Walkers had reached a turning-point in their own missionary service. Finding that his strong convictions concerning the growth of the Indian Church were not shared by the Home Committee, Walker felt obliged to resign his position as Chairman of the Council in the Tinnevelly District, and the Committee gave its blessing to the suggestion that he should move to the small town of Pannaivilai and give his whole time to direct evangelistic work. The transition from administrative work to the new assignment could not be made immediately, and thus Amy lived with the Walkers in Palamcottah during the early months of 1897, and went with them to Ooty for the great heat. As they grew in appreciation of one another, it occurred to Mr and Mrs Walker that Amy might join them in their double task of reaching Hindus in the untouched towns and villages, and helping the Christians who, if only they were spiritually alive, would shine as lights in the darkness. And thus it came about that, by agreement with the Bangalore missionaries, she was set free for work which in essence was very similar to that in which God had used her at Belfast, Manchester and Hirose.

Verses written by Walker in March, when Amy had another attack of fever, will show that by this time they were on very good terms with one another.

Who will not let me have my way,
But keeps me prisoner all the day,
And loves to tease and say me nay?
    *Annachie.**

Who plays the part of kinsman stern,
And makes my soul with anger burn?
It is that cold and taciturn
    Annachie.

Who steals my books of Tamil dear,
And hides them somewhere, far or near,
Nor will my earnest pleadings hear?
    Annachie.

And yet—who seeks my truest weal,
And does for all my sorrows feel?
It is my loyal, true and leal
    Annachie.

It was good for Amy to have found an elder brother. She
would listen to him when she would listen to no one else. He
did not hesitate to tell her if he thought she was headstrong,
following her own desires rather than the leading of the
Spirit. But when she began to wear Indian dress, he—almost
alone in the missionary community—approved and stood
behind her. Both would very gladly spend and be spent for
the souls of the people around them, and neither cared much
for the opinion of Europeans if the action for which they were
being criticized would draw one of those souls nearer to God.

It was a desperately needy area to which they had been
appointed. Friends of the C.M.S. in England, encouraged
by stories of mass conversion in the Tinnevelly District, had
begun to regard it almost as a Christian country. Even
Henry Venn, the wise and far-seeing Secretary of the C.M.S.,
spoke of it in 1861 as " in some respects the most advanced of
the missions of the Society ". But the conversions had been
confined to two castes amongst Hindus, one fairly high, the
other lower from a theoretical standpoint, though extremely
virile and progressive. There was no general breach in the
fortress wall of opposition to the Gospel presented by the higher
castes. (" Have any of the rulers or of the Pharisees believed
on Him? ") The Christian Church and the foreign missionary

* *Annachie* is Tamil for " elder brother ". Walker always called Amy
Tungachie, " younger sister ".

were alike regarded with lofty disdain, not only by Brahmans, but also by many other castes. Accessions to the Church were almost entirely from the same castes which supplied the original Christians.

Here is the substance of a letter from Walker to Amy in 1901. He was at Pannaivilai, and she itinerating with the Women's Band formed in 1898. She had asked for statistics of Christians in four villages. Of the first, called Great Lake in Amma's books because it is built on the shore of a wide sheet of water—which spreads also to the boundary of the Church and bungalow at Pannaivilai—he says that there had been one true convert in 1830. About 1850 there was another, and at the same time a number of lower-caste families " came over ". Most of them went back. There was another movement twenty or thirty years later, but when Walker wrote, only a few unsatisfactory " Christians " remained. One true believer, however, was the wife of the saintly Tamil pastor at Pannaivilai, the Rev. Isaac Abraham. Walker's notes are full of the expression " came over ", always in quotation marks, which convey his sorrowful doubts concerning the radical nature of the change.

The total number of Christian adherents might sound encouraging until it is compared with the total of the general population, or—and this is far more painful—until it is understood that many who " came over " were never born again, and that the Church consisted of second- or third-generation Christians as nominal as thousands of Church members at home.

With high courage and expectant faith the Walkers and Amy moved into the Pannaivilai bungalow in July, 1897. Amy had already visited the place immediately after taking her first Tamil examination. On that occasion the Pastor's wife had given her the words of James 1. 5: " If any of you lack wisdom . . ." Was it because of her halting Tamil, or did the old lady discover what she regarded as immaturity, or a tendency to abandon well-trodden ruts, in the adventurous spirit of this unusual missionary?

Amy seems to have been disappointed in the hope that the girl to whom God had spoken in the English Bible Class at Bangalore would be the first member of her Women's Band, but they certainly were a group whose hearts God had touched.

There was Leyal, the Pastor's daughter, Sellamutthu, a one-armed woman (called Pearl in early letters) who was Amma's faithful friend and comrade for forty-three years, Ponnammal (called Golden), one who never turned her back but marched breast forward, until she finished her course in 1915, and others who left the Band because of home duties, or, alas, because the standard was too high. But their places were filled by new converts, who grew in grace and in Christian experience by living with the team.

Ponnammal was a young widow whose father-in-law was a deacon of the Pannaivilai Church, yet he and his wife treated her as a household drudge, tolerated only for the sake of her little daughter—their son's child. But she was allowed to come to church on Sunday morning, and new life came to her through Mr Walker's preaching. After a time Mrs Walker persuaded the father-in-law to allow her to teach a Sunday School class, and so Amy met her, and, discerning her spiritual and mental calibre, coveted her for the Band. At length the old man's consent was given, but he wished he could have withdrawn it. " That *Musal* Missie "—they called her *Musal*, or " the hare ", because she moved so swiftly—" has beguiled us with folly ", he said.*

The Starry Cluster—for that was the name which Indians gave to the Band—worked in and around Pannaivilai in the hotter months, and itinerated when the weather was a little cooler. Travelling by bullock bandy they would camp near a village, and then fan out to surrounding villages. From soon after dawn until nearly midday they visited in the homes, and talked wherever there were women or children ready to listen. After the midday meal they rested and had a time of Bible study before issuing forth again. Sometimes the Walkers and the Men's Band were with them, and they joined forces for meetings in streets or open places in the late afternoon or evening.

Even before she asked it of them, they were ready to work without a stated salary. For the first month Amy had followed the usual custom of giving them *batta*, an extra allowance of money for every night spent away from home. But one day they came to the bungalow and poured out the *batta* on to the dining-room table.

* *Ponnammal, her Story*, p. 10.

They told me [writes Amy] that they had not needed it
and did not want it. At that time this was a new thing.
A new love had been kindled in those hearts—they glowed.
Thereafter it was never, " How much can I get? ", but always,
" How much can I give? How much can I do without,
that I may have more to give? " It was wonderful to see
this in a land where, as the proverb puts it, " Say *money*,
and a corpse will open its mouth." Can you imagine with
what joy we worshipped the Lord together?

This, however, was a private matter. But when, towards
the end of 1898, one after another of the Starry Cluster laid
aside her jewels, the sensation, particularly among the
Christians, was enormous. The wearing of jewels—ear-rings,
nose-rings, bracelets, necklets—is a universal custom among
Tinnevelly women. Jewels are a married woman's dowry,
and they are evidence of the husband's position and wealth.
Amy had said nothing about it. She was always chary of
interfering with Indian customs, and yet the conviction grew
that passages such as 1 Timothy 2. 9 and 1 Peter 3. 3, 4 were
relevant in India too. Then a young man whose wife was a
temporary member of the Band told her, as he walked beside
the bandy in which she and others were travelling, that jewels
were unsuitable for the kind of life which he wanted her to
live. She handed her jewels to him obediently enough, but
without any conviction that it was right to do so. But Ponnammal heard and saw what had happened, and when the
Band reached Pannaivilai, she quietly took off her jewels.
Sellamutthu did the same. " If I had loved my Saviour more,
I should have loved my jewels less," she said.

Ponnammal's relatives were furious, and public opinion in
the church was scandalized. Only the old pastor rejoiced
that there were those who would go to such lengths for Christ's
sake. When F. B. Meyer visited Palamcottah for a Mission in
February, 1899, he touched on this question without knowing
that it had become an important issue. The result was a
storm which amazed and grieved him. But there were a
few who responded, and either returned the jewels to their
families, or even gave them to be sold for missionary work in
China.

To Ponnammal it meant emancipation from the fear of
man. Moreover, it was soon discovered that, whatever
Christians might think, Hindus were not antagonized. Indeed,

they respected her the more because, as they said, there were no bounds to her devotion.

One practical advantage was that night journeys by bandy now became possible, for there was no fear of thieves. And when in later years the Dohnavur work grew, and a large company of girls were gathered there, members of the Robber Caste who, according to Indian custom, are subsidized as an insurance against attack, agreed to accept responsibility, but added, " If your girls were jewelled like others, we would not do it—no, not for lacs of rupees."

Of these results they could know nothing. They simply obeyed the Voice that spoke to them, their spirits " tender of the glory of God ".

Long my imprison'd spirit lay
Fast bound in sin and nature's night.
Thine eye diffused a quick'ning ray;
I woke; the dungeon flamed with light.
My chains fell off, my heart was free,
I rose, went forth, and follow'd Thee.

CHARLES WESLEY.

Fire-Words

" O God, my words are cold:
The frosted frond of fern or feathery palm
Wrought on the whitened pane—
They are as near to fire as these my words;
Oh that they were as flames! " Thus did I cry,
And thus God answered me: " Thou shalt have words,
But at this cost, that thou must first be burnt,
Burnt by red embers from a secret fire,
Scorched by fierce heats and withering winds that sweep
Through all thy being, carrying thee afar
From old delights. Doth not the ardent fire
Consume the mountain's heart before the flow
Of fervent lava? Wouldst thou easefully,
As from cool, pleasant fountains, flow in fire?
Say, can thy heart endure or can thy hands be strong
In the day that I shall deal with thee?

" For first the iron must enter thine own soul,
And wound and brand it, scarring awful lines
Indelibly upon it, and a hand
Resistless in a tender terribleness
Must thoroughly purge it, fashioning its pain
To power that leaps in fire.
Not otherwise, and by no lighter touch,
Are fire-words wrought."

CHAPTER XII

BATTLE

THE only language which comes near to describing the work in Pannaivilai is battle language. The enemy would not have been disturbed if the three missionaries and their Tamil co-workers had been content to sow the seed without any definite expectation of a harvest; but when he found that Mr Walker, on the men's side, and Amy, on the women's side, would be satisfied with nothing less than the deliverance of his captives, and when a few actually emerged from the dungeon, and stood forth unshackled, to the utter amazement of their relatives, his wrath knew no bounds, and his furious counter-attack was partially successful.

In the village of Great Lake, close to Pannaivilai, there was a Mission school attended by Hindu boys and girls. Their parents had little fear of any untoward result. No man of their castes, with two exceptions fifty or sixty years before, had ever confessed Christ as Saviour, and certainly no woman or girl. But the wife of the schoolmaster was a C.E.Z. Bible-woman, and she gave a Bible to a girl who had become a secret believer. She used to allow the sacred ashes to be smeared on her forehead by her elder brother, but she rubbed them off when he had gone. Gradually she came to see that it was impossible for her to be an open believer if she remained at home.* Yet family ties, and love of home, are at least as strong in India as in the West. "I cannot follow so far," was the word of one woman who heard and believed, but shrank unutterably from the inevitable consequences of accepting Christ's claims. Yet Jewel of Victory, as she was afterwards called, lay down to sleep beside her mother one night, and in the early morning was wakened (as it seemed) by the light touch of a hand, and a voice in her heart said, " Go! " It was three years since she had been outside the house, but the

* In this half-century the bondage of caste has been relaxed to some small extent, but it still remains true that there are very few caste homes in South India where a Christian girl could live if she refused to conform to idolatrous practices, and especially if she broke caste by being baptized.

103

angels were busy. No one stirred as she stepped over the
sleeping forms of her relatives, no one saw her as she ran down
the street and crossed the little river to Pannaivilai. Outside
the veranda of the Mission bungalow she cried, " Refuge!
Refuge! "

The Walkers and Amy had been established there less than
seven weeks, and of course they had never seen the girl. But
they did not hesitate. The bungalow is now a diocesan school,
and the upper room in which the Walkers used to sleep has
disappeared, but in 1898 that upper room was God's provision when the house was besieged by angry relatives. This
was only the first occasion of many when the Walkers gave up
their bedroom to Amy, and slept on the veranda at the foot of
the stairs.

The battle was on. There were stormy and sometimes
heartrending interviews, but the girl was firm, and after a few
days made her deposition to the head constable of the village.
Sometimes a rush was made, but invisible hands held back
those who would have carried her off and used any means
whatsoever to prevent her from breaking caste. If persuasion
failed, then violence would follow: beating, drugging, murder
—anything rather than the disgrace of an open confession of
Christ by a member of the Goldsmith Caste.

Jewel of Victory was preserved, but all doors were closed in
Great Lake village, and first the Mission school, and then the
teacher's house, were burned down. It was a victory for the
enemy when the Christian teacher put in a compensation
claim for an amount more than double his actual losses.

Yet within six months another girl of the same caste escaped,
and wakened the sleepers on the veranda as she clapped her
hands and cried, " Refuge! " Once again the bungalow was
besieged for days, but she would not be moved either by
threats or blandishments.

Later, when she was baptized, the Tamil Christian poet,
Krishna Pillai, chose for her the name " Jewel of Life ", even
as he had chosen " Jewel of Victory " for the first convert.

Things were happening among men and boys also, and the
first baptisms took place in Great Lake on Easter Sunday,
1899.

Jewel of Victory and Jewel of Life were sent later for safety
—and for instruction—to the C.E.Z. Converts' Home in

Palamcottah. But first of all they went to Ooty with Amy and the Walkers. It was yet another breach of missionary custom that Amy was determined to have the Indian children with her, but Mrs Hopwood of Ooty defied the conventions and made room for them. Not only in that year, but right on until she was called Home in 1912, she opened her doors to Amy and a growing number of Indian girls.

The village of Great Lake was closed, but God began to work in another village, called Uncrowned King, about seven miles to the north. The united preaching band—three missionaries and six Indians—camped on the outskirts of the village in the spring of 1899, and on the evening of March 16th a little girl of eleven, whose heart the Lord had already begun to open, heard the preaching near the main well of the village, which stands in a large open space, ideal for open air meetings. The child had been seeking for a god who could " change dispositions ", for she had a temper which flared up quickly when she was provoked, and she had tried in vain to change it. As she stood on the outskirts of the meeting, one of the Indian converts spoke of the living God. " He turned me, a lion, into a lamb," said he, and the phrase arrested the child just as she was about to go. The whole story is told in *Ploughed Under*, but Amma characteristically fails to stress the fact that Arulai (for that was her name), seeing Amma in Indian dress, was drawn to her immediately. " I knew that if only I could go to her, she would have a place in her heart for me." Could not this living God " cause the day to come that will bring us together, and she will be my mother and I will be her daughter, and she will teach me to worship Him? "

Dear Amma—she never understood how the love of God within her was so powerful a magnet that all through her life others were drawn irresistibly to her. It was little wonder that the Hindus began to call her " the child-catching Missie Ammal ", and they truly believed that she used some mysterious powder which drugged their children and made them long to be near her.

Certainly it seemed to Arulai's parents that she was bewitched, and they sent her to stay with her uncle in another village. He was a nominal Christian, but he observed caste rules so closely that they hoped contact with him would render the child immune to anything vital. When we mourn over our blunders as fishers of men, it is sometimes a comfort to remember that the devil blunders too. Otherwise he would never have allowed Arulai to know that Pannaivilai was the village next to her uncle's, and so one Sunday, as Amy sat on the floor of the church in her accustomed place by a pillar, little Arulai slipped in, nestled close to her, and came back to the bungalow after the service. And so began not only a tender and beautiful friendship, but an association of immense value to the kingdom of God, continued through over forty years, until Arulai's death.

Jewel of Victory and Jewel of Life had both been over sixteen, and therefore legally of age to choose for themselves. But Arulai was only eleven, and it was impossible to keep her at the bungalow without her parents' consent. For some weeks she was allowed to come for teaching. They could not believe that she would dream of breaking caste by becoming a Christian. Then they became anxious, and she was snatched away.

It was no new thing for Amy to pour out her love on those whom she was seeking to win, but I think she had never known such poignant pain as that which came to her when Arulai did not return, and rumour had it that she had " given up everything ", and even " rubbed ashes on her forehead ". Truly the Shepherd had found in Amy one whose persistence in seeking the lost was akin to His own, because inspired by His Spirit. She loved them—as far as an under-shepherd can—even as He loved them. It was not the formal variety of love which we, almost blasphemously, call " Christian ", for it was warm and living, the very opposite of anything mechanical or impersonal. Yet she never infringed the Bridegroom's rights. " He that hath the bride is the Bridegroom." Her love was the love of the Bridegroom's friend, but it was like His love, in that it loved to the end.

Nearly eight months passed—busy months in Pannaivilai and in itinerating with the Band. There were encouragements and disappointments. The " jewel " controversy continued to rage, but Ponnammal and a few others remained steadfast. One village girl who had responded with all her heart and was eagerly looking for a way of escape suddenly ceased to care. Almost certainly she had been poisoned, and she was never the same again. A small child was cruelly beaten and then spirited away to another village.   One of Arulai's boy cousins, about the same age as herself (who afterwards became a very valuable worker at Dohnavur), was tied to a pillar in a loft, beaten, threatened with pepper in his eyes if he did not renounce his faith in Christ.   An older cousin named Supu was also suffering persecution.

Amy was often up at night, imagining that some terrified girl had escaped and was waiting on the veranda.   But on a Sunday morning in November, as she longed rather than prayed for " some token for good ", there was a little sound at the door, the sun-blind was pushed back, and Arulai was there again.

There followed a time of serious illness.   Arulai's father was touched by Amy's care for his child, and by her honest endeavour not to make her break caste.   There were many anxious hours in the months that followed, but over and over again the father was restrained from taking the final step of removing her from Christian influence.   Amy sometimes heard her praying, " Don't let me go back to the dark, please, Lord! O let me live in the light! "   And the prayer was answered.

About this time, at the request of a missionary society, Amy wrote of her experiences.   She told of the great Undone, the thousands who had never heard, the thousands also who heard and showed not the faintest interest in the message, the Christians whose light was so dim (" if the light that is in thee be darkness, how great is that darkness! ")—in short, the facts concerning the work in south India.   But the manuscript was returned.   The Committee " wanted it altered a little to make it more encouraging ", so Amy put it into a drawer and forgot about it.   Then, towards the close of 1900, her friends from Manchester, Ella Crossley and Mary Hatch, arrived for a long visit.   They travelled with the Starry Cluster, and with the girl converts, Jewel of Victory, Jewel of Life and Arulai.   They had time to see below the surface of things, and they longed that Christians at home might have their eyes opened to the true facts.   When they saw the rejected manuscript, they begged Amy to allow them to take it home and see it through the press.   Eventually it was amended in detail, and enriched by Ella Crossley's photographs.   The book is *Things as They Are*, and Ella Crossley is the " Picture-catching

Missie Ammal" mentioned in it. It was not published till 1903, but the events took place in the years 1899–1901.

One wonders if even today the Christian Church really desires to know the truth about her missionary effort. Yet how can prayer be effective unless it is based on facts? The title, *Things as They Are*, is accurately chosen. It does not depict the "dark side", as some have suggested, nor the "bright side", but the plain truth. It was this book which made it clear to evangelical Christians the world over that a new prophet had arisen, and the burden that she saw stirred thousands to think and pray.

Meanwhile a move had been made from Pannaivilai to Dohnavur. At that time (1900) the intention was to stay for a few months only. It was a suitable place for Walker to teach a class of divinity students, and there was ample scope in the surrounding villages for Amy and the rest of the Starry Cluster to evangelize. As far as they knew, however, it was only a camping ground, and their belongings were left at Pannaivilai.

They were years of battle, but of deepening joy in the Lord, and in the work. The loneliness of Arima and Bangalore was past.

> Thy choice is best
> In Thy dear will I rest,
> And by and by
> Thou'lt satisfy.

So she had written in the margin of her Bible at Arima. But now there is another entry: " Satisfied, S. India, 1899 ".

Yet in 1899, and again in 1900, her heart was torn by letters from the D.O.M., and sometimes from his relatives, begging her to come home. He had had another slight stroke, and though his speech was largely restored, so that he took the chair at Keswick in July, 1899, yet he was becoming more and more helpless and dependent. He would write in one letter, " I hope thou wilt not let my present condition disturb any arrangements," and in the next, " Do thy diligence to come to me before winter "—words which she could never afterwards read without a pang. At Keswick, of course, there were those who felt most strongly that it was Amy's duty to return and minister to him, but one or two, such as C. A. Fox, reminded him of the desperate need in India, and of the Lord's solemn words concerning the cost of discipleship. " I could not be

sure ", Amy wrote to the Family long after, " that for me to be
with him would mean blessing or joy for him. If God wanted
me here and I was there, how could it mean that? And the
sense that He did want me here was upon me."

For instance, how could she leave Arulai? Her father
would immediately insist that she return home. She was not
yet baptized, and legally she was far too young to choose for
herself. It is easy now to look back and approve Amy's
decision. The loss to the work so soon to be initiated would
have been indescribably great if it had been deprived of
Arulai's forty years of noble service. Moreover, the D.O.M.
lived until 1905. If Amy had returned, could she have left
him again? Nay, it is even possible that her presence might
have prolonged his life.

It was an immense relief when he wrote on July 4th: " The
Master's Word was brought to me this morning early: ' He
that loveth son or *daughter* more than Me is not worthy of Me.'
' Bind the sacrifice with cords, even to the horns of the altar.'
No drawing back. Amen. May it be so in the strength He
gives. It is well to have some gift of value to present to Him
Who gave His *all* for our redemption. Praise Him." These
are noble words, and he meant them with all his heart, yet as
physical weakness increased and his mental vigour was also
impaired, the longing for Amy returned in full force. As late
as December, 1900, his son wrote, " Of course I know Father
expects you will come home, and is thinking about nothing
else, almost, all day." It was agony to disappoint him, and
she knew that in her own circle of Christian friends the great
majority would feel it was wrong for her to do so. But the
Walkers understood, and were behind her in faithful prayer.
It was another part of the training for her life-work.

PART II

THE WARFARE OF THE SERVICE

wherein Amma learned to know Christ, *in the power of His resurrection*, and in the fellowship of His sufferings.

When you have started forth towards your vision,
    When you have counted up the gain and cost,
When you have faced the old, old world's derision,
    Its scoffing tale of all endeavours lost;
When all is said, leave it the sane, wise clinging
    To proven ways you never can recall;
It has not heard your golden trumpet ringing. . . .
    O Pioneer, the end is worth it all.

When by your cause you stand, its one defender,
    And hear the jeers and anger grow more loud,
When greater men than you, grave-eyed and tender,
    Look on your lone defiance from the crowd,
Then, then the joy of battle surges in you,
    The splendour of the quite unequal strife,
And all the strength of soul and brain and sinew
    Proclaims that you will win, and this is Life!

Madness and pride?   Nay, never heed the shouting,
    The future's yours—can you not wait, O youth?
In your divine conceit you know, undoubting,
    That you have found a fragment of God's truth.
How shall you fail, how shall your faith diminish?
    —Faith less in self, than in your splendid dream?
You heard God speak to you, and at the finish
    Far in the East you saw your vision gleam.

MILDRED HUXLEY.

(Printed in the *Spectator*, 1912.   Amma loved the spirit of these
words, though they are not applicable in every detail.)

CHAPTER XIII

THE FIRST TEMPLE CHILD

On the sixth day of the month, at evening, the Dohnavur Family meets in the House of Prayer. Any little ones who have joined the Family in the preceding month are brought to the leader of the meeting and dedicated to the Lord, through Whose mighty power they have been rescued from an environment in which they could not have grown up pure and good. Then there is a time of prayer for children in danger. In quick succession, but not hastily or carelessly, members of the Family mention the names of Temple towns in southern India, and as each name is spoken all join in the petition, " Lord, save the children there! " Many hundreds have been saved in answer to those prayers, including the great majority of those who take part in them.

The custom—but the word sounds far too formal—dates back to January 6th, 1905, when it seemed as if Amma's hopes of saving Temple children were fading into nothingness. But it is linked also with an earlier date—March 6th, 1901—when the first Temple child escaped, and was brought next morning to the bungalow at Pannaivilai.* She was seven years old when she left the house of the Temple woman at Great Lake, crossed the water to Pannaivilai, and was found by a Christian woman outside the church. It was already dusk, and when the woman found that the child came from a Temple woman's house, and that she begged not to be taken back, she took her to her own home for the night. She went hungry to bed because she was a high-caste child and would not break caste by eating the kind woman's food. Preena—for that is her name—finds it difficult to remember how long she had lived in the Temple woman's house. Once already she had escaped and made her way to Tuticorin, where her mother lived. But the Temple women had followed her, and her mother unloosed her clinging arms and gave her back to them. They branded

* The story is told in *Gold Cord*, pp. 19 f., *Things as They Are*, pp. 161 f., and *Ponnammal*, pp. 32 f.

her little hands with hot irons as a punishment for attempting
to escape. Then she gradually understood that she was to be
" married to the god ", and though she was too young to
appreciate what was involved, and that the training in singing
and dancing was the prelude to a life of shame—" deified
sin ", as Amma calls it—she knew enough to shrink from it all.
Could she find her mother again and persuade her not to send
her back? The Temple women had tried to scare her with
talk of the " child-catching Missie Ammal ", and, in a dim,
confused sort of way, perhaps she felt that to be " caught " by
her would at least mean escape from the clutches of the Temple
women. But it was surely her angel who led her first to a
Christian woman, and then the next morning to Amma.
After that there was no more to be said. She loved Amma
from that moment. Fifty years later, when Amma was with
the Lord, she wrote:

> When I first came it was the early morning of March 7th,
> 1901, about 6.30 a.m. Our precious Ammai * was having
> her morning *chota*. When she saw me, the first thing she
> did was to put me on her lap and kiss me. I thought,
> " My mother used to put me on her lap and kiss me—who
> is this person who kisses me like my mother? " From that
> day she became my mother, body and soul.

Now the Walkers and Amma, and the Starry Cluster, had
been away from Pannaivilai for about a year. Walker had
paid his first visit to the convention of the Reformed Syrian
Church in Travancore, while the rest of the family had been
spending the whole time in Dohnavur and the surrounding
villages. Who planned it that they should return to their old
home in Pannaivilai on the very day when Preena took courage,
and escaped from the Temple woman's house?

The devil raged, for this was a child whom he had ensnared,
but what would have been his fury if he had known that this
incident would lead to the deliverance of hundreds of others, of
boys (eventually) as well as girls, and to the establishment of a
work whose ultimate value to the cause of Christ in India, and
in the world, only God Himself can measure?

Preena announced almost at once that she intended to stay
always, but Walker and the Tamil Pastor felt that a messenger

---

* " Ammai " means " true mother "—a more endearing term than
" Amma ".

must be sent to Great Lake, in order to verify her story, and it was not long before some of the Temple women appeared and actually announced, before they had had time to fabricate a story, that they were Servants of the Gods. But they produced no evidence that the child was theirs, and Preena herself was emboldened, after a talk with Arulai, to say before the big crowd that had gathered, " I won't go with them! " They mumbled something about writing to her mother, but the mother never appeared, and Preena has been one of Amma's Family ever since.

Miss Mabel Wade, the first European to join her in the children's work—she came in 1907—once asked Amma whether it had ever occurred to her that her life-work would be among children. At first she said " No ", but then she remembered a day long ago when she and her mother were sitting in a tea-shop in Belfast.

A little girl came and stood near the door and looked in through the window. Delicious cakes and sweets were set out in that window. As we left the tea shop we saw the little girl with her face pressed close to the glass. She was looking longingly at the cakes and sweets.

She was a poor little girl in a thin, ragged dress. It was raining, and her bare feet on the wet pavement looked very cold. (All this came back to me like something slowly floating up from under water.) Then I remember sitting by the nursery fire and writing in large letters on scrap paper. Presently this too came floating through the water, a little scrap of rhyme:

> When I grow up and money have,
> I know what I will do,
> I'll build a great big lovely place
> For little girls like you.

I had entirely forgotten this promise. But there is One Who remembers even a child's promises. And though the little girls who were to come to the " great big lovely place " were not to be the least like that little girl, yet they were in need, far greater need than she was. And the wonderful thought of our Father was far, far greater than mine. He had sons as well as daughters in His heart that day.

At first, however, the work of the Starry Cluster went on as before.

Only [as Amma says in *Ponnammal*] as evening by evening we returned from work, there was a child's loving welcome,

little loving arms were round one's neck. I remember
wakening up to the knowledge that there had been a very
empty corner somewhere in me that the work had never
filled; and I remember, too, thanking God that it was not
wrong to be comforted by the love of a child.

From that time, with Ponnammal as her constant companion, Amma began to gather facts about the traffic in
children. Preena's uninhibited stories of life in the Temple
shocked the Walkers as well as Amma, for they revealed a state
of things which few missionaries suspected. If the reader of
the foregoing chapters is beginning to form a clear mental
picture of a living person, he will not be surprised to hear that
she began to say to herself and to others, " *If these things are so,
something must be done about it* ", and, as investigations not only
confirmed what Preena had said, but unveiled an evil greater
in its extent and more grievously unholy in its character than
she had ever imagined, her attitude was rather, " *Since these
things are so, I must do something about it.*"

What things? She found that in case of illness in the home
parents sometimes vow to give one of their children to the god
if the sick one recovers, that in certain families a certain child—
the firstborn, perhaps, or the second, or the third—is regarded
as belonging to the god, that in cases of unhappy marriage a
man may get rid of his wife and dedicate his child to the god,
that a poor widow or a deserted wife may marry her child to
the god for economic reasons, or, finally, that a baby abandoned
by her parents may be adopted by Temple women if she is
" fair to look upon " and likely to be intelligent.

What things? There lies before me a note-book in which,
beginning with the story of Preena, Amma set down the
concrete evidence of the existence of this evil traffic as it
gradually accumulated. Omitting a good deal which she felt
to be unprintable, she published some of the facts in *Lotus
Buds* and other books.* Incredulity in Mission as well as in
Government circles gradually gave place to concern and, in the
case of many officials, both Indian and European, to a determination to strengthen the law against the sale of children for
immoral purposes. As a result, not only of Amma's work but
also of the efforts of a great body of reformers, it has now been
made illegal to dedicate a young child to a god.

* *Lotus Buds*, particularly from Chapter XXVII onwards

Does this mean that the *raison d'être* of the Dohnavur work has been removed? Emphatically no. If laws are not to be evaded, it is first of all essential that governments should be determined to enforce them, and that penalties for breach of the laws should be severe enough to deter offenders, and, secondly, that public opinion generally should be behind the laws. Unless these conditions are fulfilled—and surely the Prohibition Law in the United States is a case in point—the evil which the laws are intended to eradicate will continue to flourish. Sin is nowhere more powerful than where it has religious sanctions, and that is one of the most painful aspects of the traffic in Temple children. Euphemism is far too kind a word for the expression " married to the god ". What sort of god is he whose priests give to the lusts of men the girls who are trained for Temple service? If the traffic is to be stamped out, not only a brave woman of the stamp of Amy Carmichael or Josephine Butler is required. Christians everywhere in India, men and women of goodwill everywhere among non-Christians, must care until their own souls are scorched in the fire from which they determine to deliver the little ones.

I think it must amuse the devil when Dohnavur is spoken of as " an orphanage for unwanted children ". Unwanted? There are hundreds of people in South India who are on the watch for these hapless infants. Even to this day, if for any reason there is delay between hearing of a child in danger and bringing it to safety, there are almost always those who are ready to pounce upon it and make tempting offers of money for its purchase. The pitiful need of " unwanted children " must indeed be met, and fullest support given to all who care for them. But the children for whom Dohnavur exists are very much " wanted ", and their need is immensely accentuated on that account.

But now for the last time we quote from the autobiography, written with no thought of publication, but from her own heart, to the Family that was her " very heart " (Philemon 12):

For three years it was a vain search. We could not find the source from which the children, who were trained to be Temple children, were drawn. It was a bitter time. There were days when the sky turned black for me because of what I heard and knew was true. And as I went deeper in, I not only heard, I saw. Many missionaries told me it was pure imagination. But Walker Iyer wrote to trustworthy men who were in the secrets of India, and they confirmed what I heard. "Well, the proof will be the children", people said then, and I knew they meant we should never find any children. Very few were in sympathy. Sometimes it was as if I saw the Lord Jesus Christ kneeling alone, as He knelt long ago under the olive trees. The trees were tamarind now, the tamarinds that I see as I look up from this writing. And the only thing that one who cared could do, was to go softly and kneel down beside Him, so that He would not be alone in His sorrow over the little children.

When, later on, I knew of boys being in danger, it was again as if He were alone in His thought about them and His grief over them. As you know He opened the way for them at last.

But to go back to the earlier search. It became part of the itinerant work which still filled the days. Sometimes in an attempt to find the carefully guarded secret (a secret no longer) of how the children came to the Temple houses, we had curious experiences. Once we stayed in a hostel for priests and pilgrims, and sitting on the floor in the evenings round the brass lamp set on the floor, while a garland maker made garlands for the gods, we listened to the talk, and here and there picked up a clue. Once we slept in a byre (the cow was away), and heard conversation through the wall of the next house, for the wall was thin and the voices loud. This led straight to a child in danger, and also opened our eyes to one of the sources for which we were searching. The child was saved. She is in Heaven now. It was she who said, " Ring the joy-bells for me ! " The long happy friendship with Stira Annachie (Dr Howard Somervell), a friendship which has been the means of saving so many lives for service in Dohnavur, began in that cowshed, for the child he came racing in his car from Neyyoor to help, was the child of whom we heard that night, and in the mercy of God were able to redeem from the priest who had bought her from her father.

And so it went on, the search and the Gospel work in many towns and villages, till at last we tapped the source for which we had searched, and had given ourselves altogether to you, ourselves your servants, for Jesus' sake, and you, our joy and crown.

Lord, art Thou wrapped in cloud,
  That prayer should not pass through?
But heart that knows Thee sings aloud,
  Beyond the grey, the blue,
Look up, look up to the hills afar,
And see in clearness the evening star.

Should misty weather try
  The temper of the soul,
Come, Lord, and purge and fortify,
  And let Thy hands make whole,
As we look up to the hills afar,
And see in clearness the evening star.

For never twilight dim
  But candles bright are lit,
And then the heavenly vesper hymn,
  The peace of God in it,
And we look up to the hills afar,
And see in clearness the evening star.

CHAPTER XIV

"THE CLOUD RESTED"*

THERE were other events in 1901 which must have seemed quite as significant as the arrival of Preena. Early in the year five boys, including Arulai's cousin Supu, all of them products of the work at Pannaivilai, were baptized in one of the reaches of water near Dohnavur. Each of them chose a name with the word *Shining* in it, and as they stood in the water in the golden afterglow of a radiant sunset, it was as if the glory of the Lord shone round about them. But there was an immediate counter-attack. Within a week several of them were seriously ill, and two died. Was it cholera or something more sinister? One of them was Supu, and he died crying with a loud voice in the midst of his agony: " Victory to Jesus' Name! "

About a fortnight later the party was at Cape Comorin, and Walker suggested a sail in a catamaran—a float of three logs tied together. Half a mile from the shore a wave swept five of them into the sea—Amma, Sellamutthu, Jewel of Victory, Jewel of Life, and Arulai. Sellamutthu, with one arm only, seized Arulai's outstretched hand just as the child was floating off on the crest of a wave and would certainly have been drowned. Somehow all were dragged on to the raft again. Walker and the boatmen would have made for the shore immediately, but it was just like Amma to cry, " No, let us go on ", and so to enthuse the drenched little group that they sang a Tamil chorus

> Though the earth may shiver, and the sea boil,
> Whatever may happen, I will not fear.

Indeed, they sang so vigorously that Mrs Walker and others on shore, who had sensed that something untoward had happened, heard the cheerful sound and were reassured.

It might so easily have been what we call " tragedy ". A real tragedy occurred a little later, when a girl from a village near Dohnavur decided at all costs to follow Christ, and sought

---

* See Numbers 10. 12: " The cloud rested in the wilderness of Paran."

refuge at the bungalow. But there was no upper room, as at Pannaivilai, and no door that would lock. Amma took her up to the tower of the village church close by, and there they slept that night. But in the morning the church was surrounded by a clamorous crowd. At last the women from the girl's village promised Walker that if they saw her and she refused to come with them, they would be content. So Amma brought the girl down to the vestry. They crowded round, and one of them rubbed her arm. It was an aunt, one who seemed to have a mysterious power over her. Her resistance broke down, and murmuring, " I come, my aunt ", she followed her out of the church. No one ever saw her again.

> No distress of our own, no distress in the life of one beloved who has hold on the comforts of God, *nothing* can approach for sheer torture the sight of a soul that has just begun to turn towards good being overwhelmed, driven back, trampled under strong feet into pollution. . . . How long, O Lord, how long? *

But there was joy in Pannaivilai when, on the very day after Preena's arrival, Arulai was baptized in Great Lake. It was nearly two years since she had first heard the Gospel by the well-side at Uncrowned King. No one doubted that she was ready for baptism, and her father miraculously—that is the correct word—gave his consent. Ella Crossley remembers how close and intimate was the understanding between this child and Amma even then. Miss Crossley and Amma and Arulai were travelling in a bullock bandy—presumably from Dohnavur to Pannaivilai—when Amma asked Miss Crossley if she would be prepared to let her have the exclusive use of the photographs that she had been taking—many of which were afterwards published in *Things as They Are*. Unprepared for the suggestion, Miss Crossley hesitated. Now, at that time Arulai knew no English, and therefore could not follow the conversation, but she was instinctively aware that Amma was disappointed, and flung her arms round her in sympathy.

It had been an encouragement to Walker and to the others when they arrived back from Cape Comorin to find two small boys waiting for them at the Dohnavur bungalow. Like Supu, they were Arulai's cousins, though not of the same family, and one of them was Arul Dasan, who had been tied to a

* *Ragland Pioneer*, p. 148.

pillar in his own home.* So he was baptized with Arulai. Three days later, relying on the safe conduct of the leading men of Uncrowned King, Walker took Arulai and Arul Dasan back to their own village. Walker was not a man who took needless risks, but he grieved that these children should be cut off from their families, and have no opportunity to witness to them. The experiment led to a riot. The bandy was upset, the driver thrashed, and the children carried off. But the headman of the village had once received kindness from a European, and though he was old and frail he sent his son to quell the disturbance. As Walker stood silently praying, the children were produced and hustled into the bandy, the driver, bruised and moaning, took his seat, and Walker guarded the precious freight from behind. Thus two most valuable Dohnavur workers were preserved.

On their way back from the hills that year they made a pilgrimage to the grave of Ragland, Fourth Wrangler at Cambridge, the pioneer of tent itinerations in India. Both Dohnavur and Pannaivilai were familiar ground to him. Amma was never tired of quoting words that he had written fifty years before, words that she might almost have written herself, for her life was so clear an illustration of their truth:

> Of all qualifications for mission work, and every other, charity [she would have called it "love"] is the most excellent. Of all methods of attaining to a position of usefulness and honour, the only safe and sure one is to fit ourselves for it by purging our hearts from vain-glory, worldliness and selfishness. Of all plans for ensuring success, the most certain is Christ's own—becoming a corn of wheat, falling into the ground and dying.†

In September Arulai was down with typhoid and pneumonia, at the point of death. There was a night when a kind missionary, who knew something of medicine, made what he thought was the final entry on her temperature chart, "Is it well with the child? It is well," and he spoke in loving sympathy of Amma, "She will have to give her up." The child had collapsed, her temperature down to 95°, but Amma clung to the words of *Daily Light* for September 17th, "O taste and see that the Lord is good; blessed is the man *that*

---

* The other brother went back, and is still opposed to the Gospel.
† *Ragland Pioneer*, pp. 29, 30.

trusteth in Him ", and so in the end Arulai was spared once again—for Dohnavur.

By the end of the year it was clear that no one but Walker was available for the class of divinity students, and for their sakes the family settled at Dohnavur. As one by one babies in danger of Temple service were brought to her, it would have been quite impossible for Amma to travel with them, and therefore a settled home was necessary. None more suitable could have been found in the whole district than that to which they were led, as it were, by accident. It was a very quiet place, far from the main road, less dangerous for a growing family of little ones than a town would be, and much pleasanter. It was bare enough when they first came there. " There was not a flower anywhere," says Amma. " Goats wandered about and ate them if they ever dared to grow in the grass after rain." But there were trees, including a noble avenue of tamarinds just outside the ramshackle bungalow. Fifty years of loving care, and the advent of hundreds of happy children, living in simple but not unpleasing houses that look as if they " belong "—for their colour is almost that of the red earth around them, and flowering creepers soon hide their newness— have made vast changes in the old Mission compound and the area around it. Words such as Isaiah wrote (chapter 35) are applicable, literally as well as metaphorically, to that which God has done. " The wilderness and the solitary place shall be glad for them; and the desert shall rejoice, and blossom as the rose. It shall blossom abundantly, and rejoice even with joy and singing."

But the whitewashed church close by has changed but little. It was built in 1824 from money contributed by Count Dohna, a German friend of missions, and the village around it is predominantly Christian and was named Dohnavur, or the village of Dohna.* Most of the people are of the caste of palmyra-climbers.

Still less is there any change in the ancient mountains, which rise out of the plains a few miles to the west. They are the southernmost peaks of the Western Ghauts, and the last of them, called the Holy Washerman, is a precipitous double-headed mountain which seems to stand guard to Dohnavur.

* The " Dohn " of Dohnavur, does *not* rhyme with " John ". " Doh ", rhymes with " No ", " na " with " ah " and " vur " with " poor ".

It was from this mountain (says the Ramayana) that Hanuman, the monkey god who helped Rama in the search for his vanished bride, having leaped from summit to summit, took his flight across the ocean to Ceylon.

Well, that is legend, but here is truth. When God laid the foundations of the world, He knew that He would be creating the Dohnavur Fellowship for the deliverance of hundreds of His little ones from a life of shame, and so in " the fulness of time " He brought Amma to Dohnavur. Why did He bring her to a place which appeared to be largely desert? Because its substratum is in fact a sub-artesian basin, threaded by little streams wandering here and there, rivulets from an underground river. " Without the faintest thought of what was prepared for us," she writes, " we were led here and established here—*here*, where this sub-artesian basin had been fashioned, who knows how long ago? " *

* *Though the Mountains Shake*, pp. 202, 203.

Light of light, Light of light,
Lover of children, hear.
Shine, shine, through the night,
Lighten the cloudy fear.
Little boats drifting over the bar,
Little lambs lost in fields afar,
Where is nor moon nor star,
Call Thy little ones, call Thy little ones Home.

Far on fell, far on fell,
Wander the lambs that stray,
Far, far from harbour bell
Drift the small boats away.
Open to Thee are the paths of the sea,
All the world's corners are open to Thee.
Follow them where they be.
Call Thy little ones, call Thy little ones Home.

     *   *   *   *   *

Deep to deep answereth now,
Dimly I see a Cross;
Thirst, wounds, thorn-crowned brow,
Stripping and utmost loss.
Over the bar the fret of the foam,
Rain on the fell where young lambs roam,
Lord, art Thou bidding me
Call Thy little ones, call Thy little ones Home?

CHAPTER XV

"ONE INCREASING PURPOSE"

" SHE was a traveller who, starting on her journey with a clearly-marked and time-worn route before her, found herself checked by the Touch that is not human and turned to a way, very difficult and hard to find, that led to a destination which she had not desired." The words are written of a French-woman * who lived three hundred years before Amma, but certainly they describe Amma's experience, and when she read them towards the end of her life, she wrote " March 3, 1893 " in the margin against the words " a clearly-marked and time-worn route " (i.e. the call to missionary work in Japan), and " March 6, 1901 " beside the end of the sentence.

For the way was certainly " difficult and hard to find ". The search for the facts concerning Temple children continued with varying success (but the facts so hurt and burned her that the word " success " is out of place), and the search for the children themselves yielded no results at all. It was almost three years before a second Temple child was saved, and meanwhile Amma did not cease to travel with the Starry Cluster and, as always, to work beyond the limits of her strength. After one campaign Walker wrote to her in true " elder brother " style: " I fear this will find you knocked up after S——. You gave me a promise not to go unless you were really well. I wonder whether you kept your promise, and whether you really mean to try and come back here *well*." If his warnings were not always heeded, he probably did succeed in keeping her from a complete breakdown.

Thus for the next few years she was, on the one hand, following the " clearly-marked and time-worn route " of all who assault the strongholds of Satan, while on the other she was being prepared for an almost complete concentration on the task of saving Temple children. Here, for instance, is an extract from the private notebook:

* From Introduction to the *Life of Jeanne-Françoise Frémyot, known as Sainte Chantal*, by E. K. Sanders (S.P.C.K.).

In visiting in —— near Pannaivilai, found a little girl of nine or ten whose mother in course of conversation admitted was to be sold to somebody in connection with Tuticorin temple. Tried to persuade her to give her to us instead. The mother was touched and promised to give her if we would come back in a week. When we returned in a week we found she had gone to Tuticorin in the interval, and the sale of the child had been effected. The little girl was lying drugged on the floor.

And then there is a later entry:

Heard that the child had been married (to the god), had lived for a year, then died in such agony that the one who was responsible fled from the house with his hands over his ears to shut out the sound of her screams.

But she accepted an invitation to join the Walkers when they attended the annual convention of the Reformed Syrian Church of Travancore in 1902. Jewel of Victory was already married to a fine Christian man of a slightly higher caste— the Christians, alas, questioning whether it could be a satis- factory arrangement to marry " out of caste "—but Jewel of Life and Arulai accompanied the party, and they were away from Dohnavur from January 16th to March 1st, 1902. In her letter to praying friends at home she talks of the strangeness of being in an area where a language other than Tamil was spoken, for it was the first time since 1895 that she had been " out of our own good Tamil country " ! The letter is far too long for quotation, but there are comments here and there which are so characteristic as to be irresistible. She admired the " ancient Travancore style " of building—and copied it in certain respects when the Dohnavur nurseries and other buildings were being designed—but she found one of the Rajah's palaces built in " hideous English style ".

Why people should build ugly buildings when they might as well build beautiful, is as great a puzzle to me as why they should go in for ugly colours when pretty ones are to be had. But we noticed wherever we travelled that the most graceful and beautiful things flourished best out of the sphere of English influence.

In Trivandrum she " enjoyed life in spite of a furious fit of neuralgia. It was like a bit of old times " (i.e. the neuralgia, presumably). Owing to the neuralgia she missed the joy of hearing Arulai speak for the first time at a women's meeting. But Mrs Walker reported that she spoke very simply and directly. She notes the emotional responsiveness of the Syrians—in contrast to the Tamils. " We had to be very careful all along to avoid approach to the feelings "—this at the meetings under a huge awning, sometimes attended by as many as twenty thousand people. " Anything of that sort was so tremendous in its effects! Both Jewel of Life and Arulai are very reserved, and this utter absence of all reserve struck them as most astonishing." The danger was that the fruit of Walker's solemn messages might end with the expression of an emotional response to them. Of course Amma loved the women. She poulticed a woman's thumb, but advised her to go to a doctor for more drastic treatment. " She lifted her thumb heavenward and said, ' It may drop from my hand but never, no never, will I break my holy vow! ' " An eloquent faith-healer had induced " vast numbers to vow that they would never go near a doctor. . . . She has suffered agony with that thumb, and if wishes do anything, *he* has had it by this time. Both thumbs, I hope! "

She expresses herself equally forcibly about a man " dressed in light checks, boots and a hat " supplied by English missionaries, who interrupted the Christians at prayer before one of the meetings, and urged them to come out of Babylon, and join a new sect which he proposed to found with money at his disposal. Amma does not record what she said to him, but " the venom in that gentleman's face as the conversation drew to a close was a sight it would be a pity to forget. I wished I had a camera. I should have snapped him on the spot, and sent him to the *Gleaner* ".*

But there was much solid work done, and the door of opportunity was wide open for men and women like Walker and Amma, who clearly had no other purpose than to bring to these attractive but ill-taught Christians the Word of God. It was not her only visit to Travancore—there are Syrian Christians who remember her to this day, and thank God for her—but as time went on she steadily refused invitations to work for which she was strikingly fitted, and in which she would certainly have been greatly used, because the cry of the

---

* Amma might have written differently later, but she would not have ceased to be indignant concerning such disturbers of Christian unity.

children sounded in her ears, and deep down in her heart she echoed the words of Paul, " This one thing I do ".

Back at Dohnavur after six weeks' absence she was welcomed tumultuously.

> My bandy went round to my side [of the bungalow] at once, and in two minutes it was swamped. All the five children I had left behind were inside it on the top of Life and Arulai and me—such hugging and kissing! It was really Home again.

(One wonders—are Tamils so very reserved, after all?)

At that time Amma was still using a pony when she rode out to the villages, and often one of the children would ride in front of her. There are women in the Dohnavur area who remember that pony. There is no evidence that Walker advised against this unusual method of locomotion for a lady missionary—though there is a story (perhaps apocryphal) that he gave her a lecture on decorum when she rode furiously across the downs at Ooty, with her hair streaming in the wind. She herself admits that he did not wholly share her love of animals. There was the noisy dog, for instance, which so exasperated him that at last he was moved to threaten, " Either that dog goes, or I go! "—and the dog went. And there was the scandalous incident of the squirrel who, having been allowed to come to the breakfast table when Walker was absent, could not understand why the privilege was denied him when Walker returned. The squirrel landed on his shoulder, and, when he turned in surprise, dashed across the table into the butter and upset the milk-jug. Amma tried to persuade him that it was a defect in his character not to like animals. " I do like them ", he replied rather frostily, " in their own place."

But she owed much to Walker, who was like her father in his utter reliability and in loyalty to his friends. It was through the Walkers that a great joy came to Amma in November, 1902. They had been on a trip to Colombo to meet some relatives who were passing through en route to England, and decided to visit old friends at Pannaivilai on their way back to Dohnavur. But unknown to them their steps were so ordered that they reached Pannaivilai just after the arrival of a child— the little girl of Chapter XII whom Amma had seen cruelly beaten, and who had afterwards been spirited away to her uncle's house in a village three miles away. No one had seen her since, but the spark of desire for the Lord Jesus which the

Spirit had put in her heart was not extinguished after three long years. There was an old ex-devil-dancer who had found the Saviour through Amma. She heard of the child's plight, and took the risk of guiding her when she slipped out of her uncle's house, and landed her at the Pannaivilai bungalow a few hours before the Walkers arrived! Nothing but the presence of a European could have saved her when the angry relatives stormed into the compound next morning, nor could Walker have protected her from them, if God had not sent His angels so that their hands could not perform their purpose. The child—called Suhinie, or Happiness—was a much-loved member of the Dohnavur Family until she went Home suddenly in 1910.*

In the autumn of 1903 there was another happy visit from Ella Crossley and Mary Hatch, but the time for parting came in December, just after Mr and Mrs Walker had left for furlough. Mrs Walker had been seriously ill, and obviously he must accompany her, but he was torn for the company he was leaving behind—" unprotected " was to have been the last word of the sentence, but is only suitable " while we look . . . at the things which are seen ". " I can't leave you to see to all this ", he said to Amma, referring to a group of convert boys for whom he was responsible. But there was no help for it. One of Amma's children was seriously ill, and there was neither doctor nor nurse within reach. It was a challenge to faith, and no one can imagine Amma *not* responding to such a challenge. " If you didn't go ", she said, " how could we prove that God alone is enough? "

Once, while the friends from Manchester were still with her, Amma took them and the Starry Cluster by bullock bandy to Kalakadu (Joyous City), the Temple town five or six miles north of Dohnavur. By the roadside on the edge of the town is a large rectangular pool, surrounded by stone walls, in which there grow the most beautiful lotus lilies. While they stopped to feast their eyes on the beauty of the flowers, someone suggested gathering a few, but was sternly reminded, " These flowers are not for you. They belong to the Temple." In a flash, Amma saw the picture of " little buds . . . lifting innocent faces to the light ", but " sacred—*sacred to whom?* " And then the tremendous words, " All souls are Mine ", reassured

* Her story is told in *From the Forest.*

her. She saw the Temple children as " lotus buds gathered by a hand that has no right to them, and crushed underfoot ", and she consecrated herself again to gather some of those flowers and offer them to their true Owner.*

While Preena remained the only Temple child, the Lord seems to have sent other little ones, so that Amma and Ponnammal and Sellamutthu were not without training in the care of young children. There were two children from Pannaivilai, called the Imp and Tangles in *Things as They Are*, and there were two little daughters of nominal Christians who were growing up like heathen—" Lotus, aged eleven, a fair delicate little thing who looks as if a breath would blow her away, and the dear mite we call the Mouse, a perfect little darling of eight. So against our rule (if we have one) I took them." Hindu relatives plotted to kidnap them, and the compound was open to attack from all sides, surrounded only by a low mud wall. " But the Wall of Fire all round that low mud wall is a reality."

Sometimes she was tempted to question her guidance. As she lifted up her eyes, and looked on the fields, and as calls began to come from all over South India, " could it be right to turn from so much that might be of profit and become just nursemaids? " It was then that she read the words from John 13, how the Lord of glory " took a towel and girded Himself". " Children tie the mother's feet ", say the Tamils, but never again did she question whether her gifts were being wasted. She knew that the Master never wastes the servant's time. And then the babies began to come.†

* *Lotus Buds*, pp. 3, 4.   † *Gold Cord*, p. 40.

O let Thy sacred will
All Thy delight in me fulfil.
Let me not think an action mine own way,
　　But as Thy love shall sway,
Resigning up the rudder to Thy skill.

GEORGE HERBERT.

Indraneela

Dear little feet, so eager to be walking
　　But never walked in any grieving way,
Dear little mouth, so eager to be talking
　　But never hurt with words it learned to say,
Dear little hands, outstretched in eager welcome,
　　Dear little head that close against me lay—
Father, to Thee I give my Indraneela,
　　Thou wilt take care oi her until That Day.

CHAPTER XVI

"A BIGGER FLOCK"

BEFORE the Walkers left for furlough he had tried to anticipate any problems that might arise, and had given Amma carefully written instructions. He had also written a birthday letter, to be opened on December 16th, and the text chosen was, "Maketh Him families like a flock"! (Psalm 107. 41). "We will trust Him too", said the letter, "for a bigger flock." After that one should not be surprised to hear that in June of 1904 Amma was responsible for seventeen children, including the girl converts and at least six who had been saved from Temple danger. In addition, there were six or seven members of the Starry Cluster, one or two of whom were beginning to share Amma's concern for the little ones, and therefore to be willing to do less of what is commonly called "Christian work" and to help in mothering and training the children. Ponnammal was a tower of strength, and so was Sellamutthu. A third member of the Band, called Devai, was an elderly woman whose story is told in *Lotus Buds*. She proved to be God's special gift for the task of discovering children who were in danger, pleading with their relatives or guardians, and bringing them triumphantly to Dohnavur.

For her no journey was too long or arduous. She would arrive exhausted after missing one or two nights' sleep, and leave again in an hour or two if word was brought of another child in danger. She was often disappointed, and followed many false trails, but she never lost heart. She was the first of a noble band of women, including many missionaries, and scattered all over South India, who are prepared to take immediate action as soon as they hear of a child in danger.

A lovely little girl of four was the first to arrive—one who for many long years has been a responsible worker in the Fellowship. The next was another of Arulai's relatives, a child of eleven, of whom Amma wrote that "except Arulai we have never had so eager and earnest a child to teach and lead to Jesus". A little later, when her relatives came to carry her off, she faced them with tremendous courage. They planned a night assault on the bungalow, but the Hindus in the village where they were staying refused to support them. "We are on good terms with the bungalow," they said. The third was a child of eight who lived in the town where Jewel of Victory and her husband were at work. She was to be sold to a Temple woman in February. Then came the news that the father would hand over his child to Amma on payment of one hundred rupees.

Now Amma knew that if it once became known that she was prepared to bid against the Temple women for the purchase of children in danger, the situation would soon become impossible. Prices would soar beyond anything that she would feel it right to pay. Ponnammal, knowing her own people, was unhappy about the payment of money—and still more unhappy to differ from Amma, from whom she had never been out of touch for a moment. But this was one of the many occasions when Amma knew that she dared not hold back when guidance had been given to go forward. Was she headstrong? Would Walker have said, as some other missionaries certainly did say, that she was following her own desires rather than the will of God?

Well, she was not infallible, either in 1904, or 1924, or 1944. But, far more than most of us, she expected and received direct guidance from God. The event seemed to prove that she was right, for the child was saved, and lived many years to the glory of God. And Amma put out a fleece. She asked for one hundred rupees from an unexpected source. In those days such large gifts—one hundred rupees exchanged for £7 8s.— were very rare. Ten days after the child's arrival a letter came from a fellow missionary in Palamcottah, and she enclosed a cheque for one hundred rupees. The whole Family was summoned—Starry Cluster, convert girls, and the little children. "We put the hundred rupee note in the middle of the little group, and then we thanked God." But was this the sign? Had the missionary perhaps heard that Amma had paid this sum for a child? No, her answer to Amma's enquiry showed that she knew nothing.

The Lord is gracious and full of compassion. Sometimes He provides money to meet expenses which we ought not to have incurred. But to those who walk this path of faith the provision or the withholding of supplies is normally the evidence of His approval or disapproval. The conscience must be tender, as Amma's was, and the heart perfect with Him.

It was the very same week that Amma was burdened for the children as never before, for she had seen the vision of the Lord Himself under the olive trees. It was His burden primarily, yet He called her to share it with Him. At that hour a pastor in north Tinnevelly, travelling by night, had seen a group of Temple women and little innocent children with them. He was stirred to pray that something might be done, and almost immediately he heard of a tiny baby who had just then been taken by a Temple woman. He succeeded in rescuing her, and on March 1st the first Temple baby— thirteen days old—was laid in Amma's arms. Preena was allowed to choose a name for her—Amethyst, from Revelation 21. 20.

About this time Scamp the pony was sold. Amma enjoyed riding, and probably the exercise was good for her, but she felt it separated her from the Band. "You have to ride alone. I feel I can do more by being with the Band."

When the second baby arrived—called Sapphire—Amma realized that it was time to build a nursery. She was at Ooty with the older children, and one day, when out for a walk, "it was just as if a voice said aloud, ' Go forward—don't be afraid.' " So she decided to write to Dohnavur, and suggest that brick-making be begun. When she returned from her walk, the mail had arrived, and there was a gift which proved to be the exact amount needed to cover the cost of the bricks. Also, a third baby had been welcomed at Dohnavur. A strip of field was bought, and almost immediately a gift of two hundred rupees—the largest sum yet received—came anonymously through a Madras agency, but earmarked " For the nursery ".

So the " bigger flock " was given, and the " fold " in which to tend them. The year of Walker's absence slipped by, and the family was kept in peace. November brought a wonderful joy. It was a great disappointment that Mrs Walker was not fit to accompany her husband, but instead he escorted Amma's mother, Mrs Carmichael, to Dohnavur. Mrs Ardill, who entertained the two at Palamcottah, remembers Walker telling Mrs Carmichael that she could hardly wear her beautiful

English cloak and bonnet in the bandy that night, so she retired to make last minute changes in her dress. Walker was eager to reach Dohnavur in time for *chota* the next morning, and asked Mrs Ardill to tell Mrs Carmichael that it was time to leave. " Tell him he must wait. I'm peeling," said the old lady.

The visit was prolonged until March, 1906, and the joy of it was inexpressible. After she had been about a month in Dohnavur Mrs Carmichael wrote as follows to a friend in England:

> I am greatly struck by the simple childlike faith of some of these dear convert girls in God's will and way being Love. Arulai, for instance—her daily life is an object lesson. No matter what comes or goes, though God be leading in a way hitherto unknown or different from what might be naturally chosen, that it is His wish makes it all right. Cheerfulness and hope through the difficulty shows the reality of her faith. But indeed she is not the only one. An atmosphere of love and obedience pervades the compound, and in this large family of over thirty, varying in ages from thirty-four years to a babe of nine months, I have not seen an angry look, or heard an impatient word. A set of more loving, unselfish women and girls and children could not easily be found. The secret, I think, is that *everything* great and small of all kinds is done for God, and to please *Him*, and in the consciousness that Jesus is present, and that He may come today to take them to Himself.
>
> I do so often wish my friends at home could see these dear children. They could not help loving them, they are so bright and affectionate, and some of the little ones fascinating. They are specially so with their Partieammal (grandmother). For instance, I found four pretty little bouquets waiting for me on my table today. But it is not in one way only but in every way. They watch my feet lest I tread on a stone. One comes to one side, and another to the other, to hold up my skirt, and as to carrying the smallest thing for myself, that *they* may carry, it is a thing not to be thought of. If only I could speak Tamil! When I do come out with a word, and express what I want, the chorus of appreciative delight is most amusing. Sometimes I teach them a sentence of English which pleases them greatly. Yesterday they were doing a little needlework beside me, and successfully they learnt, " Please, Partieammal, give me a thread ", and " Thank you, Partieammal." This achievement passed a happy afternoon.

Amongst the women there are four or five who go to the villages round to tell the heathen of Christ, but the last fortnight sickness and death have been amongst us, and they have willingly shared in day and night nursing. Six or seven have measles badly, and have been isolated, but all are getting better now, while dysentery, that dreadful scourge of Indian life, has seized and carried off the youngest of our number, and the next little one is hovering between life and death.

Naturally she was concerned about Amy's health.

Since we came a month ago, I can truthfully say she has scarcely had leisure even to eat. She is a busy mother, doctor, and nurse day and night. Of course when all are well she does not go over to the nursery during the night, but when sickness comes she does, and during the past fortnight has often been there more than half the night. It is wonderful to me how her health stands it. Of course she is often pretty nearly worn out, but she recovers, and is as bright and vigorous again as ever.

Amma hoped great things from her mother's coming, and trusted to her experience. But even she was baffled by the delicacy of the tiny babies. There was no doctor, no nurse, and in those early days no foster-mother would help. "It is not our custom," they said. Some children thrive on artificial food, but not all. Moreover some of the children had suffered before they came to Dohnavur. So Amethyst died, and one other. But Sapphire (Indraneela in Tamil) was left, perhaps fairest and best-loved of all.

These first griefs—one must linger over them a little. This is what Amma wrote:

On the last unshadowed day before the epidemic came which swept our nursery bare, we made a feast in the new room. The children sat in rows on the floor, gay as a garden of living flowers, in their crimson and yellow and blue. "Indraneela! Indraneela!" As the laughing voices called her from side to side and end to end, the baby danced and clapped hands, and tried to walk to everyone who called. Life was bright to us that day, for the weak little babes were fairly well, and all the children were perfectly well, and the treasure babe who was always well was fuller than ever of joyousness. And the sweet ways of a baby beloved, untroubled by any hurting thing, seemed sweeter than ever that bright day, as she held out her hands to one and another, and nestled in our arms. When the feast was over we went to the courtyard garden, and the baby clapped her hands with delight when the wind stirred the leaves of the trees, and blew the flowers about. And when the children sang she clapped her hands the more. Then they made a little garland and hung it round her neck, and twined the blossoms together and crowned their queen.

On that last evening only a few weeks later, but it seemed years, the baby lay most peacefully upon my Mother's knee. She had learned to love her and to call her prettily, " Ahta ", the baby word for grandmother. That evening as she lay watching with observant eyes everything we did, we almost fancied she understood, and was trying to help us to help her, so wise were all her little ways. Then came the nearing sound of the children singing as they returned from their lessons. The baby always clapped when we sang. She tried to clap now, raising weak little hands quietly. Often during that afternoon she had looked up, far away up, with intentness nothing could distract, and had beckoned just as she often beckoned to us in a loving little way she had. But still our eyes were holden and we did not see.

So in the early morning of that last day it was as if she tried to tell us. Arulai was beside her watching. She called the little call we knew so well, then once more pointed up, holding her little hand as high as she could. Then, with that utterly joyous look that she always seemed to reserve for the sound of music and singing, she still looked up. Arulai waited, and the baby hands pointed to a musical box which we kept beside her. Arulai held it for her. She turned the handle herself till the first notes came. She had often tried before but never quite alone. Now as the notes struck out she stopped, and again looked up with those joyous eyes, so unlike a baby's eyes in steadfastness, and then she looked at Arulai.

> Let me to my heaven go,
> A little harp me waits thereby,
> A harp whose strings all golden are
> And tuned to music spherical,
> Hanging on the green life-tree
> Where no willows ever be.
> Shall I miss that harp of mine?

Then Arulai understood, felt the stab of the knife. Did the baby see the great grief in her face? She put her little hands up to be kissed, and patted Arulai's cheek caressingly, and then, tired, fell asleep.

In the few hours that followed we could not help noticing the other-world expression deepening in the baby's eyes, but even then we did not know that she was going. It is hard to let go hope. Then there was a sudden breaking of the silence, one little cry, the baby's mother-word, " Amma! "

And then so gently the Angel came, so gently touched her that she slept, and woke to the music of heaven.

One never realizes quite how many are in sorrow, or have been, until one is sorrowful oneself. Over two hundred years ago Scottish mothers sorrowed, and the letters of comfort written to them bridge those two hundred years, and bring us all together, sorrowful people needing comfort and being comforted.

"You have lost a child", wrote old Samuel Rutherford. May his words bring comfort to someone as they brought comfort to me. "Nay, she is not lost to you who is found to Christ; she is not sent away, but only sent before, like unto a star which going out of our sight doth not die and vanish, but shineth in another hemisphere: you see her not, yet she doth shine in another country. If her glass was but a short hour, what she wanteth of time that she hath gotten of Eternity; and you have to rejoice that you have now some treasure laid up in heaven. . . . Your daughter was a part of yourself, and you, being as it were cut and halved, will indeed be grieved; but you have to rejoice that when a part of you is on earth, a great part of you is glorified in heaven. . . . *There is less of you out of heaven that the child is there.*"

She was a child of kingly race, one of the royal races of India; every dainty way and pretty gesture showed it. There was something very noble about her. She was our best. The children were not prepared for what had happened. We led them into the garden where they had crowned her queen. It opens off the room where the baby lay asleep, the little head half turned upon the pillow, the little hands curled softly as in life. And we looked at all the flowers. There were some weakly nasturtiums which do not flourish here, and many blue convolvulus bells hung over the trellis. And there was one fair lily which had bloomed that morning; the children had exclaimed in delight over it only an hour before. "Jesus came to our garden a little while ago, and we gave Him two little weakly flowers, dear but very faded and sick. If He came to our garden again today what would we give Him? One of these blue convolvulus which we would not miss very much?" But the children ran to the lily. "This is our best, our one yellow lily. We would give Him this", they said.

It was January 6th, 1905, and it was as Amma gathered Indraneela's things together, and folded them to put them away, that she knew it was not the end, and that this sixth day of the month must be kept thereafter "as a day of prayer for all imperilled children wherever they may be".

"That they may be one, even as we are one."

JOHN 17. 22.

"There is, so to speak, an interchange of the energy of the divine Life (Thou in me, and I in Thee), which finds a counterpart in the harmonious relations of the members of the Church. The true unity of believers, like the Unity of Persons in the Holy Trinity with which it is compared, is offered as something far more than a mere moral unity of purpose, feeling, affection; it is, in some mysterious mode which we cannot distinctly apprehend, a vital unity (Romans XII. 5; Ephesians IV. 4). In this sense it is the symbol of a higher type of life, in which each constituent being is a conscious element in the being of a vast whole. In ' the life ', and in ' the life ' only, each individual life is able to attain to its perfection. Such a conception, however imperfectly it may be grasped, meets many of the difficulties which beset the conception of an abiding continuance of our present individual separation."

WESTCOTT'S NOTE ON JOHN 17. 22.

This is what we trust Him to cause the Dohnavur Fellowship to be to the end.

AMMA'S NOTE ON WESTCOTT'S NOTE.

CHAPTER XVII

THE PATTERN

THE pattern for the Dohnavur Fellowship was not given like the Tables of the Law, written in orderly fashion. A group of Indian women, with a European leader who felt herself to be one of them and not an alien, began to live and work together. They did not sit down and discuss the outline of the plan that they were to follow; they did not look into the future and make rules which were to govern their lives. For instance, they did not decide that love—pure, shining love—was to bind them together, for, like the Thessalonian Christians, they were taught of God to love one another. God linked them in what Westcott calls a " vital unity ", and only then did they begin to observe it and rejoice in it, and to say, " Behold, how good and how pleasant it is . . . to dwell together in unity." Amma probably said to herself scores of times, " How good it is to have such loyal comrades ", before ever she talked to them or to others of " the crystal quality of loyalty ". The Fellowship, in fact, was a thought of God before it was a thought of man. There was, of course, a slow blossoming and development. As time went on, it became necessary consciously to note and describe the strands in the pattern, but many of those strands had already been woven unconsciously into the pattern of their life together.

It seems necessary to stress the immediacy of Amma's approach to God in Christ. The pattern was given as a result of personal contact with Him, confirmed by the precepts and promises of His Word, and the example of His saints all down the ages. Later, when she began to read the lives of the mystics, she discovered over and over again that she was walking along a path already well trodden by others. God had revealed to her what He revealed to them, but she learned it direct from Him. I am not suggesting that He did not frequently give her new light through the writings of others, but, generally speaking, the pattern was first shown to her, and then confirmed by the experience of holy men—and women—of old.

To take a specific instance. Since the Lord Himself was Leader of the work, they must take orders from Him, and how were they to learn His wishes except by prayer? Amma felt that, if they were to ask expecting to receive, they must be prepared to wait and not to be hasty in forming their petitions until they were assured that they were asking according to the will of God. Their attitude was to be, " Speak, Lord, for Thy servant heareth ", rather than, " Hear, Lord, for Thy servant speaketh ". To be filled with the knowledge of His will was the pre-requisite to asking according to His will. Sometimes the knowledge was not given, and then the only possible petition was, " Thy will be done, whatever that will may be ". But often " we are meant to know our Lord's wishes ", in order that we may " lay our prayer alongside ".

Now, since this method of prayer, and this assurance that we may expect the Spirit to teach us what to pray for, had become, as it were, axiomatic in Dohnavur, we can imagine the encouragement that came to Amma many years later when she read, in a book that was ever afterwards very precious to her, the word that God gave five hundred years ago to Lady Julian of Norwich: " I am the Ground of thy beseeching: first it is My will that thou have it; and after, I make thee to will it; and after, I make thee to beseech it and thou beseechest it. How should it then be that thou shouldst not have thy beseeching? " *

The whole subject of the gradual expansion of the work, including the erection of scores of buildings, was approached from this point of view. Was it the will of God, for instance, that a new nursery should be built? Amma was sure that God would be responsible for all the work that He had planned. But funds could not be expected, and therefore could not be prayed for, unless the plan was His. Frequently the giving or the withholding of supplies has been accepted as an indication of His will.

Meanwhile, all who took part in the new work at Dohnavur were like the original Starry Cluster in that no one received a salary, but the needs of all, from Ponnammal to the latest baby rescued from Temple service, were met in answer to prayer. No money was ever borrowed, no debt was ever incurred.

* *Revelations of Divine Love*, edited by Grace Warrack. (Methuen and Co., Ltd.)

Amma did not at first adhere strictly to the principle of never mentioning a need until it had been supplied. In *The Beginning of a Story*, first published in 1908, she speaks of God's provision in answer to prayer, and gives instances of His fatherly foreknowledge of unexpected needs. The story of Elijah and the ravens was one of the earliest related to the babies. But there is one sentence in the book which could be regarded as an appeal for funds, and on that account she eventually withdrew it from circulation. It was the plain statement that " our greatest need, next to prayer, is just the simple straightforward need of money—to feed our little ones and clothe them, and to provide for the long journeys connected with their redemption ".

Now Amma loved truth and hated hypocrisy in any form. Why hesitate then to set down such a self-evident fact? Children need food and clothing, and money is required to buy them. Members of " faith " missions are nourished in the same way as other people, and must use the world's currencies to purchase what they need.

But the statement sounded too like a reminder, if not an appeal, to the reader. If it is enough that our heavenly Father knows that we have need of " all these things ", why mention the need to others? Rather let Him remind them of it, and then every gift can be received without misgiving as an answer to prayer.

In all these matters Amma was unquestionably the leader of the family, but a leader who leaned hard on their love and loyalty, and who, as in the Belfast days, knew how to use and develop the gifts of others.

Meanwhile, as Mrs Carmichael soon discovered, her daughter had truly become a mother. I think she was a little surprised to find Amy bathing the children, caring for them in sickness, punishing them when they were disobedient or untruthful. From Arulai onwards they loved her with a love which none but the best of mothers has ever called forth.

At the slightest cry by day or night she would run over to the nursery. More than once God wakened her and she went to the nursery to find an infant who would have strangled or suffocated itself if help had not come. There was one night when she was convinced that one of them needed her, but it was only on a third visit to the nursery that she discovered the trouble and saved the life of one who has for many years been a full member of the Fellowship.

The children loved the halfhour from 7 to 7.30 in the evening, when they came to Amma's room, and played on the floor with toys from her cupboard. She was never too tired to play with them. Indeed, the happiest games were those that she invented.

She taught them to love beauty, in flowers and trees and scenery, and to be gentle to every living thing. Every one of the little ones of those days, now middle-aged Christian women, has her own stories to tell of Amma's love and patience, of her unselfishness and her enthusiasm.

The children soon discovered, what the Band already knew, that Amma would ask no one to do anything that she was not ready to do herself. The tidying and sweeping and dusting on Saturdays, in preparation for Sunday, would have been dull and laborious if Amma had not come along with a broom or a rake, joined in the work, and told them stories which made them laugh till they cried.

Heedlessness of the world's praise or blame was another part of the pattern. *Things as They Are* had created something of a sensation in the missionary world of India, as in Christian circles in England. Soon after the Temple children began to come, an old man paid a passing visit to Dohnavur. A tiny child trotted up trustfully to him, and sat on his lap. Something touched him, and he turned to Amma and said, " I was the convener of the committee that met to ask that you might be sent back to England after *Things as They Are* came out. I am very sorry now—forgive! " It was the first time that Amma had heard of this committee. But already the majority of missionaries were being convinced of the need for work amongst Temple children. In May, 1905, she writes, " It was such a cheer at Coonoor to find the whole band of missionaries, 150 or more, keen and full of the warmest sympathy ". A few of them are still living, and active in the search for children in danger.

The year was notable for a breath of the Spirit of God which came to the Dohnavur Church in October. This is how Amma writes of it:

On October 22nd, to quote one of the little girls, Jesus came to Dohnavur. He was there before, but on that day

He came in so vivid a fashion that we cannot wonder that it struck the child as a new Coming.

It was at the close of the morning service that the break came. The one who was speaking * was obliged to stop, overwhelmed by a sudden realization of the inner force of things. It was impossible even to pray. One of the older lads in the boys' school began to try to pray, but he broke down, then another, then all together, the older lads chiefly at first.

Soon many among the younger ones began to cry bitterly, and pray for forgiveness. It spread to the women. Our children began, I think, simultaneously with the boys, but it was so startling and so awful, I can use no other word, that the details escaped me. Soon the whole upper half of the church was on its face on the floor crying to God, each boy and girl, man and woman, oblivious of all others. The sound was like the sound of waves or strong wind in the trees. No separate voice could be heard. Some of the older men and women were in the greatest dismay, and by earnest signs besought me to stop it. As Mr Walker was in North India, and Mrs Walker on the sea, and my mother in Travancore, and the pastor away, you will understand how, in some sense at least, one felt responsible. I had never heard of such a thing as this among Tamil people. Up in the north, of course, one knew it had happened, but our Tamils are so stolid, so unemotional, I had never seriously imagined such a thing as this occurring. One old woman seized my feet, and by signs implored me to do something, but when I looked up for direction, the only reply was, " Do nothing ". By this time, the lower end of the church, the careless part of the congregation, was staring at the other part, and talking and shouting excitedly, and the heathen rushed round the church and gazed in at the doors and windows. But nothing disturbed those who were praying, and that hurricane of prayer continued with one short break of a few minutes for over four hours. They passed like four minutes.

For the next fortnight life was apportioned for us much as it was for the apostles when they gave themselves continually to prayer and to the ministry of the Word. Everything else had to stand aside. At first the movement was almost entirely among the convert boys, schoolboys, our own children and workers, and some of the younger members of the congregation. But the older ones were caught in the current more or less, and at first it was impossible to gauge

* The speaker was Amma herself. Here is an illustration of her ingenuity in self-effacement.

its real depth. Looking back after nearly seven months of testing, we have enough of true results to make us sing with all our hearts. Almost all our children were, I trust, out and out converted. Most of our workers were thoroughly revived. The bungalow servants were greatly blessed, several backsliders were restored. Many of the schoolboys were converted, and very few, if any, of the convert boys were unblessed. In the village there were several notable conversions and the true Christians were quickened. For all this we praise God. But we want more. The congregation as a whole is as cold as ever; the village as a whole is unstirred. Nothing has happened to touch the heathen and Mohammedans in the surrounding villages. We have just seen enough to make us very hungry to see more.

To my mind the deepest joy of all was to stand still and see the salvation of the Lord. It was not our pleading, it was the touch of God, the divine apart from the human. It was as if veils were suddenly drawn aside, and Gethsemane and Calvary and the Powers of the world to come suddenly became intensely real. One trembled lest one should do anything to make the veil come between again. The result in our own lives has been, I think, a quickened power of expectation.

Mrs Carmichael returned in time to share in the blessing, and to care for Amy. " She never thinks of herself till all is done. I'm so glad to have been with her, were it only to see that she did take some food occasionally, though she is very hard to watch." But, to quote Mrs Bell once again, " The Lord cares for that sort of child ".

Before the time of blessing the family had been divided, for a new nursery was opened at Neyyoor, close to the L.M.S. Hospital. There was a general feeling that some of the infants, at least, ought to be within reach of medical care. Ponnammal was in charge, and by May, 1906, there were fifteen babies, three nurses, and five young convert girls training as nurses, in the establishment. Ponnammal was not physically strong, but she was growing continually in grace and wisdom. Mrs Carmichael—whose departure in March, 1906, ended a wonderfully happy visit—had been greatly impressed by Ponnammal, and rejoiced that God had provided such a lieutenant for Amy. She certainly was one who lived " according to the pattern ". The " illest " baby always slept in her room. She poured out her life in unstinted service for the children.

" The roads are rugged, the precipices are deep; there may be feelings of dizziness on the heights, gusts of wind, peals of thunder, fierce eagles, nights of awful gloom; fear them not! There are also the joys of sunlight, flowers such as are not in the plain, the purest of air, restful nooks; and the stars smile thence like the eyes of God."

" I do not want people who come with me under certain reservations. In battle you need soldiers who fear nothing."

From *The Spiritual Letters of Père Didon.*

CHAPTER XVIII

"THE ROADS ARE RUGGED"

IT had been a comfort to Amma that her mother was with her when news came of the D.O.M.'s Home-call on June 19th, 1905—called "Fatherie's Glory Day" in her *Daily Light*. She rejoiced that he was lonely no longer, but she missed his regular letters, even though for some years past he had been compelled to dictate rather than write them. On the other hand, her mother and her sister Ethel, who were now living in Wimbledon, had made themselves responsible for *Scraps*—the circular letter with accompanying photographs which meant so much to a widening circle of praying friends. After more than a year's stay in Dohnavur, Mrs Carmichael could speak with far more intimate knowledge of the new work which God had begun, and which was slowly being fashioned according to His pattern. *Overweights of Joy* supplemented the facts stated in *Things as They Are* but did not contradict them. Perhaps the majority of missionary-hearted Christians still preferred that missionary books and magazines should contain only stories with a happy ending, but there was an increasing appreciation of an author who dared to write of reverses as well as victories, and whose evident gifts as a writer were so clearly subordinated to a passion for truth. God was giving her the "fire-words" for which she had dared to ask.

Certainly the need of more, and more vital, prayer support was apparent enough. One petition which Amma held constantly before the Lord was for a worker, either Indian or European, who had had medical training. Ponnammal's heart was grieved by the death of another baby at Neyyoor. When the news reached Ooty, one of the younger children went away alone and prayed, "Please, Lord Jesus, quickly send Ponnammal another baby to comfort her", and on the same day a telegram arrived with the good news that a child had been saved at Coonoor, ten miles away. She turned out to be a little girl of five years old, and she was called Lala, making a third with Lola and Leela (whose names and faces are so familiar to readers of *Lotus Buds* and of some others among the earlier books). It was an added joy that a baby arrived twelve days later who was exactly the same age as the child who fell asleep.

Then the devil stirred Lala's guardian to reclaim her, and Amma had to face the terrible grief of returning her, as seemed, to the evil power from which she had been rescued. Lala did not understand; she sat on Amma's knee, stroked her cheek, and said, " Amma, isn't it bed-time? Why don't you put me to bed? " When the bandy had gone, Amma went to her room and shut the door. Then the word came, " Said I not unto thee that if thou wouldest believe thou shouldest see the glory of God? " Lala had spent only a month with the Family—within a month she was with Jesus. But how much can a five-year-old, straight from the blackness of heathenism, learn of the Light in a few short weeks? She learned enough to call her mother to her as she lay dying, and to say, " I see three people in shining white. I am going to Jesus."

The Warfare of the Service included plenty of what C. A. Fox called " holy drudgery ", but wherever Amma was there was happiness. She wanted the little ones to forget the life from which they had been saved, and as she played with them they could not guess how her heart was torn with anguish for the hundreds who were not rescued. The battle was joined; it was clear enough that she was in contact with the enemy. One day two Temple women appeared with a sad-faced baby girl. " Their wickedness seemed to smite me and defile me. I feel polluted yet by the mere memory of it. . . . At the end of five long and, to me, most horrible hours, the baby was mine." For a week she never spoke or smiled, but in the end she could not resist the atmosphere of joy and love that surrounded her. . . . Then came a lovely Brahman baby from Bangalore, but Blessing, a member of the Band, had to face threats and intimidation as she travelled with it on the train. At one of the stations, said Blessing, a Brahman official peered in. " He looked at her hands and he looked at her feet, and he said, ' This isn't your child! ' I explained, but he was suspicious, and the people closed round the door and shouted, ' Pull her out! She is kidnapping a Brahman baby! ' But just then the train started and he banged the door, and I praised God! " . . . An American missionary rescued a baby, but a woman watched the gate of the compound and shouted that the child had been stolen. So after dark the missionary arranged for a carriage to come to the back of the compound, and the woman who was to escort the child slipped over the wall with her, and was driven to a railway station outside the town.

With Christmas of 1906 cholera came to Dohnavur. Amma had none of the really effective medicines, but she was often out at night, visiting homes where all the members of the family were sick or dying, and giving them large doses of permanganate of potash. Often she had to stand outside the doors and call and wait, for the people believe that evil spirits walk abroad at night. In cholera the fear of death often makes recovery less likely, and some lives may have been saved as much by Amma's presence and heartening words as by her medicines. At the same time Ponnammal was ill at Neyyoor, and when Amma was free to visit her, she found her very worn and thin, and asking longingly when the " English Missie Ammal " of whom Amma had heard might be expected.*

The baptism of six of the children just before Easter, including several who had been very difficult, was pure joy. Almost immediately afterwards Amma was " ordered "— doubtless on medical advice, strongly supported by the Walkers —to go early to Ooty. By this time the Family numbered seventy. A dozen or more went with Amma to Ooty, a few were left in Dohnavur, and yet another group were sent down to Ponnammal at Neyyoor. The plans were carried out smoothly enough, but suddenly came the news of an outbreak of dysentery at Neyyoor.

Amma's first instinct was to leave for Neyyoor without a moment's delay, but she was very far from well, and Walker sent an urgent wire, very strongly worded, advising her to remain at Ooty. Moreover Ponnammal herself wrote brave and wise words, "You will want immediately to come down. O do not come. If you were here, all your strength would be spent, as ours is, in this fight with death. God wants you to spend your strength in prayer for us, so He has taken you up to the mountain, as He took Moses, when the people were fighting on the plain ".

* The first European fellow-worker to arrive in Dohnavur had become engaged to be married on the voyage out from England. Amma writes of her loving, unselfish help, but she stayed only a few months in Dohnavur.

It was indeed a fight with death. Telegrams were dispatched to Amma nearly every day, and before the epidemic
spent itself, ten little ones had died. Meanwhile one precious
child was dangerously ill in Dohnavur. Mrs Walker cared for
her day and night. " She is so good except at her food time ",
Walker wrote, " and then it is like a little lamb bleating. I
can't bear it, and go away and pray that she may be helped
through it."

To Amma the days seemed like years, but there was consolation too. The friends at Neyyoor were exceedingly kind, and
as for Ponnammal, her courage never failed. " Heroic is the
only word that describes her ", wrote Amma. "Weak and frail
herself, she kept all going quietly, and in an orderly fashion,
and she inspired her workers with her own beautiful courage."

Was this an enemy counter-attack? Child after child had
been snatched from him and dedicated to Another. The ex-
devil-dancer who had helped Suhinie to safety was now a
member of the Dohnavur Family. She had been Satan's
sworn servant. " Will he watch her deliverance and enrolment
in this Temple children's work without a struggle? "

One obvious lesson was that more nurseries were needed.
The children were already overcrowded, and therefore the sick
ones could not be isolated. But the need of women with some
medical training was greater than the need of buildings.
They might be either Indian or European, but Amma was
beginning to learn from rather sad experience that offers of
service must be very carefully sifted. At Ooty she was reading
for the first time *The Spiritual Letters of Père Didon*, and for the
rest of her life she loved to quote trenchant phrases born out of
his own experience, and confirmed in hers. The standard
must be kept high, and the kind of fellow-workers for whom she
prayed would then be attracted rather than discouraged.
" This sacred work ", says Didon, " demands not lukewarm,
selfish, slack souls, but hearts more finely tempered than steel,
wills purer and harder than the diamond." Amma herself
was like that—how she would have cried out against anyone
saying so!—and so were Ponnammal and Arulai and others
whose names cannot be recorded. Some were even then being
prepared in England and elsewhere for whom the Cross was
the attraction, and who knew that the pattern given to Amma
was that which God called them to follow.

The prayer for more nurseries was soon answered. "One glorious day in July, 1907", writes Amma, "a letter came which said that the writer had it on her heart to do something in memory of her mother now in glory, and a friend had joined her in the gift—and £200 was to be paid into the Bank of Madras to build new nurseries. . . . We had never once had such a gift. Even now it feels like a fairy gift which will melt away—but it hasn't. It is all turned into solid wood and brick." And the biggest joy it brought was that "it made it possible to have our dear Ponnammal home again". The Family was reunited. "On Friday, March 27th [1908], there was that sudden bewilderment of noises, bullock bells, shouts of welcome, indignant protestations from unseen infants in the bandies, delirious cries from all over the compound, and scamperings from every quarter, and we knew it had come true at last." Ponnammal and the babies had arrived from Neyyoor.

What of the prayer for fellow-workers? It was answered too. Mabel Wade was a trained nurse from Yorkshire. She was not the first fellow-worker who came to Dohnavur from England, but she was the first who took root there—and is still bearing fruit to the glory of God. Like Amma, she was a member of the C.E.Z.M.S.,* but designated to Dohnavur. It was not an easy situation. Amma regarded her as an authority in all medical matters, not fully realizing the extent to which a nurse is trained to depend upon doctors and to carry out their instructions. But she faced the responsibility bravely, and from the very first day she knew that she had come to the place that God had chosen for her.

But Tamil fellow-workers of the spiritual calibre required, women who would give themselves utterly to caring for the children, women with that sensitive regard for truth which to Amma was a first essential, were not easily found. It would have been quite simple to engage Bible women at a stated salary

---

* Perhaps it should be stated that, from the beginning, Amma had made it clear that she did not hold the Society responsible in any way for the work amongst Temple children. They might have said, "Yes, but you are our missionary, and to that extent we have a moral, if not a financial, responsibility for any work that you may undertake." But, apart from occasional gentle expostulations, they acquiesced in an anomalous situation. Probably they recognized that God's Hand was upon this unusual missionary, and so they not only suffered her to go her own way, but permitted recruits like Mabel Wade to join her.

for " Christian " work; but women of the type of Ponnammal
and Sellamutthu, ready to share with the children, not the
Gospel of God only but their very lives, were so rare in the
churches of those days, that after some unhappy experiences
Amma had to be content to wait for her own children to grow
up and take responsibility.

There were some shining exceptions. One of them was
Ponnammal's daughter, who lived elsewhere for a time, in
order that she might test her own call to the work. Today she
is a valued member of the leadership group in the Fellowship.
Another was the daughter of Christians in Palamcottah.
At the age of seventeen she offered for the work, and was
invited to come to Dohnavur for a trial period. As soon as
she saw Amma her heart was knit to her, and she has been here
ever since. A third was the grand-daughter of the Tamil
poet, Krishna Pillai. She was prejudiced against Dohnavur.
Was not the life very dull? Were not Amma's demands very
exacting? For instance, could she discard her jewels? (To
this day, there are those who, to the amusement of members
of the Fellowship, fear that an unnatural and depressing gloom
pervades the place, and that laughter would be regarded as not
quite " holy ". Having overcome their fears, however,
sufficiently to visit Dohnavur, they discover, when they begin
to analyse their impressions, that if the first ingredient in the
atmosphere is love, the second is certainly joy, and the third
peace—which agrees with the scriptural formula in Galatians
5. 22.) Pappammal—for that was her name—came " under
certain reservations ", but they soon melted away, and she
proved to be a comrade indeed, in whom her fellow-workers
could safely trust.

The need of a teacher for the growing children was met for a
time by the coming of Miss Lucy Ross, a member of the brave
group of women working with Mary Dobson at the University
Settlement, Bombay. But the adverse verdict of the doctor
in Bombay was confirmed in Dohnavur, and she was compelled
to leave for England after a short stay.

Amma was very conscious of her own limitations, fancied or
real. It was true humility and not its horrid travesty which
made her write: " My working life until the children came
has been spent almost entirely in what is usually called ' soul
work ', and I was the last person in the world to be of any use

where bodies and minds are concerned. But I had to tackle both, and felt very often that 'Jack of all trades, master of none' would be written on my tombstone—if ever I had one."

Yet to an observer it would appear that she fitted perfectly into her position as mother of the family. Here is what she wrote in the autumn of 1908, and the picture is given not primarily for the aptness of the spiritual illustration which she drew from it, but because it is an unconscious portrait of herself and her babies:

It was the hour between lights, and five little people under two years old were waiting for their food. Sometimes the cows belonging to the adjoining village from which part of our milk comes saunter home with more than their usual leisureliness, and then the milk is late. The babies, who do not understand the weary ways of cows, disapprove of having to wait, and that evening they were all very fractious. To add to their woes the boy whose duty it is to light the lamps had been detained, and the quickly gathering twilight fell upon us unawares as we sat together on the nursery veranda. The five fretful babies made discouraging remarks to each other and threw themselves about in that exasperated fashion which tells the experienced that the limits of patience have been passed. And the more depressed began to whimper.

At this point a lamp was brought and set behind me so that its light fell upon their toys—a china head long since parted from its body, a tin with small stones in it which when shaken makes a charming noise, several rattles and other sundries. If anything will comfort them their toys will, I thought, as these illuminated treasures caught my attention. But the babies only looked disgusted. One of the most sweet-tempered seized the china head and flung it as far as ever she could. Not one of them would find consolation in toys.

Then a small child endowed with a vivid imagination and a timid disposition was sure she heard something dangerous moving in the bushes outside and she wailed a wail of most infectious misery and terror, and the quick panic which comes upon birds when they hear their own particular warning call, suddenly filled the babies' hearts, and they howled.

Then I took the lamp and set it in front so that its light did not fall upon the toys but upon myself, and in a moment the whole five were tumbling over me cuddling and caressing —and content.

Are there not evenings in life when our toys have no power to please or soothe? There is not any rest in them or any comfort. Then the One Whom we love best takes the lamp and puts it so that the toys are in the shadow, but His face is in the light. And then we know that that is what we wanted all the time. And He makes His Face to shine upon us and gives us peace.

This only hope relieves me, that the strife
With me hath end; all the contest is now
'Twixt God and Dagon; Dagon hath presumed,
Me overthrown, to enter lists with God,
His deity comparing and preferring
Before the God of Abraham. He, be sure,
Will not connive, or linger, thus provoked,
But will arise, and His great Name assert;
DAGON MUST STOOP, and shall ere long receive
Such a discomfort as shall quite despoil him
Of all these boasted trophies won on me,
And with confusion blank his worshippers.
       For God,
Nothing more certain, will not long defer
To vindicate the glory of His Name
Against all competition, nor will long
Endure it, doubtful whether God be Lord
Or Dagon.
       MILTON, *Samson Agonistes.*

CHAPTER XIX

THE STORY OF MUTTAMMAL

THERE were several periods in Amma's life when tension in regard to the spiritual danger of one person was so acute and so prolonged that one wonders how she came through them without collapse. The normal work continued, there was no truce in the warfare with Satan, no relaxation in the search for children in danger, and in the soul-training of the children who had been saved. But in the background of all her thinking and praying—and often in the foreground also—was the conflict for one soul.

The story of Muttammal was dramatic according to the strictest interpretation of the word. A drama, according to the *Concise Oxford Dictionary*, is a " set of events having the unity and progress of a play and leading to catastrophe or consummation ". In Muttammal's case the " events " were sensational enough, but the *dénouement* which led to " consummation " when everything pointed to " catastrophe " was too incredible to be invented and utterly unlike anything that Amma herself had imagined to be possible.

Muttammal, a child of 12 or 13, but so small that she might have been only 9 or 10, came rushing into Amma's room with her mother on the morning of March 10th, 1909. The child was nearly fainting from exhaustion, and the mother loudly appealed to Amma for protection. Though some of her stories were false, the danger was real. The father was dead but had left fields worth some thousands of rupees to his only child. Her paternal relatives, and particularly an uncle, desired to marry her to a man of their choice, partly (perhaps mainly) because they would thereby gain control of the property, but partly because they knew that both the mother and her sister were living bad lives.

Now the child had heard of Dohnavur four years earlier as a place where " children grow up good ". She had kept this word and pondered it in her heart, for she was old enough to understand that in her mother's or her aunt's homes she could not " grow up good ". There had been an incident one night

161

when her mother had said and done something which she never forgot, though she shrank with all the force of her nature from speaking of it. So, when her mother told her that they must run away to escape from her uncle's plotting, Muttammal begged her to go to Dohnavur.

Dohnavur was "sanctuary" to them while Amma made further enquiries and prayed for light. As soon as the child gained courage to speak, she begged to be allowed to stay. "Promise me you will not give me up", she said, and when Amma explained that she was not free to do as she liked in the matter, Muttammal looked up into her face, and said, " But I have heard that your God hears prayer. Will He not hear a little girl's prayer? "

Walker had been absent from home on March 10th. When he returned he felt that the only right course was to apply to the sub-magistrate for advice, and, naturally enough, the reply was that the child must be given up. The mother had left her for a time, and she had already begun to respond to the love of Jesus. But on Easter Day the mother reappeared and de-manded her child. Amma put her off till the next day, and cried to God to work a miracle. But Monday came, and there was no miracle, only a terrible scene that rent her heart, the mother and other relatives clamouring, the child weeping and pleading to Amma to save her. For a moment she thought wildly of seizing the child and running down the lane to find some hiding-place. Walker could hardly bear it when Muttam-mal ran to him as a last resort. But the mother sprang upon her, and they carried her away screaming.

It turned out that their home was in a village close at hand, and after two days the relations allowed Amma to see her and talk to her from a picture-book of Daniel and Jonah. Then suddenly the room filled with men from her uncle's party, shouting furiously and apparently prepared for violence. Amma had to leave her like a lamb amongst a pack of wolves. Then the mother attempted to hurry on preparations for a secret marriage.

On the Thursday Amma heard that the Collector, an English official, might be on the road early on Friday morning. So at 3 a.m. she went out and sat under a banyan tree, reading from Psalm 77 the string of questions " out of the depths ", ending with, " Hath God forgotten . . .? Hath He in anger shut up

His tender mercies?" It had never been Amma's cry before, and she read on to the strong words of verses 10 and 11, and was comforted. Then the Collector's bandy arrived. He stopped to drink a cup of tea with Amma, and listened sympathetically, but assured her he could do nothing.

On Sunday came the news that the paternal uncle had kidnapped Muttammal. The maternal relations appealed to the police, and Muttammal was consigned to the care of the headman at Four Lakes—*a friend of the paternal uncle.*

After this there were weeks of silence. Just before the case was heard Amma was allowed to see her, and to give her the words, "Be thou faithful unto death. . . . My grace is sufficient for thee." Walker and Arulai and Amma had to give evidence. The child was sure that she would be tortured by her uncle if she told the truth, but under cross-examination she spoke up clearly and courageously. By this time it was July—a month, as it proved, of plots and counter-plots. The uncle feared that he would lose his case, the mother feared vengeance if he did lose it. Both sides began to consider handing her over to Amma as a temporary compromise. But Muttammal did not know this. Small wonder that she thought God had forgotten her, until she was encouraged by a dream of a Shining One Who came to comfort her.

Amma went to Palamcottah and saw lawyer after lawyer, but their answer was always the same—" wholly impossible ". But to Amma the only impossible thing was to give up the struggle. Then word came that an Indian Christian barrister had just returned from England. One of the lawyers had told her that she was between Scylla and Charybdis. But would the Christian man be a Ulysses? He listened to her story. He had been in Wimbledon, attended Emmanuel Church, had met people who believed in the power of prayer. Amma asked if she might pray with him, and as they rose from their knees, he said, " I will do my best to save that child ". Without a moment's delay he called the lawyers on both sides and talked to them before the court met. Her head in a whirl, Amma listened as both the uncle and the mother agreed to commit the child to her, and signed a *yadast* (official document) to that effect. " Amma, Amma ", cried Muttammal when they were reunited, " I did trust the Lord Jesus." The journey home was a very joyful affair. They could not but smile and salaam

to all whom they passed on the road, for they were so over-
whelmingly happy. There had been a performance of God's
promises which they could never forget.

But the *yadast* named two conditions. Muttammal was not
to break caste or to " change her religion ", i.e. she was not to
be baptized. When she was eighteen the whole matter was
to be reviewed. The keeping of caste meant that she could
never eat food with the other children. Indeed, she must have
a separate little kitchen and cook her own food. It was not
easy for her to understand that Amma's promise must be kept,
until one day she read from Psalm 40, " I delight to do Thy will,
O my God ". But the final victory was won when she read in
John 21 of the fish that Jesus Himself had cooked, and she fell
on her knees at once, and prayed, " O Lord, Who didst cook
the fish that day, forgive me for not wanting to cook, and forgive
me for doing it only with patience and not with joy ".

During the months that followed increasing watchfulness was
necessary. Either the mother or the uncle—and the latter was
more powerful—might at any time raid the bungalow or way-
lay her as she travelled—for if Amma had to go to the hills or
to Madras she dared not leave Muttammal behind. Amma
and Arulai gave much time to teaching her. Though they
did not tell her so, they were preparing her for the possibility
that she might be snatched away from them.

At the end of November the uncle lodged an appeal, asking
to be made guardian of her " person and property ". Ulysses
travelled 400 miles from Madras to be present when the case
was called on December 17th, and refused to accept any fees.
The uncle's case broke down completely, and when the judge
had heard Ulysses, and had seen the *yadast*, he gave judgment
in summary fashion against the uncle. By Ulysses' strong
advice two constables were appointed to escort little Muttammal
safely home to Dohnavur. Muttammal's first Christmas was
a very happy one.

All through 1910 there were mutterings of a coming storm.
On August 17th came definite news that the mother had made
another application to the Court. Psalm 89 is one of the
Psalms for the seventeenth evening, and the words of verse 34,
" My covenant will I not break, nor alter the thing that is
gone out of My lips ", brought solid comfort.

Every preparation had to be made at Dohnavur and Palamcottah, and by Ulysses in Madras, whenever a date was fixed for the hearing, but there were postponements from September 3rd to October 8th, then to October 28th, and then to December 21st. Once two sets of relatives came to Dohnavur and tried to see Muttammal, but were refused. " All the sets of all the relatives combined can do nothing against the LORD ", wrote Mr Price, C.M.S. missionary in Palamcottah—one of the many missionaries who stood by Amma, and behind her in prayer, through all the long months of tension.

On January 31st, 1911, the Court sat, and Amma was questioned by the Judge—an Englishman who had recently taken over from a Hindu. His very first question was, " Is it the chief object of your Mission to make converts? " and what could she reply but " Yes "? He proceeded to elicit the facts that Muttammal had no touch with Hindus and that the influences around her were entirely Christian. He questioned the possibility of her keeping caste in such surroundings. Finally, he amazed everyone by saying that he thought the *yadast* of no importance. The case was postponed again, but the opposing counsel were obviously jubilant.

Once Amma went to visit a man whom she calls the Bloodhound. A word from him would have quashed the proceedings, and she told him that Muttammal belonged to the living God, and sought to appeal to his better nature. "You appealed to what does not exist, a heart and honour ", said one of the lawyers. But if Amma was courageous, the child was courageous too. " Don't be afraid for me, Amma ", she said as they went to Court. " I am not afraid." About this time, in a moment of great anguish, Amma promised that, whatever happened, she would not give the child up to her mother. But how was she to keep the promise?

March, 1911, was the blackest month of all. At several preliminary hearings it became clear that there was only the faintest hope of a favourable verdict. On the 17th Mabel Beath came to Dohnavur on a visit to her sister Frances, whose arrival in 1910 had been a great cause of rejoicing. Amma returned early one morning from Palamcottah to find that she had arrived. She went straight to her room, looked into her eyes, and knew that she could trust her. " If everything fails ", said Amma, " are you willing to help to save Muttammal? " " Yes." " Even if it means seven years' imprisonment? " " Yes."

In their last talks together the child said quietly, " By Thy grace, whatever happens, I will not be offended in Thee." That night Walker escorted Amma to Palamcottah, and the Court opened on the morning of the 27th.   The judgment, which decreed that Muttammal should be returned to her mother on April 4th, and that all costs were to be paid by Amma, was read.   And at that very moment, as she has told in *Gold Cord*,*

> all unbidden, unprayed for, came a strange triumphant joy utterly unknown before . . . Was it the sudden shining of His Face? . . . I do not know.   But I do know that all that went before and all that had to follow, when the time came for paying the price in hours emptied of all conscious illumination, was as nothing in comparison with one moment of that joy.

But dropping for a moment to a very different level, I quote one or two sentences from Amma's circular letter of the time, simply because, like the previous paragraph, they show her just as she was.

> *Judge.*   I hope you understand, Miss Carmichael, that I am giving you most exceptional treatment?
> *Miss Carmichael.*   (looking straight at him) Yes, I quite understand that you are giving us *most* exceptional treatment. (This was a spring out of the Irish in me, I don't defend it.)

There was much dreary argument about the possibility of a stay of execution in order that Amma might appeal, but just as she was leaving for Madras to consult Ulysses, a note arrived from Walker : " When I returned home on Thursday morning it was reported to me that the child had disappeared . . . God guard His little lamb !   We have tried to do it for two years. Now God guard her ! "

On the previous night Amma had read Psalm 124 with Mrs Price.   " Praised be the Lord, Who hath not given us over for a prey into their teeth.   Our soul is escaped even as a bird out of the snare of the fowler, the snare is broken, and we are escaped."   She went straight back to Dohnavur.   No one there knew anything except that Muttammal had disappeared on the night of March 27th.   Mabel Beath had left the same day, but not with Muttammal.   To Indian Christians it seemed that

* *Gold Cord*, pp. 101, 102.

Amma had suffered complete defeat, and, as for Hindus, they openly mocked the God of heaven.

Weeks passed, weeks of uncertainty and anxiety, relieved by a postcard in an unknown hand with the words of II Chronicles 16. 9: " The eyes of the Lord run to and fro throughout the whole earth, to shew Himself strong in the behalf of them whose heart is perfect toward Him ". It suggested that Muttammal was safe. But where?

Mabel Beath was followed to Colombo, and watched there. When she arrived in London an Indian student called at her father's house, but departed when he found no little Indian girl was with her!

But it was she who had acted—and without a word to anyone, even her sister Frances. She woke Muttammal, took her to her own room, dressed her in a Muslim boy's outfit, and told her to leave the compound by a certain gate. More than that she did not feel it right to do. Muttammal must act for herself. She did so, and found a bandy waiting for her. Two Indians— from another Mission station—escorted her to it, and thence she was taken, stage by stage, through the Travancore backwaters and eventually to Colombo. There the Bloodhound traced her, and she was sent to Kandy.

But meanwhile Mrs Walker's failing health had once again made it necessary for them to go to England. No wonder he writes in his diary that he left Dohnavur " with a somewhat distraught mind." No one could say whether a case would be brought against Amma or any who might have abetted her in carrying off the child. The adverse judgment in Muttammal's case might easily endanger other children. An English solicitor who had examined all the evidence wrote, " I advise you to disappear them all and lose their tracks. . . . If you cannot do that I know of no alternative—except faith."

Faith was not lacking. Amma had been defeated, but *for that very reason*, as Milton's noble words reminded her, the contest was now " 'twixt God and Dagon ", and He would not for long

> Endure it doubtful whether God be Lord
> Or Dagon.

In this faith she went up to the hills, and one morning at breakfast she met a South Indian missionary named Handley

Bird. His wife was a close friend, but she was in England, and Amma had scarcely met the husband. When the lawsuit was mentioned, his attitude seemed to be politely unhelpful. Yet as he was preparing to leave, to her own amazement Amma heard the Voice that she had learned to recognize saying, " Follow him. Ask him to help if need arise ". So she overtook him as he opened the gate, and told him all she knew. Would he help? He promised to do so, and said as he turned away, " Don't be anxious about your bird. She is under God's wings, and God's feathers are very soft ". From that moment Greatheart * (as Amma loved to call him) spared neither time nor strength nor money in tracing Muttammal. He found her in Ceylon, and knowing that she was still in danger escorted her to Penang, Singapore, Hongkong. No one in Hongkong seemed able or willing to help, but he travelled 600 miles up the West River, following a very tenuous clue, and gained the sympathy of Dr and Mrs Lechmere Clift at Nanning, Kwangsi. And there Muttammal lived in peace and happiness for six years.

These are the facts. The explanation can only be that Greatheart was in touch with God just as Amma was. What else could account for his willingness to drop everything and spend months in taking a small Indian child to a place of refuge? But something else needs to be said. All her life Amma never hesitated to ask great things of her friends, and even from men like Handley Bird who was hardly more than an acquaintance, and only rarely was she rebuffed or disappointed. It was partly her confidence in them, the fact that she did not expect a rebuff, which evoked a generous response. Sometimes, I think, their unconscious reaction was, " I would like to be the kind of person that she thinks I am ". But, more than that, they knew that she was one who listened for God's Voice. " If the word of the Lord has come to her," they argued, " then her request is the word of the Lord to me."

This is Amma's life, not Muttammal's, and therefore her adventures cannot be related in detail. She escaped on March 27th. It was not till October 10th that Amma received what

* See *Pilgrim's Progress*. While conducting pilgrims to the Celestial City, Greatheart encounters Giant Maul, who thus accuses him: " Then said the Giant, Thou practisest the craft of a kidnapper, thou gatherest up women and children, and carriest them into a strange country, to the weakening of my master's kingdom."

she always called the "Joy and Comfort" letter, which told
her where the child was, and with whom. After that there was
regular correspondence by circuitous routes. To Amma " her
letters were a sweet delight. . . . Every letter was a honey-
drop".

But for what purpose had God stretched forth His Hand of
power to deliver her? Was she to remain an exile in China to
the end of her life? Most people thought so, but Amma never
quite accepted the inevitability of such an ending to the story.
And then came—not for the first time or the last—a "shewing"
which the chronicler does not attempt to explain.

> On the night of August 15th, 1915 [writes Amma], I seemed
> to see in a bright dream Muttammal being married to Arul
> Dasan, the eldest son of the Dohnavur Family. The wed-
> ding was in Galle Face Church, Colombo. The one who
> was marrying these two was the Secretary who had helped
> Greatheart four years ago. The lady . . . who had suc-
> coured Muttammal in her need was with her, taking my place,
> giving her away to Arul Dasan.

She tried to put the dream away from her, but found there
was something in her which would not accept her own common-
sense admonitions. At length she spoke to Arul Dasan, who
was much impressed and agreed that Arulai should be consulted. To Amma's great astonishment Arulai said that she
had been praying about this suggestion for a whole year. So
letters were written to China, and the two were engaged.

After that there was much writing to and fro. It was suggested that Arul Dasan should go to China and be married in
Nanning. Then it seemed that the Clifts ought to take furlough, but what could Muttammal do? Dr Clift joined the
Chinese Labour Battalion in France as a medical officer.
Should Mrs Clift take Muttammal to America, where she would
be safer than in war-torn Europe? Amma tried to be willing
for anything, but the dream was always in the back of her mind,
and at last she wrote suggesting that, if only Muttammal could
be brought to Ceylon, she believed all would be well. No one
would dream of suggesting that a film be made of Muttammal's story, but there was sufficient of melodrama in the excite-
ments of the journey and the landing in Colombo to provide
good material. It so happened that Mrs Clift had to continue
her journey before the wedding could take place, and thus the

dream was fulfilled in every detail, for the lady whom Amma had seen took her place and gave Muttammal away, and the Secretary conducted the service—in Galle Face Church. Arul Dasan and Kunmunnie (Muttammal's new name) are living happily together to this day in a pleasant little house close to Dohnavur.

On the night of April 4th, 1911, there was to have been a jubilant celebration in the temple of Muttammal's village. But God, and not Dagon, was conqueror. The verdict in the courts of earth was reversed in the courts of heaven.

It need hardly be said that throughout the long months and years of tension Amma was supported by the persistent, fervent prayers of a growing number of friends. To one who sent her a poem with the title " For one in peril pray ", she wrote:

> I shall never forget the hour when your poem flashed through me like a living thing. The Judge was against us. The opposing lawyer had determined to get him to order the child to be handed over to a " neutral guardian " then and there. The Judge hesitated. We waited simply breathless. Then the Judge said he would not hand her over for the next few days. During the tense silence of waiting your poem *spoke*.

But there was no one who followed all the twists and turns of the story more closely than Mrs Carmichael. When the news came of the first decision in Amma's favour, and the safe return of Muttammal to Dohnavur, she was staying with her son Alfred and his wife Kathleen in British Columbia.

> She slipped out of the room [he wrote to Amy] on to the veranda. I happened to look through the sitting-room window and saw her holding on to a veranda post, her face radiant and turned up to the sky, her eyes streaming and closed, and words of praise and thanks being formed by those sweet lips. I drew Kathleen to my side, and we watched her, feeling very close to heaven. It was beautiful to see how her first thought was to give thanks. She just stood there unconscious of anything save God.

Amma's trust had been in " God Who raiseth the dead ", and her testimony was that of Paul, " Who delivered us from so great a death, and doth deliver; in Whom we trust that He will yet deliver; ye also helping together by prayer for us, that for the gift bestowed upon us by the means of many persons thanks may be given by many on our behalf ".

I have no word,
But neither hath the bird,
And it is heard;
My heart is singing, singing all day long,
In quiet joy to Thee Who art my Song.

> For as Thy majesty
> So is Thy mercy,
> So is Thy mercy,
> My Lord and my God.

How intimate
Thy ways with those who wait
About Thy gate;
But who could show the fashion of such ways
In human words, and hymn them to Thy praise?

Too high for me,
Far shining mystery,
Too high to see;
But not too high to know, though out of reach
Of words to sing its gladness into speech.

CHAPTER XX

FOR convenience' sake the story of Muttammal has been told right through to its happy ending. But the years between her escape and her return to Dohnavur as the bride of Arul Dasan were full of other happenings. Faith was tested in that period through the prolonged illnesses of some members of the family, and the death of others. But the collapse of faith, which would have given free entrance to the devil, never took place. To this time belongs the story of a mud wall which "fell in solemn crashes", all through a night of heavy rain. When the children saw the ruins next morning, one of them said, "Amma will be sorry", but another corrected her. "No," she said, "Amma will say it is the trial of our faith." The phrase became proverbial, and was applied to circumstances which scarcely deserved it, but it did describe Amma's attitude to the whole of life, including events far more painful than the incident which gave rise to it.

By God's gracious ordering the months which followed Muttammal's departure were relatively peaceful. No charge was preferred against Amma or her accomplices in the disappearance. Even the bill of costs was delayed for some months, and just when it was presented Amma received a cheque for the exact amount, to a rupee. It came from the head of a London publishing house which transmitted funds for various missionary societies. On a certain morning three weeks before, he had been constrained to send for his cashier as soon as he reached the office, and to enquire what funds were in hand for Dohnavur. He could not rest until he had written the cheque and dispatched it. When Amma acknowledged it he knew why the urge to take immediate action had been so strong upon him.

There was no sting in one of the griefs of those days, but it was a sore grief none the less. A little Brahman child called Lulla, five years old, was particularly precious to Amma and Ponnammal, indeed to the whole family. In August, 1912, she was taken ill, and medical help arrived an hour after she had fallen asleep in Jesus. But the manner of her passing was such as they could never forget. Her breathing had been so distressing that Amma left the room and besought the Lord to take her. When she returned Mabel Wade amazed her by saying, " She has been smiling ", and as they looked—Mabel and Ponnammal and Amma—a smile lit up the lovely little face, she looked up and clapped her hands as children do when welcoming someone whom they love dearly. Then she turned and tried to kiss them, as if to say goodbye, but in a moment she was holding out her arms to Someone else whom they could not see. Amma always felt that the three who watched her had been given a glimpse into heaven. " You have sent the Lord a beautiful flower ", said the old woman who kept the gate of the compound.

During that same month Mrs Hopwood of Ooty went Home. It was she who had received Amma and her convert girls fourteen years earlier, and every year since 1898 Amma had spent the hot weather with her. She was " part of our Indian life ", wrote Amma. " She was like a mother to me."

But a heavier blow was to fall. On a very joyful day in October, 1911, Walker had returned to Dohnavur. Amongst other things he brought a microscope from England for the use of Amma and the children. " It has added a new room on to life ", she said, " a wonder-room full of delights ", and of course they were delights which she was never weary of sharing with the children. A special table had to be made for the microscope—the very table at which this biography is being written.

In August, 1912, before Lulla's illness and before news had come of Mrs Hopwood's death, Walker was to leave for a series of meetings in Masulipatam.

> One evening [writes Amma], we were all resting in our deck chairs under the stars. We had been talking of work and workers, and of those (to me) most wonderful women, who seem perfectly self-reliant, needing no strong arm alongside. I remember how, suddenly startled at the bare thought of working alone, in the sense of having all the burden of responsibility, I exclaimed that I never could do it. Mr Walker laughed. " Well, you don't have to ", he said, and I remember the quick sense of joy and relief.

He left Dohnavur on the 12th, and Lulla saw the face of Jesus on the 18th. On Saturday the 24th came two telegrams from Masulipatam. The first, delayed for two days, stated that Walker was " dangerously ill "; the second contained only the words, " Revelation 22. 4 "—" They shall see His Face." How little they had imagined that he would enter the Gate so soon after little Lulla! Amma pictured her amongst those who were waiting to welcome him.

But the shock was very great, for there had been nothing to prepare her for it. Yet her first thoughts were for others, and especially for Mrs Walker in England. Then she thought of Ponnammal.

I knew her poor heart, still bleeding after the parting with Lulla, would be very sore, and I went to comfort her. But she turned and comforted me, telling me how God would be more to me than ever, for He knew I had now no arm but His, no help but in Himself. She was so brave—her courage greatly strengthened mine.

Yes, they all knew what Walker had been to Amma—" a strong arm at all times, such a wise counsellor, such a true friend ". Mr Carr came over from Palamcottah, and every evening he played the organ while the children sang. It had become a custom to sing " For all the saints " as the closing hymn each Sunday evening.

Now [writes Amma] all through the days, and often through the night, now as I write, that song sings within me:

And when the strife is fierce, the warfare long,
Steals on the ear the distant triumph song,
And hearts are brave again and arms are strong,
　　Alleluia! Alleluia!

The girls spent their September holidays in going to the villages around us in little bands, and we hope to keep the 24th, Mr Walker's Glory Day, sacred for this work, as we keep the 6th,* Indraneela's Day, for prayer. . . . We have seen our God's fore-thinking care for us proved in very many ways since that day of sudden desolation.

* It has long been the custom in Dohnavur to hold a special consecration service on August 24th, when God's challenge, " Whom shall I send, and who will go for us? " is brought before the Family, especially the older boys and girls. In recent years it has been necessary to change the date of this gathering, because so many of those for whom it is intended are away at boarding-school in August.

One of those "ways" was this. Two sisters, Edith and Agnes Naish, after many years in Palamcottah, where Agnes had been teaching in the Sarah Tucker College, had established themselves very recently in Sermadevi (the nearest railway station to Dohnavur), intending to give themselves to evangelistic work in the villages. As soon as they heard of Walker's death they felt they must offer to help Amma through the months of pressure which would follow, and the call seemed so urgent that they broke their usual custom and travelled over to Dohnavur on Sunday the 25th. Was it not a work of necessity and of mercy, and therefore lawful on the Sabbath? Their coming brought immediate relief, especially in the school, but it led to something far more wonderful, for in the following year they joined the Fellowship, and from that time until her health began to fail Agnes Naish was in charge of the children's education. Her love for teaching is as evident as her gift for it, and Amma rejoiced that she could hand over responsibility to one so well qualified to bear it.

Yet another of God's mercies was that Arul Dasan, who had been working for Mr Walker, agreed to work with Amma. He helped in writing, both in Tamil and English, and in the superintending of building work. This was important because, as the work grew, there was scarcely ever a time when some new building was not in course of erection, and others were being planned. The Family, which numbered seventy in 1906, had doubled itself by 1913.

There was spiritual gain too, especially among the older children who had been helped unconsciously through Walker's life amongst them. "Those who were earnest are more earnest, some who were chilly have been revived, and one most difficult child, never touched before, has been completely changed."

Thirty-three little ones were baptized on August 30th "after months of waiting for sure light". A letter from Mr Price of Palamcottah was a great cheer: "I am not worthy to be a praying father of any of those little ones, but if you will send me seven names I will pray for one each day."

There had been serious anxiety concerning Arulai's health, but by the spring of 1913 she seemed to be much stronger. But Ponnammal, the other of the two Indian sisters on whom Amma chiefly depended, was taken seriously ill. Mabel

Wade, the one trained nurse, was away in England—she left with the greatest reluctance, but Amma insisted that she ought to go—and the kind doctor in Neyyoor, on whom they had often relied, was also absent on furlough. So Ponnammal was taken to the Salvation Army Hospital at Nagercoil, and Amma went with her and nursed her through two operations. For the diagnosis was—cancer, and even after the operations the doctor could give no assurance that it would not recur.

When the second operation delayed the longed-for return to Dohnavur, Arulai was in danger of being overwhelmed by a rather unusual epidemic of malaria. Seventy of the children were ill at the same time, and some were sent in batches to Nagercoil. But she wrote in one of her letters to Amma, " Are you tasting the sweetness of this time? I am." Truly Amma was comforted by her friends' devotion to herself, but she was comforted far more when she found that they shared her devotion to Him Who is altogether lovely.

After a few months in Dohnavur there was a third operation at Nagercoil in October, followed by such relief that Amma began to hope again for full recovery. Sometimes Ponnammal was able to walk a little, but then there would be another long period of pain and helplessness.

But meanwhile—on July 14th—Mrs Carmichael was called Home. She had written letters of strong loving consolation when Walker died, and the news of Ponnammal's illness and apparent recovery was much in her thoughts. On July 4th she begins her letter to Amy with the words, " My own most precious earthly possession ". " Over and over again ", she says, " I have pictured your triumphal entrance with dear Ponnammal into Dohnavur. . . . You are being carried along in God's mighty protecting Arms of love and care." Her last loving letter was written on July 10th, and her last act was to post a cheque which had been received for the Dohnavur work to *The Christian* for transmission. To her friends in Wimbledon she was known as " the Beloved ".

The cable telling of her death did not reach Dohnavur till the 17th, and Amma notes in the margin of *Daily Light* for that evening the words, " Blow upon my garden, that the spices thereof may flow out." The very next morning *Daily Light* contained the verse which had been especially her mother's verse ever since 1885, " The Lord is good, a stronghold in the

day of trouble; and He knoweth them that trust in Him."
Amma writes in the margin, " Opened *Daily Light* this morning
with an almost wish that mother's verse might be given to me,
and here it is."

The home in Wimbledon had been in some ways a centre
for the Dohnavur work. Now it was broken up, and Amma's
sister moved elsewhere. But that same year Irene Streeter,
wife of Canon Streeter of Oxford, agreed to become Home
Secretary. A few months before her marriage in 1909 she had
visited India with a friend, and they arrived unexpectedly at
Dohnavur, as *Gold Cord* relates.* Just before Mrs Carmichael's
death Mrs Streeter had paid another visit, and in view of her
love for Dohnavur and her deep concern for the children in
danger, Amma rejoiced when in October she accepted the position of Dohnavur representative in England. She became, as
Amma says, " the dearest friend that a work like this could ever
have ".

There were other friends. At the Durbar of 1912 Lady
Lawley had privately told Queen Mary some of the facts which,
at her request, Amma had compiled, and the Queen sent a
message of sympathy. It was a great distress to Amma that
this story was printed in a missionary magazine, for she had
mentioned it only to a few of her inner circle of friends, on the
understanding that it was strictly private. But by this time
there were not a few in high places who recognized the need
and the value of the Dohnavur work, and though she shrank
from publicity Amma was comforted by their sympathy, and
emboldened to hope that the Government might take more
drastic action to deal with the traffic in children's souls.

It was during this difficult period that many of the songs
sung in the House of Prayer and at the Fellowship prayer
meetings were given to Amma. " They began to come ",
she says, " during the weeks of night nursing in April ", when
she herself was suffering from " that variety of neuralgia which
stabs its victims with patient persistence ". But they continued
to come at the most unlikely times. " In a hot bandy crawling
along a hot road, when everything in one is gasping, they come
so persistently that it is quite a trial not to be able to sit up then
and there and write them down." Two songs were written

* *Gold Cord*, pp. 137, 138.

on the brown paper wrapped round a huge bottle of medicine which she was bringing back to Dohnavur from Nagercoil. Dr Turner, who worked so hard to save Ponnammal, proved to be musical. " You have only to give the doctor words, and he finds music for them which expresses all they want to say but cannot."

What she calls " the song of the time ", printed at the beginning of this chapter, expresses her " quiet joy " throughout these days of sickness and bereavement. Many years later she wrote to her sister:

> I am finding a good deal of honey in the word " through " in Psalm 84. 6 and Isaiah 43. 2. We don't stay in these places—we are always " passing through ". Like the one who cometh up from the wilderness leaning on her Beloved (Song of Solomon 8. 5) we are only " passing through ", " coming up from ".

Right to the end of Amma's journey there was One Who gave her " songs in the night ".

He said, " I will forget the dying faces;
The empty places—
They shall be filled again.
O voices mourning deep within me, cease."
But vain the word; vain, vain:
Not in forgetting lieth peace.

He said, ' I will crowd action upon action,
The strife of faction
Shall stir me and sustain;
O tears that drown the fire of manhood, cease."
But vain the word; vain, vain:
Not in endeavour lieth peace.

He said, " I will withdraw me and be quiet,
Why meddle in life's riot?
Shut be my door to pain.
Desire, thou dost befool me, thou shalt cease."
But vain the word; vain, vain;
Not in aloofness lieth peace.

He said, " I will submit; I am defeated.
God hath depleted
My life of its rich gain.
O futile murmurings, why will ye not cease? "
But vain the word; vain, vain:
Not in submission lieth peace.

He said, " I will accept the breaking sorrow
Which God tomorrow
Will to His son explain.'
Then did the turmoil deep within him cease.
Not vain the word, not vain.
For in acceptance lieth peace.

CHAPTER XXI

"GOOD, ACCEPTABLE, PERFECT"

In December, 1913, a child called Kohila, which means Cuckoo, celebrated her first Coming Day. For those who do not know Dohnavur the words "Coming Day" require explanation. The actual birthday of a child rescued from Temple danger is rarely known, so the anniversary of arrival in Dohnavur is observed instead.* Amma always loved to mark special days, and that was one of the many traits in her character which appealed to Tamils. As the Family grew larger it became the custom for all whose Coming Days fall in any particular week to celebrate them together on the preceding Sunday. Each child's room is decked with flowers on that day, and small presents are given, always including a card and a tiny piece of scented soap. On Sunday morning the *Annachies*, and *Sitties* and *Accals* † and others make a joyful progress through the compound, visiting each "Coming Day" child, offering congratulations, viewing the tiny gifts, never forgetting to smell the soap and comment on its fragrance. At the evening hymn-singing in the House of Prayer the "Coming Day" children, or, rather, the smaller ones amongst them, sit specially dressed and garlanded beside the one who is conducting the gathering.

These customs were only in embryo when Kohila ‡ joined the Family, but to a child of about five years old the first Coming Day is a great event. Some weeks later her guardians wrote demanding that she be returned to them, and they threatened to charge Amma with kidnapping if she refused. With Muttammal's case in mind, Amma did not hesitate for a moment—except to tell Ponnammal, who all through this year

---

* But in recent years, for the purpose of entries in official forms, great efforts are being made to estimate the actual date of birth.

† *Annachie* (older brother) is the word used for all the men workers, Indian and foreign. *Sittie* (mother's younger sister) might be translated "Auntie", and is used for all the foreign women workers. *Accal* (older sister) is used for Indian women workers.

‡ The book *Kohila* gives her full story.

was slowly dying, of the risk that she was taking. Supposing the verdict in the criminal court went against her, it might mean seven years' imprisonment. But Ponnammal did not hesitate either. " Do not think of me ", she said. So plans were made to " disappear " Kohila, and missionaries were found hundreds of miles away to give her sanctuary until the storm blew over. It would have been folly for Amma to escort her, but Arul Dasan was willing to take the risk, though he might easily have suffered as an accomplice. As they travelled in a house boat in Travancore, two men recognized her, and spoke of the case to be tried in Madras. But they were restrained from going further.

On February 6th, 1914, as Amma writes in the margin of *Daily Light*, " we all faced prison as a probable end of little Kohila's case ". She told the *Accals* that she did not expect to be with them a week hence. Pappammal asked, " But will it not be possible to have a *buthil* (substitute)? ", and in a moment they were all pleading for the privilege of being *buthil*, of going to prison instead of Amma.* Arulai, Rukma, Lola, Leela, Preena, and Purripu, Ponnammal's daughter—all would gladly have taken Amma's place. The fact that the law would never have accepted a *buthil* does not affect the fine quality of their love and loyalty. But the very next day came a telegram, " Criminal case dismissed ", and they breathed again.

Is it necessary to explain that neither on this occasion, nor at any subsequent time, did Amma carelessly or willingly flout the authority of the law? The law against kidnapping was a good law, a very necessary law. Out of respect for it Amma would not have appealed if she had been convicted. But it was not framed with such children as Kohila in mind, and Amma could not send her back to destruction without sinning against a higher Law. So the risk had to be faced, and " God arose to judgment ". That was Amma's explanation, and no other reason for the failure of the charge was ever forthcoming.

Just before the outbreak of what we called the Great War —never dreaming that there could be a greater—in August, 1914, Amma had been guided to purchase more land. *Nor Scrip* † tells the story, which followed the happily accustomed lines—the prayer for guidance and then for a sign, the

---

* The story is told in *Gold Cord*, Chapter XVI.
† *Nor Scrip*, Chapter V.

coming of the "sign" gift from an unexpected quarter, and
the completion of the transaction with all necessary funds in
hand. A large field was to be used for a market garden, and
through the kindness of the Director of Agriculture Arul Dasan
was given some months of intensive training in the cultivation
of vegetables. Of course the Lord knew how the value of such
a field would increase as the war progressed. It was not that
Amma's friends ceased to give, but an adverse exchange
diminished the value of their gifts until the purchasing power of
£1 had dwindled to 4s. Mails were sometimes lost by enemy
action, and months would pass before donors realized that
Amma had not been remiss in acknowledging their cheques,
for the cheques had never arrived.

Yet all needs were met, and of course no child saved from
Temple danger was ever refused admittance. As Amma said,
she could not believe that the War turned God's word inside
out and made it read, " It is the will of your Father that these
little ones should perish." God was the Treasurer of the work,
and the War did not affect His resources.

Meanwhile Ponnammal's cancer had returned. Whenever
the pain was less acute she would beg Amma to take her round
the compound, and she would give advice as she had always
done. " Amma, it is the season now for buying cotton seed
for the bullocks," or, " Amma, this or that kind of vegetable is
in season now." But the time came when movement was
impossible, and the friend and counsellor of eighteen years
could only suffer. For some months she heard heavenly music
from time to time. When it came she needed no sleeping
draught, no medicine to relieve her pain, for she was sleeping
peacefully before the music ceased, and woke in the morning
refreshed. But for the last seven or eight months of her life
the comfort of the music was withdrawn. Then she was
encouraged by a dream in which, after she felt herself sinking
in a deep stream, the Lord appeared to her in radiance un-
speakable, and she woke praising Him.

Occasionally it was necessary for Amma to leave Dohnavur.
Once, for instance, she was in Madras at the invitation of Canon
Sell, the C.M.S. Secretary. He had often urged her to bring
a few of the girls to the great city for an educational, sight-seeing
trip. Frances Beath was of the party, and in Madras they met
also Mr and Mrs Beath senior, and Mabel, who had been

staying for some time at Ooty. Mabel tells how the Canon determined that Amma should speak at a drawing-room meeting. He overcame her opposition only when he suggested that courtesy demanded her compliance in return for his hospitality. She shrank from the limelight, and even feared it for the children's sake. Moreover, she knew that some would be present who resented her wearing of Indian dress as a blow to British prestige!

The day before the meeting was a very full one. She wanted the children to see everything—the beach, the harbour, factories, shops. At a jeweller's, for instance, they were allowed to see a number of uncut stones. "How do these girls know about such things?" asked the jeweller in amazement, and Amma replied, "Through reading the Book of Revelation." That night she had one of her bad headaches, and Frances sat up with her trying to alleviate the pain, until at length she slept.

In the morning the weight of the meeting had gone, for she had had a dream, and knew how to begin her address. A big crowd filled the bungalow, and after a hymn Canon Sell introduced the speaker.

> The atmosphere of that room [writes Mabel Beath] was in the main frigid. This little dark-haired, dark-eyed lady in Indian dress began to speak, and her first sentence was, " I had a dream last night."

Now one of the amusements of her critics was to poke fun at her as a dreamer of dreams, and so at her first words they looked at one another as if to say, " I told you so."

> I had a dream last night [she said]. I thought I had come to this gathering, and an aged child of God with many years' service behind him was asked to pray. " O Lord ", he said, " here we are gathered together for yet another meeting, and Thou knowest how tired we are of meetings. Help us to get through this one."

The frozen atmosphere melted, and a ripple of laughter spread over the audience. They were ready to listen as she spoke with great simplicity and power of the work which God had committed to her trust.

Sometimes it seemed as if she could not continue that work if Ponnammal were taken. Kind friends wrote and said that they were praying for " another Ponnammal ", but the Dohna-

vur village pastor was wiser. He smiled and shook his head so
expressively that Amma knew exactly what he was thinking.
Women of character, ability, and spiritual insight such as
Ponnammal possessed were not easily to be found in the
churches of South India. They are rare in any land.

Her love for Amma shone out in look and word to the very
end. A few weeks before her passing she said rather wistfully,
"I had hoped to be able to stay with you and help you to bear
the burden, but it is not to be." The pain increased, and
Amma spoke often to her of the joy that lay beyond, the joy of
perfect service unhindered by pain. "Yes," she said, "I
greatly desire it, but I could bear as much pain as I have now.
If only I could stay to help you. I think I could continue to
endure it up to this limit."

Frequently throughout the illness Amma was "assailed"
(as she puts it) by letters and tracts suggesting that if only she
would pray the prayer of faith, healing would be granted.

> But our little children had taught us many things. We
> knew they did not always know what was good for them,
> and we should have been very grieved if they had persisted
> in imploring for something, after we had let them understand
> that we could not give it. . . . Not, "Thy will be changed"
> but "Thy will be done", is the prayer we are taught to
> pray.

Remembering that He is our Father, Who yearns to give us
His very best, she felt it was "inconsiderate to press Him
further". The words that face the opening of this chapter
were given by Ponnammal's death-bed.

For Ponnammal entered into Light on August 26th, 1915.
Her last conscious thought was for her daughter Purripu. "I
give her to you", she said to Amma. "You will be a Mother
to her." And Purripu has been a very precious legacy.

The funeral gave Amma the opportunity of establishing a
new tradition. If death has lost its sting, should not even a
funeral be evidence that Christ has overcome him who had the
power of death?

> We filled the room with flowers, it was a perfect bower of
> flowers of all bright triumphant colours; and round her
> in great sprays we laid white jessamine. The children came
> in groups; and the village people, quiet for once, came too;
> and when all was ready for the sowing of the seed our own

kind servants came and carried the light cot with Ponnammal
sleeping among the flowers, out through the garden and the
compound, and into the village street; and the children
and girls followed, a hundred or more of them—two good
Sitties stayed to care for the babies and set the nurses free—
while the village people crowded round and wondered.
For never before had they seen such a sight. Nor indeed
had I, for never before had we quite such an opportunity to
strip off the dull sheath from that despondent function—is not
a Christian funeral too often just that?—and show what is
within, even the hope of glory; and cause it to appear what
it surely is in the angels' eyes, a Triumphal Procession. And
that was what we wanted, God helping us, to do. So the
little ones were in their happy blue, and the girls in their
white and yellow; and all who could, bravely tried to sing;
even the children who would have been broken-hearted if
left behind, and yet were too small to enter into it perfectly,
controlled their sobs and tried to do as Ponnammal *Accal*
would wish; and the sight of this controlled grief spoke, I
think, to the people as nothing else did, for till grief has
worn old with them it is very uncontrolled. Ponnammal's
father, who had been with us for some months, could not
find words to express his surprise. In all his seventy years,
he said, he had never seen anything like it. And I praised
our God Who had enabled us to hold up the things that are
not seen and show them to all who would look.

But oh the dreary emptiness of the compound when we
returned! And yet even that desolation was good, and joy
was set in it. She is not here, she is risen, it said—not here—
far hence; and yet near in a new way. " I believe in the
Communion of saints." And we prayed to be delivered
from all selfish sorrow, and returned to our work again.

But before the year ended it seemed as if Arulai might be
taken too. When she returned from a happy holiday with
Frances Beath's parents at Ooty she was suffering from nephritis.

One day—it was one of the worst days—I faced for the
first time a possible parting with this treasure of all treasures.
It was not only her own preciousness which made it a tremendous thing to part, it was her preciousness to the whole work.
The Iyer, Ponnammal, Arulai—our three strongest spiritual
influences, the three upon whom I could always count for
strength of character as well as for spiritual power—Lord,
must Thou take them all?

On December 6th Arulai was at the Gates. She was able
to tell Amma later how she had seen Walker Iyer and Ponnam-

mal, and then it seemed as if the children and their *Accals* gathered round, so that she could go no further into the heavenly Land. Amma sent a wire to one of her old friends in Palamcottah, Mr Ardill—" Come. Arulai dying "—and, at the risk of a good deal of misunderstanding, for important diocesan meetings were in progress, he travelled by bandy through the night, and arrived on the morning of the 7th. Through the night of the 7th he travelled back again, and Mrs Ardill greeted him with the question, " Did you take the funeral? " " No," he said, " there was no funeral "—for Arulai had been given back. She lived for twenty-four more years, growing all the time in grace and wisdom, and the long strain of her illness was lightened for Amma by a new understanding of the words of Romans 12. 2, " Good and acceptable and perfect ". The words were painted in blue on a piece of rough teak over the doorway of Amma's room. Arulai's room was just opposite, and one day when both doors were open Amma looked across and saw her, as it were, framed in the door, with those words written above her. " Those three words hallow pain," she wrote. " They take from it all bitterness, all that stings and rankles; they leave it, still pain indeed, but somehow sweetened, chastened." And in Tamil " acceptable " is rendered by a word meaning " lovable ".

O thou beloved child of My desire,
Whether I lead thee through green valleys,
        By still waters,
        Or through fire,
Or lay thee down in silence under snow,
Through any weather, and whatever
            Cloud may gather,
            Wind may blow—
Wilt love Me? trust Me? praise Me?

No gallant bird, O dearest Lord, am I,
That anywhere, in any weather,
        Rising singeth;
        Low I lie.
And yet I cannot fear, for I shall soar,
Thy love shall wing me, blessed Saviour;
            So I answer,
            I adore,
I love Thee, trust Thee, praise Thee.

CHAPTER XXII

"THROUGH ANY WEATHER"

"Had torn up all the rest of this note-book when Arulai came in and begged me to stop, and remembering difficulty in verifying dates, I did. When finished with, *destroy*." This is the kind of difficulty that Amma's biographer faces. In the later years Mary Mills (the Perfect Nurse) and Neela, Amma's secretary and right-hand, salvaged much valuable material. Courage and wisdom were needed, for sometimes it was necessary to find safe hiding-places for old letters and diaries which Amma would have destroyed. By the time that she had become accustomed to the thought that something would be written—since the stories of God's working in her life were His if He wanted them—much had already been lost. But part of a diary of the years 1915–1929 is extant, and some of her inner experiences during the war years are here set down.

In 1915—the year of Ponnammal's Home-going, and of Arulai's dangerous illness—Amma herself was far from well. She writes on October 10th:

> Looking back—Shining things: Love and goodness of all to me when ill. Bless them for it, my God. Shadowed things: Distress of thought of doctor being called to leave far needier people for me. Distress of finding some dear ones overburdened because I had given way. Distress because I did give way. Lord, teach me how to conquer pain to the uttermost henceforth, and grant this my earnest request. When my day's work is done, take me straight Home. Do not let me be ill and a burden or anxiety to anyone. O let me finish my course with joy and not with grief. Thou knowest there could be no joy if I knew I were tiring those whom I love best, or taking them from the children. Let me die of a battle wound, O my Lord, not of a lingering illness. Father, hear me, answer me. Forgive this prayer if it be wrong, and grant it if Thou canst turn it to Thy glory.
>
> *October* 26. Had children in field weeding. Told them of need of money—a new idea to them. Explained a little to older girls about our way of working, and what it involved of careful sensitiveness towards God. Finally got them, and

all, to the point of willingness to give today (Festival Day) to weeding. Girls splendid over it, children very sweet and good. Inwardly prayed for a quick assurance from our Father that He was pleased. It would be like Him to do this.

October 27. Mail in today, and £50 from a friend of Irene Streeter, her soldier brother's money left to her. Took letter up to field where children were weeding, and we all praised God standing in shadow of cactus hedge. There was other money too—more in one mail than has come for many months. All much cheered, and much awed too.

Most of the entries until the end of the year are concerned with Arulai's illness.

December 28. The Life [*Walker of Tinnevelly*] came today. Too ashamed as I read Dr Stock's words on the paper wrapper to take any pleasure in the book. O my God, I am ashamed before Thee.

Here a word of explanation seems to be necessary. The Life of Walker had been finished before the outbreak of war, but Amma had held it back from publication because she doubted if anyone in England would want to read anything but war news. Hidden away in a remote corner of India— for that is how Dohnavur was regarded by anyone who knew of it—she was never isolated in spirit from world events. Indeed, there were few who agonized as she did over the suffering of Belgium, and at a much later date the rape of Abyssinia, and all the manifold griefs of the Second World War. Letters and newspapers were delayed, but she had a breadth of mind and sympathy which astonished those who imagined that her concern for the Temple children was a passion which absorbed all her thinking, to the exclusion of the " great world's anguish ". In 1915, however, she consented to allow *Walker of Tinnevelly* to be published. Dr Eugene Stock had not been asked to write a foreword, but he had read the whole book in manuscript, and it was no wonder that the publishers should ask him to write what we should now call a " blurb " for the jacket of the book.

Doubtless his eulogy was both sincere and well deserved, but Amma was equally sincere in her grief concerning it. True humility, " a deep sense of one's own moral littleness ", is so rare that we tend to question its sincerity, but right on to the end Amma was truly amazed at the success of her books, and wondered that more than a very few people should care to read them.

After this a number of pages have been torn out.

October 10, 1916. My friend of friends with Christ [Miss Nugent], but know it is as one knows things in a dream. Now at home, of dear old days, there is only one left who has room in her heart for much of me. Lord, give it to me to live in the joy of those who are gone, and not in my loss.

January 4, 1917. Went to —— for festival. At night Dorothy Waller, who was staying with me, and I unexpectedly found ourselves in a Temple house. Dorothy stabbed to the heart. That night I knew she could never be the same again. . . . She had heard her call and must join us.

January 15. I never knew spiritual assaults could be so tumultuous. They are like a noise of shoutings within me. Trials of voices about K—— who left us today, and V——, whose heart is not right with God. Is the work for these girls going to end in dust and ashes? And—God forgive me —most subtle and wearying voices about what I did last year as regards money, giving up dear old Mr B——'s gift, fears lest I was not sincere in it. If I deceived myself, then all was vanity. Burn, burn out of me any insincerity that lurks within.

January 16. Relieved. Hold Thou me up and I shall be safe. And O forgive me, but I *must* ask it : take me quickly when my work is finished. Do not, I beseech Thee, let me be disabled by pain or inability and live on a burden to others. Have been more than usually in pain these last few days.

January 20. The taunting voice this morning said, "Wast thou not a fool to wreck thyself thus on thy God? " Lord, was it ever foolish to wreck oneself on Thee?

May 30. The Two arrived [Arul Dasan and Kunmunnie]. O what great troubles and adversities hast Thou shewed me. And yet Thou didst turn and refresh me. Therefore will I praise Thee and Thy faithfulness.

Then follows the story of the Forest, which demands a chapter to itself, and after that there is another great gap. In 1919 Irene Streeter visited Dohnavur again, and dug the first sod of a new nursery.

August 12, 1919. Letter from X—— (a new recruit) sure of her guidance, and by the same mail one from Miss C—— about the £100 she sent, hoping it would not lose by exchange too heavily, and giving it for any need. Her letter had been delayed a fortnight, so came with X——'s. Flashed

in my mind—" This is the £100 for X——'s passage."
Nothing will be lost by exchange if it is used at home. This
is the Seal and Sign. It is also, to my heart, the Lord's seal
upon the whole forward movement. He Who knoweth the
heart knows the thoughts that are in mine, the temptation to
fear for the others who may be left to carry burdens heavier
than mine have been, the inward *terror* sometimes. He knows
how under the joy of each new nursery built has lain this fear.

    September 16. The fourth of the new nurseries begun.
Irene digging first sod as before. She left us that same
evening. A hard goodbye.

    There followed a time of strange and new distress. No
news reached us from home. [Mrs Streeter's substitute
apparently misunderstood what was expected of her.] So
for the first time, guidance being uncertain, we stopped
work begun. A huge rice bill had to be paid—unexpectedly
large, as it was hoped rice prices would fall. This left us
with barely enough for two months more. Still no news
from home. With this inward strain upon us we went to
Madras to find the atmosphere there saturated with money
talk. Exhausting and depressing. E. McDougall took me
to the sea. Glorious, soul-strengthening, was reinforced in
faith.

Dr Eleanor McDougall is widely known as the founder and
first Principal of the Women's Christian College, Madras.
Their friendship began in this way. Amma had seen in a
magazine or newspaper a fellow-missionary's sweeping criticisms of the new College, and she wrote to Miss McDougall
expressing her sympathy. The criticisms had meant nothing
to Miss McDougall, and she was rather puzzled, for she did not
know, or did not remember, that she had been attacked. But
she did appreciate the sympathy of a stranger, and in 1916 they
met for the first time. Amma calls it " an unforgettable hour".

    All the time I was with her I seemed to see a field under
the plough, and to hear one of the finest of our Tamil pro-
verbs, " Better is it to plough deep than to plough wide ".
She is going to plough a deep furrow.

It was a friendship based on mutual appreciation and on
common intellectual interests. The two women were of similar
mental calibre, for Amma, with fewer opportunities of formal
education, had a taste for good literature which she never
ceased to cultivate, She knew well that the Way of the Cross
is a narrow Way, but she had none of the small-mindedness

that mars the testimony of some whose basis of belief is identical with hers. It was Dr McDougall who introduced her to Saint Teresa and other mystics, for she respected Amma's faculty for distinguishing essentials from externals, for refusing to ignore the pure wheat because it required sifting from the chaff. She was quick to recognize and be challenged by the depth of spiritual insight in some from whom she differed even in important matters. Indeed, she and Dr McDougall often crossed swords in argument, and though neither would admit defeat, each recognized in the other a foeman worthy of her steel. As time went on, Amma was inevitably surrounded by colleagues much junior to herself, and though she was utterly sincere in her appreciation of their gifts, and would often defer to their judgment and try to make them feel that even in the early days they could make a valuable contribution to the work, yet she was their leader, and drew forth their reverence as well as their love. From this point of view it was both salutary and refreshing when someone from outside, who was more nearly her equal in years, argued with her and chaffed her as few others could do.

For several years, from 1921 onwards, Dr McDougall came annually to Dohnavur, and spent some weeks in the Forest with Amma. She conducted a class in Latin, Greek New Testament, and some other subjects, for a few of the older girls. Her first visit coincided with a time of great spiritual tension, and it was a refreshment to Amma to talk with her. One of the girls, quick to note anything that was comforting to their dear Amma, came to Dr McDougall with her New Testament, and pointed to the words of II Corinthians 7. 6: "God, that comforteth those that are cast down, comforted us by the coming of Titus ", where she had crossed out the word " Titus " and substituted " McDougall " for it. Dr McDougall went to Amma with a solemn face, and said, " I am sorry you do not teach your children to have a proper respect for the Scriptures ". Amma looked so horrified that Dr McDougall hastened to explain, and to this day she is known in Dohnavur as Titus!

We have wandered a long way from the record of " new and strange distress " in the autumn of 1919.

November 25. Mail in—only £80. Lord, what does it mean? Instead of fresh help, heard from Miss V—— that she is ill and can help no longer.

December 1. Half awake, half asleep. I was in a great Bank. Thought it was Barclays Bank. Looked up and saw on a kind of frieze running round the wall: " Casting all your care upon Him, for He careth for you ", and " Your heavenly Father knoweth that ye have need of all these things ". Seemed too other-worldly for earth. Rose refreshed. Remembered thing shown at Sengelteri—stormy sky, clouds tearing across in wild confusion and behind them a hand holding a little nest with eggs in it. Lord, we are still waiting upon Thee. Remember Thy Word unto Thy servant, upon which Thou hast caused me to hope.

December 2. Yesterday the mail came unexpectedly. Cheque for £52.10.4, royalty on books. Tremendous surprise, as I had not thought books were selling much. Cheque from the heavenly Bank that I saw in my dream.

December 4. Today cheque. " From ' *He careth for you* ' " written on the envelope.

December 31. Many other gifts this month . . . I feel like writing them every one down, so doubly precious and reassuring have they been. Dorothy did accounts roughly, and found the year cleared. My God, my God, I thank Thee.

And in January of 1920 a Keswick speaker, Dr Charles Inwood, spent two days at Dohnavur.

January 28. When I went over to Mr Inwood's room with roses he told me he had been praying, and the Lord had told him to give us £50. . . . Much heart-strengthening talk about the ways of the Lord with those committed to Him as we are.

January 29. Getting further and further into the heart of this brave dear man. He added £6 of his own to help in the loss through exchange. When I demurred he said, " The Lord has told me to do it. Don't you think I know His Voice when He speaks to me? "

These were Dr Inwood's impressions:

The two days spent here have no parallel in my experience. Everything in this work has the touch of God so naturally upon it that I lived in one unbroken act of wonder and worship and adoration. . . . The visit was to me a sacrament, a new contact with the Spirit of the Master that enriched my own spirit for all coming time.

It is thus that the hearts of God's true soldiers warm to one another. But there was a concrete result of the visit. Dr Inwood had imagined that the work had behind it a group of wealthy and influential friends. When he learned that it was not so, he remarked, " You ought to tell it. It is keeping back something that belongs to God if you don't ". Thus was sown the seed of *Nor Scrip*, *Tables in the Wilderness*, *Meal in a Barrel*,* *Windows*, and *Though the Mountains Shake*, the series of books which tell something of God's provision for a work that is wholly dependent upon Him.

So the War years passed, and Amma and her fellow-workers learned to trust their Leader " through any weather ". At the beginning of 1919 the sun of public approval shone upon the work, and that was almost more bewildering than the storms which Amma was accustomed to face. For early in January she received a telegram from Lord Pentland, Governor of Madras, congratulating her on the inclusion of her name in the Royal Birthday Honours List. The award of the Kaiser-i-Hind Medal for her services to the people of India was well deserved, but to Amma the shock was very great. At first she even wondered whether she could refuse it, and she wrote to Lord Pentland:

> Would it be unpardonably rude to ask to be allowed not to have it? . . . I have done nothing to make it fitting, and cannot understand it at all. It troubles me to have an experience so different from His Who was despised and rejected—not kindly honoured.

At length she was persuaded that it would be ungracious to refuse it, but nothing would induce her to go to Madras in March for the presentation ceremony. His Majesty's advisers had done wisely in putting forward her name, and her friends were right in pressing her not to refuse the honour, but they appreciated her scruples, and loved her the more because she was so transparently honest in seeking only the glory of God.

* " Doesn't Miss Carmichael choose strange titles for her books? " said someone. " *Beer in a Barrel*, for instance "!

Dim green forest
Of a thousand secrets,
When you were planted
Did the angels sing?
Many things I wonder,
Are they all your secrets,
Won't you ever tell me anything?

Great white waterfall
Breaking through the forest,
Where do you come from,
Where do you go?
Had you a beginning,
Will you go on for ever?
For ever and for ever will you flow?

Great black, glistening wall
Veiled in shining glory,
Piled among the waters
Rock upon rock,
O to have stood and seen
Hands at work upon you,
Shivering you and shattering shock on shock.

Deep, dark, silent pool
Hollowed at the water's foot,
What do you think of
All the long day?
Do you hear the thunder
Of tremendous waters?
Do you hear the laughter of the spray?

CHAPTER XXIII

THE FOREST

AFTER Walker's death Amma rarely went to Ooty. It was not merely that he and Mrs Hopwood were gone, and the place constantly reminded her of them both; the cost of conveying an increasing number of young people there, and providing accommodation, had become formidable, and moreover the distance involved too long an absence from Dohnavur. So she experimented for a year or two with an empty Forest Department bungalow at Sengelteri, in the mountains above Dohnavur. It was near, it was sufficiently cool, and there was a river and a waterfall " specially contrived for bathing ". The artist in Amma was never weary of watching the children " in their blue and yellow clothes so perfectly harmonized with the colour scheme of the place, with its shadowy greens and browns, that wherever they went they made pictures ". But she was first of all a mother.

To me the joy of joys was to have the opportunity of getting to know them in new ways, and Mother-work requires that constantly growing knowledge. It gave me a new touch with some of the most difficult characters, a new hold upon their affections which is of priceless value.

They saw tracks of tiger and elephant and deer, and they found bears' holes.

One evening we gave the Family a shivering half hour. Four of us were returning from a walk up the forest, when we saw the others coming back from the river, and we hid behind a tree and growled. There was a wild rush up to the house, and then, to our immense gratification, we saw the whole household turn out with sticks, led by Sellamutthu horribly alarmed but valiant. The coolies followed, their eyes and mouths wide open with terror. More growls from behind the tree. The coolies fell back; but the children made a dive for the wood where, as they imagined, we were being devoured whole, and with the faithful Sellamutthu at their head rushed on, resolved to rescue us or perish; and the coolies ashamed at their terrors flourished their weapons and whooped. Then we emerged calmly, and enquired what was the matter? " Bears ! Bears ! Hasten ! Hasten ! " shouted the whole assembly, and Sellamutthu was in the act of offering devout thanks to heaven for our deliverance, when a small girl behind me giggled, and the game was up.

Amma always loved to play bears or tigers with the children. Very exhausting? Yes, but also relaxing. You cannot be concerned with the state of the world, the problems of exchange, or even the perils of Temple children when you are on all fours impersonating a tiger, or growling like a bear.

But Sengelteri, though delightful, could accommodate only a fraction of those who needed the change, and moreover it was not their own. So Amma, accompanied usually by Frances Beath or Helen Bradshaw, began prospecting for a site on which they could build houses for themselves. She was told that she was expecting the impossible, but that was nothing unusual for Amma. It was disappointing, however, to toil painfully through forest undergrowth for hours, and then find that the journey was in vain—there was no water, or no view, or no flat place on which to build. Once they slept 4,000 feet up on the floor of a mud cottage on a coffee estate. It was so cold that two of the older girls kept a fire burning all night. But it was land that belonged to a temple which would not sell. On the way down they found a lovely little dell with a stream running through it, and a kind Brahman who knew the forest thought they would find no better site. But he casually mentioned a place called the Grey Jungle.

" The moment we saw it we * knew we had found our heart's desire. How can I describe it? It sets you singing however dull you are." She admitted, however, that " some would find its front door prohibitive. It is a straight cliff up which you climb as best you can. It will have to be made safer, as at present a slip there would mean a funeral ".

There was a good deal of talking, and much more praying. " Lord, we only want to do Thy will," says the diary. " We do not want to run before Thee, and embark on costly follies." A Mr Bell, " one of those experienced saints whose word carries

---

* The " we " of Amma's letters is often like the " we " of Paul's Epistles. It was probably Amma whose instinct told her she had found the place of her desire, and the others were infected by her enthusiasm.

weight ", visited the Grey Jungle and " looked with longing on
the upper hillside, where there is a splendid open grassy place
backed by mountains, just the place for the forest house, and
he felt it would be worth much to secure it ". The owner was
there that day—an old Mohammedan—and he asked £100 for
37 acres of hillside, with a river running through it that never
ran dry, and waterfalls and bathing pools, great trees and
luxuriant vegetation. There was a view right across the plain
to the eastern sea coast, though Dohnavur itself was hidden by
foothills.

Then we sat down, with wild pineapples looking up at us,
and wild oranges looking down at us, and the great mountains watching from afar, and we prayed for a sign. That
night we found our mails waiting. I opened mine next day.
One letter was from a lawyer in Cork saying my dear friend
Florence P—— had left £100 to me. . . . On Frances
Beath's birthday, September 14th [1917] the Grey Jungle
became ours.

With enthusiasm which was not of the type which the Chinese
call " five-minute hot-heartedness ", but which persisted
through all kinds of unimagined difficulties, the building of the
Forest House began. " The carpenter proved untrustworthy
and in all ways troublesome. The masons were not much
better. There were many delays. Rain came before the roof
was on, and twice the walls fell." Both for the Forest House
and for later buildings the children themselves helped enor-
mously, carrying heavy loads of mud or of bricks or tiles, and
often putting the workmen to shame. The men were of several
castes, and therefore could not eat or sleep together. Amma
slept with the children, first in a ramshackle hut and then in the
unfinished house, with coolies sleeping close at hand. When
the rain came, gang after gang of men would attempt to pick
up their tools and small belongings and make for the plain.
But by prayer and patience and courage and indomitable
cheerfulness Amma would either circumvent them, or draw
them back to work after they had sworn they would never
return.

The second house was eventually built on a site that no
builder or engineer would have passed. Once the corner of
the veranda, painfully built up with stone and bricks, fell with
a crash. All were horrified, but Amma only laughed. " We

must build again," she said, " but stronger and deeper," and somehow inspired the workmen to begin again. This was the Jewel House, which later proved so unsafe that something had to be done. Expert advice favoured complete rebuilding. But as Amma went up with a party that included the expert, they saw the arc of a perfect rainbow spanning the very site, and a way was found whereby the loads on faulty foundations were lightened without the rebuilding which became necessary at a later date.

But we are anticipating. As time went on, God gave Amma fellow-workers with a great variety of gifts, who caught her enthusiasm and with immense patience worked to translate her dreams into realities. She would be intensely grieved if they were not given the credit that is their due. But it was she who conceived impossible plans, and persuaded men with practical gifts to achieve what they would hardly have attempted of their own volition.

At a very early stage the difficulties seemed overwhelming. One set of men would fell a tree, but the set which ought to be there to raise it and prop it up for sawing were away at a festival, and the sawyers would not touch it. So the carpenters had no work, for the sawyers would not saw. They all hated rain. The walls were built of stone set in mud.

> The masons were provided with palm mats to cover the wall tops before the roof was on, but they scamped this if they could, and many a time we (i.e. Amma and Arul Dasan and the children) stood in drenching rain handing up and laying the mats on the bare wall tops, while the masons, huddled in their huts, shivered and wished themselves and us in Jericho—if Jericho be dry.

" There really did seem something diabolical in the character of the difficulties." Diabolical? It was an immense cheer to Amma when she realized that the opposition *was* spiritual, and therefore could be met and overcome with spiritual weapons.

One moonlight Sunday evening Arul Dasan led a service, and read the 27th Psalm.

> By the time he had got to verse 6 I could say the words aloud, and did so, turning to the listening men, who with their big saws on their shoulders stood around. I told them whether they came or went the house would be finished. It was God's house and He would see to it. From that night

on things went forward as never before, and by the good Hand of our God upon us the roof of this house was on before the rains.

Why did the enemy rage? Partly, perhaps, because in adjacent valleys on both sides of the ravine lie temple properties, and the temples would have purchased the land if Amma had not done so. Partly because a cast-iron idol, which they found there, called " the devil of the chain ", was removed, and an idolatrous stone symbol was built into a fireplace. Partly, too, because the Hindu workmen attended an evening meeting for several months, and two carpenters from Travancore (who had taken the place of the first unsatisfactory drinker and opium-eater) asked for baptism. Paradesi and Devadas were baptized, at their own request, in the Pool below the Forest House.

The Pool looked its very loveliest. A rock runs into the heart of it, and on it we can stand. This rock was coloured a sort of dull gold that day because of the way the light caught it. On either side the water was jade green, till it reached the rocks which are grey, splashed and veined with crimson, brown and yellow, and their colours were brokenly reflected in the water. A little waterfall tinkled at the other end. This is the pool of many joyful swimming hours. . . . But never was it so happy a pool as on that day when those two men confessed Christ crucified. The toil of the house was as nothing then—the very remembrance of it fell off. . . . Arulai is continuing the Bible teaching that new converts so much require.

Amma had learned to swim and to dive at Millisle and in Strangford Lough. She was determined that every child should swim, not only for the enjoyment of it but because the pool— ten to fifteen feet deep, according to the time of year—was dangerous until they could do so. There was one occasion in the early days when she herself was nearly drowned. A child who was learning to swim suddenly seized her and dragged her under, and she could not free herself, and possibly was too tired to swim ashore. But as soon as she had been rescued, as she lay on the rock, she cheerfully told the anxious little group around her how much she had enjoyed the sensation of drowning, and adjured them not to frighten the Family in Dohnavur by describing the incident. The record in the log-book is limited to four words: " Adventure in the Pool ".

There was a lower pool which Amma called the Death Pool. Its banks were so slippery and shelved so steeply that it was difficult to climb out, so the name was chosen as a warning against possible danger. Years later a younger worker, not liking the sound of it, suggested another name. But he had to face insuperable opposition. " Amma named it," he was told. Incidentally, there was another occasion when he was teaching the children to sing a certain hymn. They made two or three mistakes, and persisted in them after the correct version had been played several times. " Why could you not sing that hymn correctly? " he asked someone afterwards, and the reply was, " Amma taught us that song."

How summarily she would have dealt with this particular evidence of their loyalty, if she had known of it! But there is something very moving about the staunchness of their love for anything which reminds them of Amma.

The servants, like the children, would do anything for her. In the Forest she delighted to have meals out of doors. She used to sit reading or writing in the shade of a great over-hanging rock throughout the hours of daylight. But she loved to have tea in a different place each day. " Let's have tea on the top of that rock," she would say, and, however inaccessible the place, one of the servants would do her bidding, at the risk of broken china or even a broken limb. Before paths were made and graded, she would climb straight up the side of a hill, taking some of the children with her, a servant with a large knife cutting the way before them through almost impenetrable brushwood. Where she wanted to go she would go, and the servant would blaze the trail without murmur or complaint.

Those of the children who were left behind in Dohnavur loved to write and keep her in touch with the day-to-day happenings. In May of 1918 one of them wrote:

Last Sunday God gave Kunmunnie [Muttammal] a baby boy and our mother cat had three kittens on that same day. Amma, last Sunday when I got up from my bed a wind came rushing to me from the east, and I thought I would send a message through it to you. I want to sit on your knee and give you two big kisses.

The first-born of Arul Dasan and Kunmunnie was called David, and a great rock towards the summit of the mountain to the east of the Forest House is called David's Rock because it was discovered on the day of his birth. To this day it is one of the places to which the children resort as soon as possible after they reach the Forest, because the Dohnavur Compound can be seen from it.

"Your room is crying without you, and I cannot wipe its tears, and it have made a pool," writes another child. "All the nurseries and children are saying, 'Ammai, come quickly, we want to see you so very badly.'" "As much imagination as the pool," writes Amma, for she knew that "the nurseries go their way with the true philosophy of babyhood. No sensible baby is going to break its heart over my absence."

"I can see you with my inward eye taking * a song about all the things that God has made," says the same child. Amma was far too busy for song-making at that time, but in the years that followed, when she enjoyed almost perfect happiness in the Forest, she "took" a great many songs, grave and gay, and all of them were meant to be sung. As one and another provided music to fit the words, they were added to the scores of songs which all the children (in those days) learned by heart.

They clamour to be quoted. From uproarious week-day songs like "The Golden Oriole", who died of eating too many caterpillars, and "The Elephant"—well, this is "The Elephant":

> The elephant comes with a tramp, tramp, tramp,
> The elephant comes with a stamp, stamp, stamp,
>   Through forest and over marshy ground
>   His great big flat feet pound and pound
>   With a rumpety—dumpety—crumpety sound.
>
> See, here's a tangle of maidenhair,
> Among the pandanus spikes down there;
>   And right through the very middle of it
>   He's trampled exactly as he saw fit
>   With his blundery—wondery—dundery wit.
>
> A fool, do you think? No he's no fool,
> Look at the track, it leads to a pool,
>   And on and on to a shady place
>   Where he can fan his beautiful face
>   With a jungelly—tumbelly—scrumbelly grace.

---

* This is the way that Dohnavur always describes Amma's verses, and she approved it. "They believe one listens and then *takes*, and I don't think I could describe what happens better."

—to the imaginatively descriptive, such as " Dim Green Forest ", and the lovingly worshipful, such as " Mountain Lilies " :

> God, Whose glory fills the sky,
> God, Whose glory fills the sea,
> God, Whose Name is very high
> Lifted up in majesty,
>
> Here among the hills afar,
> By Thee planted, by Thee fed,
> Lonely under moon and star
> Lo, a shining lily bed.
>
> How didst Thou take thought to plant
> Such a garden in the wild?
> Say to it, Thou shalt not want,
> Just as to Thy human child?
>
> Dressed like queens in white and gold,
> Through all weather here they be,
> Singing, singing as of old,
> Lord of lilies, unto Thee.

" Hush " sounds best at a Sunday morning service on the veranda of the Jewel House, which commands the widest view of the plain:

> O hush of dawn, breathe through the air
> And fill the heart in me;
> Still is this mountain-land, as where
> God's footsteps be.
>
> And can it be He walks these woods,
> These paths that we have swept?
> Then may my heart with all her moods
> Be holier kept.
>
> Ah, not to this dear place belongs
> Aught but the good and gay:
> Be all my thoughts like wild birds' songs
> On this Thy day.

For " Moonset " one must choose an early morning before dawn, preferably when the moon is where Amma saw it when she " took " this song.

It was a great full moon
  That hung low in the west,
But the dear little birds sang everywhere,
  And the unborn dayspring blest.

Not one singing bird could be seen,
  But every bush and brier
Was astir with the sound of the music they made,
  That sweet invisible quire.

The hills in the wonderful light
  Sat listening, grave and mild,
And they folded the plains in their gentle arms
  As a mother might her child.

And high in the still, white air
  All in the soft moonshine,
They rose and rose to a pearly peak
  Like a far-away holy shrine.

If thus it can be with the world
  In the setting of the moon,
With what riot of joy will it welcome Thee back,
  O Sun that art coming soon.

Amma wrote an introductory page to the first Forest Log-Book, taking as her text the words: "They shall not hurt nor destroy in all My holy mountain." There was room in the Forest, she said, for all the other creatures as well as ourselves. The only exceptions were snakes and scorpions—if they came into the house. "Then I am afraid we must slay them, as they are where they ought not to be." She taught the children to treat all God's creatures kindly and with reverence. To this day they grieve if they see a donkey ill-treated, and a bird with a broken wing is safe with them. They have eyes for the great moths that fly over the Emerald Pool in which they swim, for the great horn-bill that flaps across the valley, for the black long-tailed monkeys swinging from tree to tree, as well as for the peculiar beauty of what Amma called an Alleluia sunrise.

Not a few of the books of the middle period were written in the Forest. She continued to go there year by year until the journey became too painful and exhausting. When Wordsworth wrote

Oft when on my couch I lie

he could rise from it unaided whenever he wished. There came a time when Amma lay on her couch and could rise no

longer, but Forest memories were not unlike the poet's recollections of the dancing daffodils:

> They flash upon that inward eye,
>   Which is the bliss of solitude.
> And then my heart with pleasure fills,
> And dances with the daffodils.

One can hardly over-emphasize Amma's love for the Forest.
She would lay her hand caressingly on the great rocks and trees.
She would stop to remark on the beauty of a red leaf or a wild
fungus. She loved to be within earshot of the running water.
To those who were with her the Forest is still full of Amma.
But this chapter would leave an utterly wrong impression if the
Forest is pictured only as a place that Amma loved. Its
practical value to the whole Family during these thirty-five
years has been immense. Year after year, throughout the two
hot seasons, groups of workers, Indian and European, and of the
older boys and girls go up in batches and return refreshed.
The journey costs almost nothing, yet mind and body are
renewed. It is not everyone whose eyes are opened, and ears
attuned, to see and hear what Amma did, but even the least
imaginative appreciate the rest and the quiet and the beauty
of the place. There must be hundreds today to whom the
Forest is sacred, not because of memories of Amma, but because
the living God has spoken to them. His Voice is heard in the
cool of the Forest, as in the cool of the garden long ago.

Rock of my heart and my Fortress Tower,
   Dear are Thy thoughts to me;
Like the unfolding of leaf and flower
   Opening silently;
And on the edge of these Thy ways,
   Standing in awe as heretofore,
Thee do I worship, Thee do I praise
   And adore.

Rock of my heart and my Fortress Tower,
   Dear is Thy love to me;
Search I the world for a word of power,
   Find it at Calvary.
O deeps of love that rise and flow
   Round about me and all things mine,
Love of all loves, in Thee I know
   Love Divine.

CHAPTER XXIV

"IT'S A BOY"

It was late evening on January 14th, 1918, when a bandy unexpectedly jingled up to the Dohnavur bungalow, and all of us on that side of the house flew out to meet it. A tired woman was crumpled up inside, in her arms was a bundle. It held out thin little arms to me, and dropped a weary little head contentedly on my shoulder. It looked round once and smiled and cuddled down again. I remember thinking, " I wish you were a boy ", as the nice round brainy little head cuddled close. Then Mabel carried off the bundle to the nursery, to return five minutes later racing breathless, " It's a Boy! "

That was how the boys' work began. But in the margin of *Daily Light*, in recording Arul's arrival, Amma adds, " First-fruits of seven years' travail." For at that time Amma had seen in a Temple court, not far from the idol, a row of little boys from eight to ten years old playing musical instruments. She discovered that, like the girls, they were frequently adopted as babies by Temple women. But as she made further enquiries, she found that boys were wanted by the dramatic companies (and, later, by cinemas) as well as by the temples, and that it was almost impossible for them to grow up good and pure. Whenever a boy who seemed likely to be intelligent or good-looking or both was left unprotected, there were " scouts " on the look-out for him. " Not once ", she wrote later, " have we heard of such a boy without finding others had heard of him first." Like the girls, then, these are not unwanted children; there are those who are prepared to pay large sums of money for them.

Walker was on furlough when there came to Amma the inward pressure to begin work for boys as well as girls. She was uneasy about waiting for Walker's return, but allowed common-sense arguments to prevail. She and her Tamil helpers were overstrained already—how could they undertake new work? Moreover, how could she dream of defying all the conventions by having boys and girls in one compound? After they had left the nursery stage, boys would require men to train them, and would men workers, either Indian or European, come to a place which was known far and wide as a home for girls?

When Walker returned at the end of 1911, she spread the matter before him. While he could not but sympathize, and appreciate both the need and the opportunity, he urged that she ought to expect God to find someone else to carry this burden. "You haven't strength enough for both," he said. "It is bound to grow into a big work. It would be better done in touch with you, but apart. Boys' and girls' work should be kept separate in India."

It was sound advice, and though Amma afterwards feared that she had stifled the voice of conscience, I think the Lord's time had not come. Walker's death, Ponnammal's long illness and death, Arulai's illness, engrossed Amma and her friends to the exclusion of other things. In later years her mature judgment was that it had been right to wait, but for a long time she had "a scathing inward memory" that she thought she could not forget, even in heaven.

In any case, the burden became heavy again in August, 1917, and she told the Family. They were ready for anything that the Lord might ask of them, but one of them urged that, if the Lord were leading along the new road, surely He would send them a doctor. It was quite true that boys are more difficult to rear than girls. Amma went up to the Forest in September with her burden unrelieved. Then in the Grey Jungle she stood one day after rain, watching the mighty rush of vehement waters flinging themselves over the rocks in a miniature Niagara. And as she watched the endless flow of water God spoke to her again. What if war-time made it more impossible than ever to plan new projects? What if the supply of adequate funds and suitable workers seemed to be problems more insoluble than any that she had faced before? What, after all, were they in the light of God's resources? *The water flowed on*, and the burden left her.

Then swiftly came the news that her fellow-worker was prepared to withdraw her objection, even if no doctor were forthcoming, and the very same month a medical student in England offered her services to Amma for Dohnavur.

But Arul arrived in January, 1918, before it had been noised

abroad in any way that Dohnavur would receive boys. So
when he appeared Amma first surveyed a field alongside the
girls' compound where there was plenty of room for boys'
nurseries, and then, having received a pattern for the buildings,
she asked for £100 " as sign and seal on the new endeavour ",
and she bravely told the Family that she had done so.

" Has it come? " was the question at the breakfast table
on the next mail day. " Not yet," said Amma, " but it will."
And then appeared one who had already left the table. " Has
your sign come? " she asked. " No, but I think it will come
tomorrow with the registered mail." " It has come," said the
other. She herself had received a legacy of exactly £100, and
she gave it for the first boys' nursery.

To Amma's eager spirit it seemed as if boy babies came very
slowly, and again and again the company of friends whom God
had raised up all over South India to assist in the children's
rescue were forestalled by the enemy. " There was always
someone on the ground before we got there." But was it not
also God's merciful overruling that they did not come in overwhelming numbers before He had prepared the workers? The
lady doctor came, was welcomed, began the study of Tamil, and
—was ordered home on health grounds.

In *From the Forest* and *Gold Cord* * Amma has described her
visit to a place in Madras where boys were being trained and
to the theatre where they acted. Her diary for November 15th,
1919, gives the story telegraphically but vividly enough.

> Spent from 9 p.m. till 2 a.m. in the city. Went to a house
> where boys trained for the drama are kept. Saw about
> twenty-five of them, charming little fellows from eight years
> old upwards. Spent twenty minutes or more with them
> before I was discovered and turned out. A specially dear
> child led me in. K——, who took me, followed astonished,
> for the child stood as if waiting for us, and ran to meet me
> with outstretched hands. " Amma, Amma, come in ", he
> cried. Heard much from the boys about their lives. . . .
> Then to theatre. Saw the boys act. The little fair lad who
> led us in was the attraction—that lovely lovable boy. " O
> to save these, to perish for their saving! " Lord, show the
> way.

Arul was a year and a half when he arrived. He remembers
how Amma would take him on her lap on his Coming Day, and

* *From the Forest*, pp. 116 f. *Gold Cord*, pp. 211 f.

say, " You are my very first son." It was her love, he says, that drew him to the Lord. Quite early he showed an unusual interest in nature, both animate and inanimate. When Amma heard it, she gave him the words of Psalm 111, verse 2, " Sought out of all them that have pleasure therein." Today both boys and older people look to him as an authority, and he has a wonderful collection of birds' eggs, stuffed birds, birds' feathers, a stuffed mongoose, a stuffed leopard, etc. With patience and gentleness and love for all God's creatures, he has " sought them out ", and others as well as himself " have pleasure therein ".

It was June, 1918, before the second boy arrived. A Christian schoolmaster 200 miles to the north of Dohnavur saw in a dream a baby lying on a tray, and heard a voice ask, " What shall be done with it? ", to which another voice answered, " Let it be brought up well." A week later he passed a woman holding a baby, and was reminded of the dream. He found that the boy was in danger, and persuaded the woman to abandon her purpose of selling him to a dramatic company. Then he brought the child to Dohnavur himself, even though he did not know that boys would be admitted.

It was eight years and more before God gave to Dohnavur in Godfrey Webb-Peploe the man whom He had chosen and called to be leader of the boys' work. The two boys of 1918 had increased to seventy or eighty in 1926. Once the door had been opened it could not be closed. But it required immense faith and courage to go on receiving the boys when there was no one in view to train them. The first man to join the Fellowship arrived in 1922. He was a true gift of God, and did valuable work in many directions, but he would have been the first to admit that he lacked the special qualities that were needed for leadership on the boys' side.

So against hope Amma believed in hope. The need had been shown to her, and apparently to no one else. At least, the search for someone else to rescue boys in danger had yielded no results. The difficulty was increased because Amma aimed high.

We are trying to form a new mould so that the type of character evolved may be different from that which for so long has been the grief of every man and woman missionary who thinks deep thoughts. We are trying to see to it that

the training is of the kind which may be expected to produce
new results.

It was an aim which some did not understand, and which
others frankly regarded as unattainable. "Shall we succeed?"
she wrote in 1918. "I do not know. We can only try to do
that which has been shown to us, and pray from the depths of
our hearts, 'Lord, prosper Thou our handiwork.'"

Amma had seen in her own father the pattern of hard work,
incorruptible integrity, generosity to all who were needier
than himself, and burning zeal for the glory of God and the
spread of His kingdom, which she desired to see reproduced in
the boys whom He sent to Dohnavur. When her youngest
brother Walter died in South Africa in 1925, one of his friends
wrote of him in terms which Amma might have used in describing the pattern at which she aimed. He wrote of

> his personal character, so sincere and so transparently honest,
> and of his simple and reverent faith . . . his wonderful
> courage and indomitable will. . . . He was patient and
> courteous even in provoking circumstances. . . . There was
> something very generous in his attitude to others. I never
> heard him say an unkind word of anyone. Of one who had
> wronged him he spoke without a trace of bitterness. . . .
> Always full of dignity he loved a joke as much as anyone. . . .
> He had an almost childlike faith in prayer and a passionate
> belief in immortality. . . . I have never met a purer-
> minded man. I have never met a man with a higher ideal
> of love and service.

Occasionally someone suggested that the character-training
of boys and girls which might have such results, or, still more,
the erection of buildings to house them, was not evangelistic
work, and therefore not worthy of support.

> Well [she wrote], one cannot save and then pitchfork souls
> into heaven—there are times when I heartily wish we could—
> and as for buildings, souls (in India, at least) are more or less
> securely fastened into bodies. Bodies cannot be left to lie
> about in the open, and as you cannot get the souls out and
> deal with them separately, you have to take them both
> together.

Did she succeed? Is the Dohnavur Fellowship, which has
the same standards, succeeding today in producing such men
and women? Amma lived long enough to see men and

women in various departments of the work whose lives are lived according to the pattern. The devil still works overtime in the attempt to prove that it cannot be done. " Sometimes I felt she was wrong in her judgment of character," said one who loved her. " I would have dealt summarily with some whom she believed in. But I often found that they came through in the end, and justified her refusal to accept defeat." Remembering the inheritance with which many of these children are born into the world, we can only marvel at the grace of God, which so often overcomes weak or evil tendencies, and makes a rock-like Peter out of an unsatisfactory Simon. On the other hand, there are some over whom Amma agonized in prayer, who are eating husks in the far country today. " Lost ", as she used to say, may mean " not yet found " for them also. As to the product of today, there is no member of the Fellowship who is not humbled in the dust by the percentage of apparent failures. But all alike would look within themselves for the reasons, and seek again the cleansing of the precious Blood, and the renewing of the Spirit of power and love and self-discipline. Not one would change the pattern or lower the aim. And when members of the Family in Dohnavur or elsewhere in India overcome the temptations of unrighteousness, laziness, impurity, greed, selfishness, and self-pity, and show forth the life of Jesus, then those who watch for their souls are humbled still more, because they well know that not one fraction of the credit is theirs. Only, they would say, let Him be praised Who gave the pattern, and provides the supernatural power to live in accordance with it.

Rose of my heart, what seek I now but Thee?
And dost Thou say, Thorns grow upon My tree?

Thorns tore Thee, Fairest; what if I be torn?
Where Thou dost blossom who would stay for Thorn?

I hold Thee fast: I will not let Thee go,
For me doth this dear Rose of roses blow.

And so I say, Rose of my heart, to Thee,
Close by my Rose would I Thy lover be.

CHAPTER XXV

SISTERS OF THE COMMON LIFE

THOMAS À KEMPIS' *Imitation of Christ* was a little book which Amma read, and on which she fed, during most, if not all, of her life in India. Through Thomas à Kempis she was introduced to Gerhard Groot, who about the year 1380 founded a religious community, called Brothers of the Common Life. According to Thomas à Kempis, "They humbly imitated the manner of the apostolic life, and having one heart and mind in God, brought every man what was his own into the common stock, and receiving simple food and clothing avoided taking thought for the morrow. Of their own will they devoted themselves to God." The Brothers were quite distinct from the monastic orders, for they took no vows and were free to leave when they chose. The majority were laymen, of all kinds and degrees. They met for worship in the morning, and then scattered for the day's work, for it was one of their principles that they continued to live and work in the world, to earn their living and not to beg. They were not to be isolated from everyday life—hence their name.

Amma describes in *Gold Cord* * how, as she puts it, " a new thread was added to our gold cord ". On the evening of Saturday, March 18th, 1916, she met with seven Indian girls, and suggested that they form themselves into a Sisterhood of the Common Life, after the analogy of Groot's foundation. The aim was " to help and strengthen in most inward ways those who earnestly desired to follow their Lord with no reserves, no limitations, and with no ends of their own ". All these seven girls, including Arulai and Preena (the first Temple child), had already considered the question of marriage and reached the conclusion that the will of God for them was that they should remain single and, as Arulai was fond of saying, " attend upon the Lord without distraction ".

On the other hand, since they were bound by no " vows "— at least in any technical sense—it was understood that there would be no stigma upon them if they should afterwards decide

* *Gold Cord*, pp. 158 f.

to be married. In that case, however, they would cease to be Sisters of the Common Life.

They met every Saturday, as Amma put it, " in Jonathan's wood ", i.e. to strengthen one another's hands in God. The meetings were conducted in English, for Amma longed to introduce these Indian girls to the men and women whose words and lives meant so much to her—Samuel Rutherford, Gerhard Tersteegen, John Bunyan, Bishop Moule of Durham, Lady Julian of Norwich, Richard Rolle, Raymond Lull, Brother Lawrence, Thomas à Kempis, and many others. If the word " mystic " was used, it did not convey to them the popular misconception—that mystics are unhappy people whose heads are always in the clouds. They discovered that mystics were men and women to whom God had revealed Himself so clearly that the only practical thing was to follow hard after Him in the everyday things of life, practising His presence in school or kitchen or field or nursery no less than in so-called sacred buildings. " The Cross is the attraction " was one of their favourite words, and a Sister of the Common Life could always be asked to do a task from which the flesh would shrink. Two of the seven are with Christ, and one, to Amma's sore grief, left Dohnavur. The other four are still following on, and have been joined by many others who, of their own volition, have chosen this way.

Writing to Kunmunnie, then far away in China, in July, 1916, Amma suggests that

> there are many girls who feel called to spend themselves for the people of India in this special way, but they are forced into worldliness by their parents and see no way out.

She speaks of Sisterhoods in other parts of India, where vows were taken, and asks for prayer that

> some may be led to us and in our much simpler life (which has no vows but only free and happy service) find what they are wanting, liberty to follow their Lord.

In a little manuscript book prepared for the Sisters, Amma sets forth a few guiding principles. It is a life of joy.

> There is nothing dreary and doubtful about it. It is meant to be continually joyful. . . . As Sisters of the Common Life we are called to a settled happiness in the Lord Whose joy is our strength.

It is a soldier's life.

The nearer the soldier is to the Captain the more he will be attacked by the enemy. . . . To belong to the Sisters of the Common Life will certainly bring the devil's fire upon us. . . . When a soul sets out to find God, it does not know whither it will come, and by what path it will be led; but those who catch the vision are ready to follow the Lamb whithersoever He goeth. . . . As Sisters of the Common Life we are trusted to be very careful about our inner discipline, and continually to expose every part of our inward life to the searching light of God. . . . Let no least thought of unkindness move in me there. Let such a thought be impossible to me. Let it be intolerable. If I have given room to any least feeling of unlove, show me the seriousness of that sin. Break me down before Thy face because of it. . . . We are trusted *to spread the spirit of love*. Tenderness in judgment, the habit of thinking the best of one another, unwillingness to believe evil, grief if we are forced to do so, eagerness to believe good, joy over one recovered from any slip or fall, unselfish gladness in another's joys, sorrow in another's sorrow, readiness to do anything to help another entirely irrespective of self—all this and much more is included in that wonderful word *love*. If love weakens among us, if it ever becomes possible to tolerate the least shadow of an unloving thought, our Fellowship will begin to perish. Unlove is deadly. It is a cancer. It may kill slowly but it always kills in the end. Let us fear it, fear to give room to it as we should fear to nurse a cobra. It is deadlier than any cobra. And just as one minute drop of the almost invisible cobra venom spreads swiftly all over the body of one into whom it has been injected, so one drop of the gall of unlove in my heart or yours, however unseen, has a terrible power of spreading all through our Family, for we are one body—we are parts of one another. If one member suffers loss, all suffer loss. Not one of us liveth to herself.

We owe it to the younger ones to teach them the truth that united prayer is impossible, unless there be loyal love. If unlove be discovered anywhere, stop everything and put it right, if possible at once.

More than once Amma stopped a prayer meeting because she sensed that there was some hindrance of this sort, and resumed it when love had been restored.

In the early days all who came to Dohnavur from abroad joined the Sisterhood automatically. But as the Fellowship grew, and included men as well as women, and particularly

as the number of married workers increased, it was only by
their own free choice, and after an opportunity had been given
to face all that might be involved, that newly-arrived *Sitties*
became Sisters of the Common Life.

What of the men?   Amma undoubtedly hoped that, from
amongst both Indian and European *Annachies*, there would be
those whom God would call to remain free from the joys and
responsibilities of marriage, in order to give themselves wholly
to the boys.   Before the boys' work began, indeed, she had
written of the need of a British married couple, and at that
time her thought was that the boys should remain in Dohnavur
until they reached school age, and then be transferred to a
hostel in charge of the married couple, to be situated near a
school which the boys would attend.   But this plan did not
come to fruition, perhaps because (as we shall see) Amma felt
that no outside school provided the wholly Christian education
which she desired for her children.   Moreover, in India there
were difficulties about a married woman living in a boys' compound, especially as the boys grew to adolescence and beyond.

Since misleading statements have been made from time to
time concerning Amma's attitude to marriage, it would seem
that this is the place to attempt to interpret that attitude.
She heartily endorsed the scriptural statement that " marriage
is honourable in all ", and she knew how powerful can be the
testimony of a truly Christian home.   She did not hesitate to
assume the responsibility of Indian parents, and to seek to
arrange suitable marriages for many of the girls.   The practical
difficulties are much greater than might be supposed.   It is not
easy to find Christian men whose standard of consecration is
anything like that of Dohnavur.   On the other hand, girls who
have grown up as members of the Dohnavur Family find it hard
to adjust themselves to life in an ordinary Indian town or village,
even though Amma occasionally sent them to live with married
people as a preliminary preparation.

This is only one of the problems to be surmounted.   After the
boys' work had developed, marriages within the Family naturally
became common, but unless a married couple was fitted to work
in Dohnavur, and felt the call to remain, a home and a means
of livelihood must be found outside.   Excellent, says someone.
Surely the best Dohnavur products should be for export, scattered far and wide over South India.   With their knowledge of

the Scriptures, their sterling character, their ardent evangelistic zeal, should they not spread the Light in many a dark corner?

This also was Amma's vision. If it has not been translated into action on a large scale, the reasons are manifold. For one thing, the Family has been growing continuously, from 130 in 1913 to over 900 in 1952. Thus it must absorb an increasing number of the very best amongst its products. Secondly, the hospital work must be staffed, and to Amma's mind this was to be regarded as the main outlet for evangelism. Third, if both husband and wife are from Dohnavur, they naturally have no relatives in the place to which they go, and in many places it is still dangerous for a girl to be left in a house alone while her husband goes out to work. Members of the Fellowship are constantly asking themselves—as Amma asked herself—whether there are defects in the Dohnavur training which account for some of the disappointments—yes, even tragedies—over which they grieve and ponder and pray. But difficulties there always will be, to be met and overcome by the grace of God.

On the other hand, Amma felt strongly that the Dohnavur work required the life-service of a substantial number of women, and perhaps a smaller number of men, who would remain unmarried " for the kingdom of God's sake ". On the women's side she was not disappointed. Today there are three groups of Sisters of the Common Life who meet regularly for fellowship—an English language group (i.e. a group in which the English language is used), and a senior and a junior Tamil group, whose knowledge of English is inadequate for the appreciation of the kind of books which Amma originally introduced to the Sisters. On the men's side, however, while it is recognized that there is a need of some workers upon whom the boys (especially the older boys) can count to stay with them right through the difficult years, yet the number of men, whether Indian or European, who regard abstention from marriage as a Divine call is at present very small, and a Brotherhood of the Common Life has not yet been formed. This is simply a statement of fact, with no comment except that it is a matter about which lovers of Dohnavur should be constrained to pray that the will of the Lord may be done.

To sum up, it would not be fair to impute to Amma a bias against marriage in any general sense. There may have been specific cases of men and women who, in her view, were called to remain unmarried, and therefore were disobedient to the heavenly vision if they turned from the call. But she was eager to avoid any suggestion that marriage should be regarded as God's second best for those who were not so called. The truth is that she did not exalt celibacy as a higher state than marriage, but she knew that from a purely practical point of view the risk of losing valuable workers may conceivably be increased if they marry. It happened occasionally at Dohnavur, as it happens on every Mission field, that the health of one partner, either husband or wife, necessitated retirement from the work, and because the sick man or woman was married, two workers were lost instead of one. Still more poignant is the problem when children arrive, unless both husband and wife are at one in the conviction that God's calling is without a change of mind, and therefore He can be trusted to care for the children when separation becomes necessary. Friends? He can provide those who will make a home for the children if there are no relatives willing and able and spiritually fit for the tremendous responsibility. Funds? He can see to it that the children are not handicapped by the lack of suitable education. The one essential is that the parents should be of one mind concerning a life call to the work before ever the situation arises.

The booklet for Sisters of the Common Life contains the following extract from a poem of Tersteegen—but the life which it describes is not for a select company only, but for all the children of God.

> Across the will of nature
>   Leads on the path of God;
> Not where the flesh delighteth
>   The feet of Jesus trod.
> O bliss to leave behind us
>   The fetters of the slave,
> To leave ourselves behind us,
>   The grave-clothes and the grave!
>
> We follow in His footsteps;
>   What if our feet be torn?
> Where He has marked the pathway
>   All hail the brier and thorn!
> Scarce seen, scarce heard, unreckoned,
>   Despised, defamed, unknown,
> Or heard but by our singing,
>   On, children, ever on!

Mender of broken reeds,
 O patient Lover,
'Tis love my brother needs,
 Make me a lover.
That this poor reed may be
 Mended and tuned for Thee,
O Lord, of even me
 Make a true lover.

Kindler of smoking flax,
 O fervent Lover,
Give what Thy servant lacks,
 Make me a lover.
That this poor flax may be
 Quickened, aflame for Thee.
O Lord, of even me
 Make a true lover.

CHAPTER XXVI

"IMMANUEL MY HELP"

THE battle for the soul of Jambulingam, who called himself Red Tiger in the days when the English newspapers dubbed him the Robin Hood of South India, was one of the fiercest and most prolonged that Amma ever fought. For nearly two years he and his friend Kasi were scarcely ever out of her thoughts.

Life was filled as to foreground with its thousand calls and claims and duties crowding one on top of the other; but the background was always the same. The figures of two men stood there; and, all but visible, was the form of the accuser, all but audible the noise of his laugh. "Rejoice not against me, O mine enemy." That was our day; and at night our very dreams were prayers.

The first nine months of 1921 were normal enough—if Amma's years could ever be so described. In the spring she was writing *Nor Scrip*, and therefore it was no wonder that faith in regard to the financial methods there described should be sharply tested. In February she returned to a certain organization a sum of Rs. 2,500. It had been reported to her that a kind old friend had " fought the Committee to get this grant for us ". Could she be happy about retaining money which had been secured in this way, while stating publicly in *Nor Scrip* that Dohnavur looked to God alone for supplies? One early morning " in the peace of full moonlight ", she wrote in her diary:

Dear Lord, wilt Thou kindly confirm this action by some comforting token for good? Rs. 2,500 is a great deal of money to give away, as it were. There are many things we could thankfully use it for. People will misunderstand. Mr X—— does. " As you have more money than you know what to do with," is his attitude. Dear Lord, comfort and help.

On May 5th she was in the Forest when the accounts for the first four months of the year were sent up by Dorothy Waller.

The ordinary expenditure, quite apart from the purchase of land, was higher than ever before, and in January and February it far exceeded the income.*   But the total gifts for the four months came to over Rs. 22,000, " enough to pay all expenses and leave over the Rs. 2537 which was returned ". " They called upon Thee and were holpen," is Amma's comment.   " They put their trust in Thee and were not confounded."

Then in August the same God Who had given material blessing did something far greater.   There was a new touch of His Hand in spiritual blessing upon the Family.   It was not that special meetings were planned in the hope that He would bless; the meetings simply had to be held in order to give the recipients of His blessing the opportunity to testify to it.   " It has been and is a time of the blowing of the Wind," writes Amma.   " Straight into our hearts blew the wind of the Spirit."   " Amma," said one of the girls, " many children have heard the Word of God in their hearts and they want to tell the others."   So they met each Wednesday evening.   " The work goes on," is the diary entry for September 22nd.   " Yesterday evening a joyful torrent.   My God, how can I thank Thee. X——, Y——, and many others about whom we have been very anxious."

The very next entry tells of coming down from the Forest on October 3rd, and after that for two years little else is mentioned but—Robin Hood.

> Days full of thought about Robin Hood, for details of his doings told me by the men as we came down [i.e. the coolies who carried her chair] made me want to get at him some-how, and help him to a better life.

For Jambulingam was the talk of the whole countryside—a man who gave to the poor most of what he took from the rich, and who was loved on that account; who jumped clean over a well more than twenty feet across, a crack shot who never missed a bird on the wing if it were anywhere within range; a jester who escaped from the police and sent his guard back with the handcuffs, saying, " Take these iron bangles back to the police station, for to that place do they belong "; one who was gentle

---

* The Fellowship never goes into debt. Bills are always met when they are presented. On this occasion there were, of course, " Baskets " (or reserves), as explained in *Nor Scrip*, p. 33, to meet the need.

to little children and old people; a man of his word, who con-
fiscated a cartload of rice, and said to the poor driver, "Return
this day week, and look among the roots of that tree yonder,
and thou wilt find the money." And so it was.

India, like England, loves a sportsman. When we read of
Robin Hood in the greenwood, do we remember that he was a
robber chieftain, breaking the laws of the land, and deserving of
condign punishment? Amma was attracted, and being what
she was, her next thought was, "Could I see him, and tell him
of the Saviour?" The coolies thought it impossible, but that
was a word which did indeed occur in Amma's dictionary, but
whose presence there she always ignored.

So the incredible happened, and on October 12th she writes,
"Saw him." How? Had she contrived to discover one of his
retreats in the mountains, and send him a message? Not at all.
She prayed, and as she prayed God gave Jambulingam the
desire to see her. She had been in the Grey Jungle overseeing
building work, and he and his men knew it, and had watched
for her for eight evenings. On the 12th he and two of his
men waylaid her as she came to view some land near the foothills and salaamed to her. They talked together, and Amma
shared her tea with them while Jambulingam told his story.

It was the tale of an honest man, falsely accused, who had
fled to Penang when word of a police summons reached him,
who had returned because he was anxious about his wife and
children, only to find that an enemy was blackening his name
and that the police were terrifying his wife. Instead of facing
the charge and proving his innocence, he had fled to the
mountains, and his wife had died of shock. He was convinced
that his case was hopeless, for the police would be deceived by
false evidence, and many of them would accept the story of
him who offered the largest bribe. Since there was no hope of
justice, he had become an outlaw, and salved his conscience by
generosity to the poor and weak. It was a healthy life, full of
excitement—but what of his three little children?

At his request Amma promised to welcome the children to
Dohnavur. He on his part promised that he would never use
his gun except in defence of his life. She urged him to surrender to the police, and offered to do her utmost to see to it
that the surrender would be made to an Englishman. But
they feared *himsa*. This is a Sanscrit word used in South India

to describe anything unjust done in the name of justice, and particularly pain or torture inflicted to extort a confession. They had suffered *himsa* already.

There was time for a few words about the Saviour and Friend of sinners, and then they knelt in prayer. How marvellously had God timed their meeting! Five days later they were trapped, tortured, and finally carried to hospital under guard. The news reached Amma when Dr and Mrs Schaffter were with her, and they took her straight to the hospital where Jambulingam lay. After some delay she was admitted, and he listened like a thirsty man who drinks of cool waters. Amma was well aware that she was in contact with the enemy. " Now for a battle against the cruel powers of hell," she wrote that evening. " Lord, whose battle is it? Surely Thine. Lord, save."

For a time she was allowed to pay occasional visits, even after he had been moved to the district jail, and between the visits he studied the Bible that Amma had given him. One of the verses that he marked was Deuteronomy 32. 10, " He found him in a desert land," and as time went on it became clear that the Good Shepherd had found His lost sheep.

In January, 1922, Amma was in the Forest again, and her thoughts sleeping and waking were of Jambulingam and Kasi, his friend. One night she dreamed that she was outside the gate of the jail. The gates, outer and inner, opened without delay, and she walked straight to the hospital ward where the Red Tiger lay, and asked him, " Do you wish to be baptized? " He answered, " Yes." " When? " And he said, " Now." Then she was conscious of someone passing, a missionary who had no connection with the prisoner. She asked him to baptize Jambulingam, and he did so, giving him the name Jebamunnie, or Jewel of Prayer. She rose and worshipped, and only then did she realize that it was a dream.

Now the facts must be stated without explanation, for the chronicler has none. He can only say that there were times when God showed His servant things that were to happen, and that this is one of the most striking instances. He is not qualified to discuss whether Amma possessed unusual psychic powers, or what is commonly called " second sight ". She was God's child, and He sometimes spoke to her in unusual ways.

For the dream was literally fulfilled. On January 30th she

drove to Palamcottah with the Bishop's wife, who was a close friend. A C.E.Z. missionary (Miss Bennett) came with her to the jail, and as the Superintendent was just about to enter, the gates opened of their own accord. Jambulingam was standing by his bed. She asked him the two questions, and he answered as she had heard him in the dream. Then she asked him to write a statement, expressing his wish to be baptized. The Superintendent initialled it, and Amma prepared to give it to the Rev. E. A. L. Moore,* the missionary of the dream. " But he is in Calcutta," said Miss Bennett. Amma went with her to the Ardills' home to ask for Mr Moore's address, and then learned that he was expected back in Palamcottah that evening. " He may be passing now." *Passing*—it was the very thing shown in the dream.

Five minutes later Amma met him as he passed, but he very naturally demurred—he had never even seen Jambu-lingam. So Amma was compelled to tell him the dream, and that was enough. Jambulingam and Kasi were baptized the next morning, January 31st. " Present there—my dear Irene (the Bishop's wife), Nellie Bennett, several prisoners and the warder—and many invisible presences, and the Lord our Redeemer." On the way home she read concerning an incident in the Life of Florence Nightingale: " There was a perfect co-ordination of events."

After that great day visits were forbidden, except that a Tamil clergyman was allowed to teach the prisoners once a week. Sometimes he could not go, and they were left un-taught. Only once in four months was Amma allowed even to write to him, enclosing a letter from his little daughter. But when he was examined he told the truth, and his witness in the jail was clear and bright.

His feet were bound with a type of chain specially reserved for dangerous criminals. Every time it was fastened he took it as a challenge to escape if he could! At his trial he pleaded guilty. Day after day he stood in the dock, while evidence was given. He admitted all that was true, but found that his con-fession did not seem to hasten the end of the tedious trial. No wonder he was depressed—until on a Sunday afternoon the Tamil clergyman read to him from Acts 12. Poor ill-instructed Red Tiger! On August 1st, the following Sunday morning,

* Afterwards Bishop of Travancore and Cochin.

he and Kasi and two others escaped. "Alleluia!" he exclaimed as he clasped hands with Kasi on the free side of the prison wall. And thus began a long year of outlaw life for them, and of indescribable tension for Amma.

She blamed herself for relaxing in prayer. The margin of her *Daily Light* is full of references to this time.

> *September* 16. *Let everyone that nameth the Name of Christ depart from iniquity.* Prayer of all prayers for Robin Hood. . . .
> *September* 25. *And experience, hope.* After a night full of temptations to anxiety about Robin Hood I have experienced the loving-kindness of the Lord. Experience *worketh* hope.

Would he go back to the old life, and begin highway robbery again? He utterly refused to wreak vengeance on his betrayers. "I have been forgiven," he said, "and must I not forgive?"

Friends of Amma frequently risked their lives to get in touch with Jambulingam and Kasi, to urge them to keep straight and to give themselves up to the police. The other two criminals left them when they found that they were determined not to rob. "Several highway robberies that have taken place since", said the *Madras Mail* in October, "have been attributed to him, but it is generally believed that they are the work of his imitators."

But the number of such incidents increased. Jambulingam's reputation was so great that other dacoits were inevitably tempted to use his name. The police began to spread the story that he was robbing again, and gradually those in authority believed it. Amma was called to Palamcottah in November to meet one or two British officials, and utterly failed to convince them that the men were living honest lives. Indeed, they were distinctly doubtful as to whether she was wholly free from blame. For instance, when she offered to produce two witnesses who had seen Jambulingam and Kasi in the Forest on the very night when they were supposed to be robbing and murdering in the plain, the natural rejoinder was that if these two men knew where they were, it was criminal on their part not to inform the police immediately.

Amma persisted in urging them to trust the British authorities and to surrender themselves. Night after night in December she watched for their coming. Indeed, all through this period she kept a light burning all night, on the chance that they might come. But as the false charges multiplied, and the virtual impossibility of clearing themselves from complicity became more and more apparent, she could hardly wonder at their hesitation. In regard to many of the charges she could have found plenty of witnesses to prove their innocence, but could the witnesses be sure of protection? During these months a number of men from the village of Caruniapuram, near Jambulingam's home, had professed conversion, mainly through their knowledge of the change in him, but not a few of them were imprisoned on false charges, and some came to Dohnavur for protection.

It was a most delicate situation for Amma. All through she steadily kept in view that she had no status at all in the matter, except as one whom God had called to give spiritual succour to the two outlaws. From every other point of view they were escaped jailbirds.

Meanwhile in November, 1922, Alec Arnot had arrived, and in January he secured the first Dohnavur car—a Ford. The roads were execrable in places, and it was a miracle that no serious accident occurred, but from January, 1923, onwards Amma could be driven to Palamcottah or Sermadevi or Neyyoor, and there was a great saving of time and strength.

At length in June the Sub-Collector (an important official) asked Amma to try to see the men and persuade them to come in. It was known that they had friends all over the district who supplied them with food, and warned them of danger when they came down into the plains—as they frequently did. The police were becoming a laughing-stock, and higher authorities were seriously annoyed.

On the night of July 11th Amma was at Caruniapuram when someone told her that the two outlaws were not far away. She stained her face and arms, put on her darkest *seelie*,* and about midnight two men half led, half carried her through the jungle to an appointed rendezvous. The two dangerous criminals, terrors of the countryside, " took my hands (writes Amma) and fondled them as children would a mother's ". The Sub-Collector had said that he believed Jambulingam would speak the truth. " If he tells you that he has not been robbing, I shall believe it." " No", said Jambulingam, " I

---

* The *seelie* or *sari* is the main garment of an Indian woman.

have kept my promise." But the temptation to despair, and then to do what they were accused of doing, was very great. They knew who the men were who were robbing in their name.

Amma pleaded with them to surrender, in spite of everything, trusting God to protect their friends. But they felt it was too late. " It was like putting a horse to a jump just beyond him," she writes, and at length she ceased to plead, and they talked of other things, of daring follies such as two daylight visits to Tuticorin, of the generosity of those who supplied them with food. (Incidentally, Amma had never given them anything whatsoever except books, though often she had longed to help them when she heard that supplies were low.) They recognized now that their escape from jail was " vain folly ", but " we lost heart ". Now, like David, Jambulingam said, " I shall now perish one day by the hand of those who are hunting for me." " If only I heard that you had died without a weapon in your hand ", said Amma, " I could bear it. But I don't know how to bear the thought of your going to God with blood on your hands." Jambulingam caught her hands again in his. " Do not fear for us," he said. " Will God forsake us ? "

Then they prayed, and repeated parts of Psalm 23 and Psalm 27. " Very, very hard to say good-bye. They were like loving children. Lord, Lord, to Thee I commit them."

The next entry in the diary is, " Thursday evening, September 20, 1923. ' With Christ, which is far better.' " They had been invited to a feast in Caruniapuram, but there was treachery.* The house was surrounded by the police. Edith Naish and two other members of the Fellowship heard the shooting. They had been in the very act of praying for Jambulingam and Kasi, though they had no idea that they were in the village. The two men fired from the windows but, crack shots as they were, they only wounded two of the police. Clearly they were attempting to scare them off, and then break away. But when the police began to set fire to the thatched roofs of the surrounding houses, they knew they must leave if the village was to be saved.

So, while all was pandemonium, they emerged, and Edith

---

* " Treachery " is Amma's word, but she saw both sides of the case, and knew that, from the police point of view, anything which would ensure their capture was justifiable.

Naish and her friends saw them running in almost a leisurely fashion out of the village. But Kasi slipped as they were crossing a stream, and was shot. Jambulingam ran on, unaware that his friend had fallen, and then turned to wait for him. He took cover, and fired one or two more shots to delay the pursuit. If he had not waited for Kasi, he could have escaped easily enough. Then suddenly he drew himself up, sprang on to a bank of red earth, and threw his gun away. Several of his friends saw all this, and said that he " looked as if he remembered something ". Surely it was Amma's last word to him. He looked up to heaven, raised his hands in worship, and then walked slowly backwards, and stood under a tamarind tree. Then the police were upon him, forcing him to the ground, breaking his arm—one of them actually bit into his neck in order to drink the blood of one so valorous— dragging him by his feet to the nearby tank. At last someone shot him through the head, and after that there was no more that they could do.

One of Amma's friends came up to the Grey Jungle next day with the story. " Have they sinned? " she cried when she saw from his manner that the news was serious. " No, no. They died clean." And after that nothing seemed to matter.

That same night in a village twelve miles away two men were robbing. " We are Jambulingam and Kasi," they shouted. It took a little time for the many impersonators to learn that that game could be played no longer.

For a time Amma hoped, and almost believed, that the authorities would accept the evidence which cleared the names of the dead men. But it was not to be. Even concerning the manner of their death a false version of the story was officially accepted, and, to Amma's grief, some of her close friends believed it. " I'm really sorry for Miss Carmichael," said a British official to one of them. " She will be expecting to meet Jambulingam in heaven, and she will be disappointed." Critical comments on her own attitude were made in high places. She suffered public obloquy for daring to maintain that since their escape from jail God had kept the two from falling.

Meanwhile God used the testimony of some who knew the two men and had been brought to the Lord through the change in their lives. An evangelistic band visited a good many towns in southern India, and the Name of Him Who died to save His people from their sin was exalted. Believing that publicity might be used of God to strike a blow at the practice of *himsa*, she wrote the full story in *Raj, Brigand Chief*, and, with this end in view, secured forewords from the Bishops of Travancore, Tinnevelly and Madras, and also from Dr Howard Somervell.

In a day when *himsa*, called by other names, is practised in every totalitarian state, and the so-called democratic countries are not wholly free from the stain of police corruption and cruelty, the facts which Amma helped to uncover may seem less important because the evil is so widespread. But she was one who could not hear of the wrongs of the poor without burning indignation—and shame, whenever responsibility attached to the British Raj. " Lord, how long shall the wicked, how long shall the wicked triumph? "

On the night of December 15th she was much distressed, and felt that she had fought in vain, and to no purpose. " Then waves of light flowed round me—I was in Paradise, content, sure. ' O rest in the Lord ' . . . Mabel and the sweetest of the singers were in the dining-room singing it for my birthday." So she encouraged herself in the Lord her God. " Immanuel my help " were the words which the hunted fugitive used to write at the foot of his letters to Amma. Immanuel is a Prince Who has never failed to help His subjects in the time of their need.

Father, hear us, we are praying,
Hear the words our hearts are saying,
We are praying for our children.

Keep them from the powers of evil,
From the secret, hidden peril,
Father, hear us for our children.

From the whirlpool that would suck them,
From the treacherous quicksand, pluck them,
Father, hear us for our children.

From the worldling's hollow gladness,
From the sting of faithless sadness,
Father, Father, keep our children

Through life's troubled waters steer them,
Through life's bitter battle cheer them,
Father, Father, be Thou near them.

Read the language of our longing,
Read the wordless pleadings thronging,
Holy Father, for our children.

And wherever they may bide,
Lead them Home at eventide.

CHAPTER XXVII

MOTHER AND CHILDREN

ONE of Amma's brothers tells a story which we would call libellous but that he is an honourable man and is prepared to swear that it·is authentic. When they were very young (as he says), Amy, who was of course the eldest of the family, would sometimes pinch him and make him cry, because when he shed tears his eyes were such a lovely blue. Her tender heart must have smitten her, as she secured this æsthetic joy at the cost of her brother's pain. Once on a rainy day, says her mother, she was standing by the dining-room window with tears running down her cheeks. Asked what was the matter, she could only reply, " Poor gardener! poor gardener! " Apparently the gardener did not run for shelter in every storm, and his bedraggled figure stirred her sympathy.

But the pinching story, which hagiolaters will regard as apocryphal, is a reminder that several of Amma's grown up " children " have vivid recollections of a day when Amma was tired, and two girls lay on either side of her. One pinched the other, and the other, intending to retaliate, found to her horror that she had pinched Amma instead. How was pinching to be eliminated? Amma told the child to promise that she would never pinch again, and on the spur of the moment invented a catchy tune to the words:

> A promise is a sacred thing
> And I
> Will try
> To hold sincerely to my word,
> And keep my promise.
> I, Amma, I.

Soon there was a group of little girls round the baby organ, all singing the words together, and then taking turns with the last line. " The one who covets the distinction will pat herself invitingly, and all the others will fall into line and singsong her name at the end." This would go on till each one had been, as it were, the " Amen " to the chorus. One cannot be sure that the promise was never broken, but certainly no one ever forgot the occasion.

With no Froebel or Montessori training, Amma used her fertile imagination to impress the minds of the children. Each of them was a separate personality, and was treated accordingly. A small boy who had not seen very much of Amma was summoned to her room after some misbehaviour, and a friend told him exactly what Amma would say or do. But nothing happened according to his expectations. She spoke differently, and punished differently, because, while the cases might be parallel in other respects, he was a separate little person. Canings were not uncommon, but Amma's handkerchief wiped the tears away, and few children left the room unhappy or aggrieved. She could be severe, especially with anyone who had been untruthful, but she never nagged. Her children could not bear to think that they had grieved her, and with most of them it was an easy step from that realization to true sorrow for having grieved God.

For many years she gave each child a good-night kiss, and even when the Family was numbered in hundreds she knew the characteristics of each one, and made it her aim at least to see, though not necessarily to speak to, every child every day. Right up to the time of the accident in October, 1931, the old name of Musal Ammal (the Hare) fitted her well, for at one moment the children would see her busily typing, and then the next she was overseeing a new building or visiting a remote corner of the compound. Towards the end of this period she purchased a tricycle. The children loved to push her, but often the pace was too hot for them, and she had several spills as she tried to round corners too sharply.

Chellalu was the kind of mischievous child about whom so many stories were written that Amma's friends may have imagined she was typical, which was not the case. Amma always reminded her that she began by pulling off Amma's sun-helmet as soon as she took her into her arms. Once her teacher gave her a chit to take to Amma. She knew it was a report on her disobedience, so she swallowed it. But when she saw Amma she acknowledged the offence. Amma first prayed that the punishment might help her, and then inflicted it. When Chellalu howled she gave her a glass of water—an effective way of silencing her. But it was Amma's love that held her back from any real evil. One night the children heard the attractive sound of a band outside the compound.

They guessed there must be a wedding in the village, and Chellalu persuaded the girls in her room to get up at midnight and climb on to the garden wall to see the fun. Their *Accals* woke to find the room empty, and were frightened, and then, when they found them, considerably annoyed. Chellalu knew that they would be reported to Amma, so she got up very early, went to Amma's room, and confessed. Did Amma remember the comet of 1882? Anyhow, she promised that when there was another wedding she would take the children to see it, and she kept her word.

One of the boys grew restive and discontented. " Go and talk to Amma," said Arul Dasan. " Tell her all that you have been telling me." But when he entered her room and saw her face, the words died away on his lips. His grievances were forgotten. " Did you tell Amma ? " asked Arul Dasan when he returned from the interview. " No," he said, " those things slipped my memory when we talked together."

The children learned a good deal of English from the rhymes that Amma taught them about birds and beasts and flowers. Many of their games were action songs. For instance, in " The Butterfly " most of the children stand round in a circle singing, while a few in the centre, representing the butterflies, act accordingly.

> Our mother was a butterfly,
>   We are her little eggs,
> Inside us caterpillars lie,
>   Young things with many legs.

> I am a little caterpillar,
>   Very soft and fat,
> I'll change into a chrysalis,
>   What do you think of that?

> I am a little chrysalis,
>   And very still I lie;
> For folded up inside me
>   Is a little butterfly.

> I am the little butterfly,
>   I want to fly about;
> I'm so tired of being here,—
>   Oh, now I'm out! I'm out!

> O kind wind, come and fan my wings,
>   O sunshine, make them dry,
> O flower, I come to you! Away,
>   Away, away I fly.

Often the words and simple music came to Amma simultaneously. In the later years, during periods of great tension,
she would appear at the breakfast table with the most
ridiculous rhymes. On the other hand, " The Donkey "
owed its origin to a night of physical pain and anxiety. Amma
had only one good eye, and on a long railway journey a smut
was blown into it, and nearly blinded her. For a few hours she
seriously wondered whether she would ever be able to read
again; but she appeared fresh and cheerful the next morning
with a production entitled " Donkey's Bray ", purporting to
tell how in Noah's ark the animals who had given way to
depression were cheered and enlivened by a donkey's comical
" Hee-haw! "

Once when she was planning to take some of the children to
Madras, Amma thought she would test Chellalu's power to
keep a secret, and confided in her. Alas—within an hour the
children who were to go flung themselves upon Amma. " We
know," they said, " Chellalu told us." Close behind them
came Chellalu. " I keep my promise, Amma," she said. " I
keep it very hard. I said, ' We are not going to London; we
are not going to Calcutta; we are not going to Bombay; we
are not going to Palamcottah.' Then they guess and say, ' We
are going to Madras ', and I say nothing at all."

Amma herself used to take prayers with the children nearly
every day. Her talks were illustrated from the beauty of
Nature around them, or from the habits of birds and animals.
But it was not easy to find time for preparation, and yet she
felt it would be even worse to ask the *Sitties* to speak without
sufficient notice. As she walked across to the school with
Helen Bradshaw one morning, she confessed that she had no
idea what she was going to say in the few minutes' talk. But
then she picked a withered rose from the path, gazed at it, and,
turning again to Helen, said, " Now I know what I am to say."

But there was nothing careless or haphazard about the
spiritual or mental nurture of the children, even though there
might be technical deficiencies along certain lines. Some of
the finest women in the Family today are those to whom Amma
was mother and nurse and teacher, all in one. Then God gave
her the gift of colleagues qualified in various directions, and she
leaned hard upon them. She was not happy about sending the
children to outside schools, even Christian schools. Some-

times the teachers were Hindus, often they were merely nominal Christians. Could they lay the spiritual foundations of the kind of education that Amma had in mind? Had they the delicate regard for truth which she regarded as the first essential?

At one time a government grant was offered if only the Family could be brought within the general scheme of national education. But it would have been necessary to employ outside teachers, and, of course, to use the school books issued by the government. If only they were straight and true and hard-working, Amma was not greatly concerned about the academic standards to which the children might attain. Certainly their minds were opened through their study of Nature, whether in Dohnavur or in the Forest, and the microscope gave them access to a new world.

At the same time it was recognized that if some of the children were eventually to give their lives to the service of others as doctors or teachers, they must be prepared to pass government examinations, and Dr McDougall's vacation classes in the Forest were planned partly with this thought in mind. It would appear that the need of women to train the Family that was growing so rapidly at that time, and, secondly, the need of the newly opened medical work, absorbed those who might have had the mental equipment for other tasks.

Nothing has happened in the last thirty years to alter the basic aim that Amma always kept in view—to train good soldiers for Jesus Christ. Groups of children, both boys and girls, are now attending Christian High Schools elsewhere, and there are a number of men and women training as teachers and nurses. Owing to the change of government which took place in 1947, it is essential that the schools and hospital run by the Fellowship should be staffed by workers who possess the qualifications recognized by the authorities.* It is of course arguable that these changes might have been made sooner, and the infallibility of Amma (or of those who, with her, laid the foundations in years gone by) is not a dogma which all members of the Fellowship are compelled to accept. What they do regard as vital, however, is that the purpose of the children's education is not the passing of examinations but the training of spirit, mind and body for the service of the King of kings. To this purpose all else must be subordinated.

* See p. 371.

Amma was determined that the children should grow up in an atmosphere of love, and therefore of happiness. In the case of those who were old enough to remember their pre-Dohnavur days she would pray that the Lord would erase painful or polluting memories from their minds, and often the prayer was answered. She did not encourage them to ask questions about their origin. " Where did I come from, Amma? " asked a boy, and when she said, " You are my son," he found that answer sufficient. But as they grew older she did, of course, tell them something of the danger from which they had been rescued, and sometimes on their Coming Days she would recall the circumstances of their arrival.

> It is a wonderful day for me as I look back [she wrote to one who is now a fellow-worker]. Ponnammal was in the attic of the little room in Neyyoor praying for a child in danger (she did not know what child). As she prayed a woman was carrying you to the big temple near Nagercoil, but our God sent His angel to stop her, and you were saved. When Ponnammal rose from her knees, a bandy drove up to the door, and soon you were in her arms, and then in mine. How we rejoiced, she and I, together . . . I am seeing you as I saw you first, [she wrote to another] a tiny sad child who did not know how to smile. But one day under the tamarind tree near my room I was running up and down with you in my arms, and at last you smiled and I was happy.

" When I arrived," said one who came at four years old, " Amma bathed me, and as she did so she told me that the Lord was my Shepherd. I slept in the room with her."

One of the boys was saved by a missionary in the Telugu country, but a wealthy man offered Rs. 1,400 for him, so she sent him to Dohnavur. The would-be purchaser followed him here, and told Amma that with Rs. 1,400 she could save many other children. But she refused to part with him, even though a court case was threatened. She packed a basket in which he could be sent at any moment to another Mission station, where friends had promised to " disappear " him. On his Coming Day she used to tell him this story, and say, " You were saved from grave danger for a very special purpose."

All her letters—and many of her books—show how thoroughly Amma enjoyed the children. They knew that she was never weary of them, that there was nothing that she would not do to help them. She had a very strong sense of duty, but it was not that sense which impelled her to spend every possible minute with the children. She simply loved to be with them, and they to be with her.

I only met Miss Carmichael once [writes someone]. A friend introduced us in a street in Madras, and I so well remember it. I had never even heard of Dohnavur before. She looked so loving and the three small children with her were so friendly and un-shy and clung to her, and were just like little blue butterflies in their blue *saris*—quite different from the usual staid children that I knew.

When the time came that Amma could no longer be in several places at once, but lived in one room, and saw only those who were privileged to come to her, she loved to share with them—especially with the little ones—the thoughts that came to her. Often they were suggested by the friendly birds which lived in a caged-in part of the veranda, and were allowed to fly round her room. Here are a few samples, chosen because they may help just a very little to show why her children loved her.

Are you Raggles or are you Taggles? Raggles and Taggles are two Indian robins which Vineetha *Accal* gave me. Raggles was called Raggles because he was always untidy. His feathers hung about like rags. He did not take the trouble to tidy himself, and so Taggles had to try to tidy him, which he did by pulling those loose feathers out. But the great difference between the two is this: Raggles expects to have his food put into his mouth, and Taggles, though he likes to be fed, takes the trouble to feed himself. Raggles, you see, likes everything to be done for him, while Taggles does things for himself and even tries to help his lazy brother. Also Raggles doesn't come when he is called, and Taggles gladly does. I like Taggles' disposition very much. Don't you? Are you Raggles or Taggles?

Are you a barbet or are you a bulbul? One day Pilipu, the barbet, had eaten as much *papali* as he could swallow, but he wouldn't leave the tray where the *papali* was, though he knew Mr Fluff, the bulbul, wanted some very much. He just sat there like the dog in the manger made into a bird, and he watched Mr Fluff out of the corner of his eye, and when poor Mr Fluff ventured nearer he made a little growly noise. What do you think Mr Fluff did? He gently spoke in a soft little warble, and that was all. For a whole long

quarter of an hour that patient bird waited, never saying a
cross word (he doesn't know how to be cross), and at last
greedy Pilipu got tired of sitting there, and flew off and then
Mr Fluff had his *papali*. Are you a bulbul or are you a
barbet?

I have two baby mynahs. They are called Huz and Buz.
They are not like other mynahs. They are black. Their
feathers have not come properly yet, so they are downy,
sooty balls. But the special thing about them is that they
have immense mouths, and these mouths are continually
opening wide, so wide that you could easily put three fingers
in, and all day long they cry in their own language, " Give!
Give! Give! " Even after Neela *Accal* has fed them, they
begin again, " Give! Give! Give! "

This is Holy Week because it is full of thoughts about the
holy suffering of our Lord Jesus. Some people, when they
think of Him and of all He has done for them, never think
at all of how much they can give to Him. They are like
Huz and Buz, their one cry is " Give! Give! Give! Give
me joy. Give me an easy time. Give me all I want. Give!
Give! Give! " Do you want to be like Huz and Buz? I
do hope not.

When Huz and Buz grow up, I think that they will be like
Jock, who does all he can to make people happy. Often
when we are feeling tired, his brave whistle cheers us, or his
funny talk makes us smile. He doesn't say, " Give, Give,
Give." He gives to us who give him food and everything he
needs.

What can you give, you little lovers, to the One Who gives
you everything, and, more than that, gave His life to make
you good and happy? You can give Him a grateful heart.
If anything has gone wrong, you can give Him what the
Psalm calls a humble and contrite heart. You can refuse
to cover wrong things as if they didn't matter much; you
can confess them, and like David accept the fruit of your
doings (Sittie will explain that), and humbly and lovingly
begin again. You can give your Lord Jesus all you have to
give. Then your word will be, " I give! I give! I give! "
and He will hear and He will be pleased with His little
lovers.

The mention of Amma's birds suggests that this chapter
should end in an anti-climax. When she was in Madras she
used to visit a market where birds in cages were for sale. On
a certain occasion in 1923 she was grieved to see so many little
creatures in cages that allowed them no freedom of movement.
She bought as many as she could, and her kind friends, the

Leghs, arranged for them to be taken to the station. She was accompanied on the journey by Mary Mills, with a baby just rescued, and by a girl, who was returning to Dohnavur because the Christian family who had adopted her refused to keep her any longer.

Alec Arnot met them with the Ford at Sermadevi station, and immediately Amma began to discuss with him some phase of the Jambulingam affair. Mary tried to care for the baby and the birds, but the girl was carried on to the next station, and had to be retrieved later. The car was crowded and covered and hung with bird cages, so that when it reached Dohnavur the human freight was scarcely visible. It was already late at night, but room had to be found for all the birds, and all had to be fed. Arulai vacated her room for the night in their favour. It really seemed to be doubtful whether in Amma's eyes a human being was more important than many Java sparrows!

There is a strange little mammal called the loris, but there is a conflict of opinion as to whether two of these creatures arrived that same night, or on a different occasion. At any rate, their diet is live cockroaches, and one of the *Sitties* remembers searching behind cupboards and on hands and knees in dark corners, in order that the lorises might not go to bed hungry. Francis of Assisi would have had a point of contact with Amma in regard to birds and beasts as well as more important things.

Strength of my heart, I need not fail,
  Not mine to fear but to obey.
With such a Leader who could quail?
  Thou art as Thou wert yesterday.
Strength of my heart, I rest in Thee,
Fulfil Thy purposes through me.

Hope of my heart, though suns burn low,
  And fades the green from all the earth,
Thy quenchless hope would fervent glow,
  From barren waste would spring to birth.
Hope of my heart, O cause to be
Renewals of Thy hope in me.

Love of my heart, my stream runs dry;
  O Fountain of the heavenly hills,
Love, blessed Love, to Thee I cry,
  Flood all my secret hidden rills.
Waters of love, O pour through me;
I must have love: I must have Thee.

Lord, give me love, then I have all,
  For love casts out tormenting fear,
And love sounds forth a trumpet call
  To valiant hope, and sweet and clear
The birds of joy sing in my tree,
Love of my heart, when I have Thee.

CHAPTER XXVIII

"STRENGTH OF MY HEART"

THE nineteen-twenties were years of rapid expansion. It was not only that the main task, the saving of children in danger, was pursued with unremitting zeal and determination, so that even in 1923 there were thirty nurseries in Dohnavur, and throughout this decade there was never a time when new buildings of one sort or another were not in course of erection. But concurrently there was a more regular and sustained reaching out with the Gospel to towns and villages around and, not only at Caruniapuram but elsewhere, places were found where a little Starry Cluster could shine for a time and "show the life of Jesus". But it was as " pilgrims " rather than " stars " that Edith Naish, May Parker, and others sallied forth, visiting Temple festivals, camping as Amma had been wont to camp, and giving many of the older Dohnavur girls a taste for village work which they have never lost.

At the same time the Light that shone in Dohnavur itself was attracting men and women to it. It was a warm Light which brought comfort to the sad while it illumined their darkness. Have we given an exaggerated impression of the extent to which Jambulingam's affairs absorbed Amma's mind and heart? Certainly she always had leisure for needy souls. One of the great joys of this period was the coming of Arulai's sister, called " Mimosa " in the book which was published under that name in 1924. Was there ever a clearer instance of the power of God's Spirit to keep a tiny flame of love burning in the heart of a woman, with so little fuel to feed it that nothing but a miracle of His working can account for its survival? The immediate cause of her coming—after more than twenty years' separation from her sister—was that Arulai had a day's fever, and spent it mainly in praying for Mimosa. No one could have guessed that in Mimosa's sons, who were lovingly welcomed to Dohnavur at that time, God was preparing some of His finest instruments for the future leadership of the work.

Expansion to " other cities also " was made possible partly

by the growth, in grace and experience, of some of the older girls and boys, and partly by the arrival of reinforcements from the United Kingdom. One must not say " England " or even " Britain ", because Ireland supplied an astonishing percentage of the earlier workers. At the beginning of the *Dohnavur Letter* of November, 1923 (for in spite of sentimental protests the old title *Scraps* has been scrapped after twenty years), it is delightful to read the names of twenty-seven " Dohnavur workers ", headed by Sellamutthu, Arulai, and Mabel Wade, all jumbled happily together under the heading " Indian, English, Scotch and Irish ". By the end of 1924 the thirteen non-Indian workers had become twenty, and " The New Seven " are listed as studying Tamil. Amma, now fifty-seven years of age, writes of slight anticipatory apprehension before their arrival.

> The older one grows the more one realizes what such things [as a forward movement] may contain, and how sensitive all concerned must be towards God and one another, if a sudden large increase of numbers is to bring abiding joy and strength.

But soon she was reassured by " that strange lovely knitting of hearts together, that instant understanding that needs no words ". So they entered upon the year 1925 with great hope and confidence.

It was a year that held many things for Amma and for Dohnavur. One very happy thing was the guidance to build a House of Prayer. Amongst the New Seven were three doctors, and the first Dohnavur hospital, though it has very sacred associations, was a makeshift affair. Surely a new building was needed. But on her birthday in December Amma had received some small money gifts, and, though a hospital had seemed the greater need, she was given a swift clear sense that the House of Prayer must come first. Next day came a gift from missionaries in Algiers towards a House of Prayer, and then a letter suggesting that a Mr and Mrs Dann and a Mr and Mrs Jackson would like to spend Christmas in Dohnavur, if it were convenient. Convenient? Mr Dann had designed the Chapel of the Women's Christian College in Madras, " so simple, so Indian, so satisfying " that Amma could think of no one in the world to whom she would rather entrust the task of designing the House of Prayer. Mr Jackson had been the builder, and at this juncture when, as Amma says, he might have been in England or Timbuctoo, as far as she knew, Mr and Mrs Jackson had actually taken up residence in Palamcottah.

Thank God, He plans these " coincidences " for all who listen for His Voice, and they happened so often in Amma's experience simply because her heart was perfect towards Him. There were delays and tests of faith, but the House of Prayer was dedicated by Bishop Tubbs * on November 16, 1927. Already " the climbing flowers that are like glorified violets " were nearly forty feet up the prayer tower.   A church or chapel used to be called a " place of worship " in an almost technical sense, but the words truly describe the House of Prayer.   There are no pictures, no stained glass windows, no symbols, to induce a sense of awe, but it is a building in which it seems natural to obey the injunction to " worship the Lord in the beauty of holiness ".

Another joy of 1925 was the visit of Godfrey Webb-Peploe. He was en route to China as a missionary of the Children's Special Service Mission.   He and an older friend, R. T. Archibald, conducted a mission in Dohnavur, and the Spirit of God was at work. " We joyed together," says Amma, " according to the joy of harvest."   But Godfrey left Dohnavur on March 31st, and the margin of *Daily Light* for that day has the words: " Good-bye to G. W. P.   A broken day ", and then a couplet from Alfred Noyes' poem, *The Torch Bearer*:

> Let me not live in vain, let me not fall
> Before I yield it to the appointed soul.

The words bear record that even then Amma had seen in Godfrey one to whom she would willingly hand the torch if she were called away from the Dohnavur work.   But at that time the thought went no further.   How could she covet for Dohnavur a man who had heard the call of God to China?

Meanwhile a vague sense of anxiety concerning one of the new workers had arisen in Amma's mind.   She read the words of *Daily Light* for May 21: " Strengthened with all

---

* Her background in Millisle and Broughton helped Amma to understand the hesitation in the minds of some of her friends concerning Dohnavur's intercourse with Bishops!   In her *Dohnavur Letter* of March 1928 she introduces Bishop and Mrs Tubbs with an explanatory parenthesis: " Who, you know, belong in spirit, and are far from being what the words connote to some of the *Dohnavur Letter's* very varied readers."

might, according to His glorious power, unto all patience and longsuffering with joyfulness ", and then she writes of the possibility of disappointment in regard to this new worker, and of anxieties concerning some others, both Indian and European. " A dreadful time of distress," says the diary, " never such known here before. I am beginning to sink. Lord, save me. . . . He has stretched forth His Hand, He has caught me. My Lord and my God." Thus she fought with her fears. Yet uncertainty remained. "What of guidance? Was it all a mistake? And yet we waited long and prayed much. Lord, undertake for me. I do not know what to do." She calls May 30th " the most painful night of my life. The coward in me quails." She prayed often for a renewal of hope. Would not the perplexities be resolved? " Keep me from looking back on what appeared to be guidance."

In July there was a " strange and dreadful prayer meeting ". (How strange that the sentence should ever be written of Dohnavur!) A guest who had obviously heard reports from someone " prayed distressingly, and I could not be crystal clear that there was nothing in his prayer. He prayed about *friction*. We had never heard or used or thought of the word before, in connection with ourselves, and could hardly bear it."

At length something happened which seemed to make action necessary. " One of the very saddest nights of my life " is the marginal note in *Daily Light* of November 28, but even then the words, " Let not your heart be troubled ", brought comfort. The next day the severance took place. A Life of Amma would be incomplete without reference to a trial which cost her so much. Perhaps the principles on which the Dohnavur Fellowship was established in the following year owe something to the experiences of 1925.

In August there was a strain, severe enough, but of a different kind. Another of the New Seven, Dr Marguerite Stewart, the daughter of missionaries in Madras who were very old friends, was taken seriously ill and went to Neyyoor for a series of operations. Amma loved her very dearly, and wrote as the illness proceeded:

> This letter goes out to you from under the shadow; and deep within all that is, and under all the stir of a new campaign, there is a very silent place where one seems to live, holding Marguerite up to God.

The middle of August was the most critical time. On the morning of the 15th Amma writes in the margin of *Daily Light*: "All day with God for Marguerite", and on the next page:

> In the night saw Marguerite attended by a bright presence, a boy. Extraordinary sense of joy and liberty. Tried to think who it could be and remembered her little brother taken long ago.

She wrote these words in the early morning of Sunday the 16th, and on the 17th she wrote to Marguerite:

> On Sunday night I was shown just one of the invisible forces that have been round about you—"sent to minister". I was not sure at first what that look into the unseen meant, but on Sunday morning at 7 o'clock the assurance came that a great attack had been met and defeated, and at 10.15 the hopeful letter came.

From that day onwards recovery was steady though very slow, but a long time of convalescence was necessary, and so another new worker was removed from Dohnavur.

"And now are you ready for another story of the doings of Him Whose name is Wonderful?" It is thus that, in a letter of 1925, Amma introduces the subject of Three Pavilions.* Through the good offices of a Syrian Christian, an official of the Travancore Forestry Department (whose cousin Koruth became a full member of the Dohnavur Fellowship in 1928), sixty acres of land on a rocky hillside, overlooking the Pilgrim Way to Cape Comorin, were purchased in July. Three Pavilions, so-called because it is close to a place where centuries ago the kings of Tinnevelly, Travancore and Tanjore used to meet, has proved to be a splendid investment. Amma had foreseen that, as the Family grew, some might need to hive off to avoid overcrowding, but when the cheque was signed—and she signed it on her knees, looking to God for guidance concerning the use to which the property should be put—she could hardly have foreseen whereunto this would grow. Three Pavilions now houses about seventy girls. For the most part they are either less robust than others, and therefore needing special care, or mentally less well endowed, and therefore unfitted for normal school life in Dohnavur. It is a happy place, with wide views of both mountains and sea,

* A fuller account is to be found in *Gold Cord*, pp. 249–252.

swept by winds which are healthy and invigorating though sometimes inclined to be violent.

Amma went there often while building was in progress, and, as always, gathered the workmen together for prayers. One who helped there as a lad is now headman on the farm. In his village not far from Three Pavilions seven families have been won to the Lord.

It is only fifteen miles from Three Pavilions (which is just over the Travancore border) to India's southernmost point, Cape Comorin; and in this same year, and through the help of the same Syrian Christian, Amma bought a small plot of ground by the sea, and built a little house which she named Joppa, believing that God would make it a place of vision to tired workers from Dohnavur. More than that, she saw it as a place of witness to pilgrims. For there is a temple at India's " Land's End ". In the years that followed Amma and many a group of her fellow-workers found refreshment by the sea, but she never forgot the challenge of the temple, representing unseen powers that hold sway over the people whom she loved.

> Down on the shore below the striped temple wall I stood one day, desperate because of things seen in the court above, broken by the sense of my own impotence. . . . And my heart cried out to my Lord, " O Lord, how long? "

How could anyone who loves God, and who loves India, as Amma did, be content until He reigns without a rival there?

Christ our Captain, hear our prayer,
  Warriors we ask of Thee,
Comrades who shall everywhere
  Stand for love and loyalty;
Servants who with souls aflame,
  Kindled from Thine altar-fire,
Live to magnify Thy Name,
  Live to meet Thy least desire.

Lovers who in love abide
  In the Secret Place of rest,
Yielded to be crucified
  That Thy life be manifest;
Labourers who joyfully
  Choose rewards unseen today.
Cause us, O our Lord, to be
  Like to these for whom we pray.

CHAPTER XXIX

THE DOHNAVUR FELLOWSHIP

In the year 1925 Amma and Mabel Wade ceased to be missionaries of the Church of England Zenana Missionary Society. There was no breach of fellowship, but the Dohnavur work had been virtually independent for many years past, and it did not seem fair that anyone should be allowed to think that the C.E.Z. was responsible for it. Amma had always tried to make it clear that the Society would never be asked to meet any financial liabilities incurred by her, but it was an anomalous situation, especially as new workers came to Dohnavur who were not attached to the C.E.Z. or to any other organization.

What was the next step? It never occurred to Amma to establish a new " mission ", but in order to hold land and property it was necessary that an association should be formed in legal fashion, and thus the Dohnavur Fellowship came into being in 1926, and was officially registered in 1927. When this process was accomplished the C.M.S. generously handed over some of its property (i.e. the old bungalow where Amma had lived with the Walkers and some surrounding land and buildings) to the Fellowship.

In the official " Memorandum of Association " the object of the Fellowship is stated as follows:

> To save children in moral danger; to train them to serve others; to succour the desolate and the suffering; to do anything that may be shown to be the will of our Heavenly Father, in order to make His love known, especially to the people of India.

It is interesting to note that while legal requirements are properly safeguarded, the language of the Constitution breaks away from the purely formal. For instance, the regulation which deals with the leadership of the Fellowship states that

> the Leader with the help of the Council shall direct the conduct of the Fellowship according to the plans that God shall reveal. It is agreed that *the supreme Authority is vested in the Unseen Leader, the Lord Jesus Christ,* while the human

Leader seeks, in co-operation with the other members, to carry out the mind and will of the Divine.

With regard to candidates, " only those shall be received into membership whom the existing members have reason to believe their Unseen Leader has chosen ".

It is noticeable that the words " Indian ", " European ", or " foreign " are never used. The Fellowship consisted from the first of men and women of several nationalities. Since it was an outgrowth of the Starry Cluster, Indians were naturally included in it from the very beginning. On the other hand, the number of workers from the United Kingdom and Australia, and later from Switzerland, Canada and New Zealand has increased from a mere handful to between forty and fifty, many more than Amma anticipated in 1926. But the pattern, with its keywords of love, loyalty, unity and service, is no different from that already outlined in Chapter 17. Indeed, the expansion of the work and the growth of the Fellowship only emphasized the supreme importance of each of these words. Since the members are part of one large Family, they *must* be knit together in a love by which they serve one another, and in a oneness that is based on utter loyalty.

One of Amma's deepest desires was that Dohnavur might be a place where the Lord Himself would feel at home, because here was a group of people living in literal obedience to His new commandment, who believed that they " could be held fast to loyal love, to the kind of loyalty that would be ashamed to think an unworthy thought of a fellow-lover." She refused to believe that our Lord had given a command which could not be obeyed. Was it not an intolerable thought that nowhere in the whole world the Beloved could find a company of His lovers who loved one another with a pure heart fervently?

From this high ground she never moved. But she recognized, too, that, from what men are pleased to call the " practical " aspect of things (as if literal obedience to our Lord's command is not a practical matter!), any lack of inner harmony in the Family at Dohnavur would be more obviously dangerous than elsewhere. Where, as in the case of a large missionary society, there are many centres of work, a misfit can at least be moved from one to another—there are both round holes and square holes, and a peg which does not fit into one may perhaps be happily adjusted to another. A breakdown of happy relations between fellow-workers is a tragedy anywhere, but the harm of it may be minimized by redistribution. But in a community whose members live and work and eat together, unlove (as Amma called it) is literally fatal. It means that the cement has fallen out without which the whole building may collapse.

The Fellowship does, in fact, consist of men and women who earnestly endeavour to preserve the unity of the Spirit in the bond of peace, and who do actually live together in free and joyful comradeship. But disservice is done to Dohnavur by those who speak or write of it as a Garden of Eden without the serpent, or a heaven from which all strife and malice and envy are excluded. Visitors to Dohnavur are charmed by the spontaneity of the children's happiness, and if they could spend months in the compound, rather than days or hours, the first impressions would be confirmed. Only they would discover that this love, this harmony, is constantly under attack, that there is not a moment when the adversary is not seeking to undermine it. It is God Who makes men to be of one mind in a house, and they would cease to be of one mind if the members of His household ceased to be in touch with Him. The long-term visitor would find no complacency in the Fellowship today, any more than it existed in Amma—only a great longing to press toward the mark, a burning desire on the part of this company of ordinary men and women to exceed the ordinary in faith and hope and love and courage and patience.

Perhaps it was inevitable that many who were attracted to Dohnavur by reading Amma's books should think of it as a place where the ideal had been attained, and overlook the frequently repeated warnings not to fall into this error. " Not as though I had already attained " was her eager disclaimer, and " I follow after " her equally eager resolve. The prayer, " Make us what we seem to be ", was often on her lips.

Reference has already been made to many of the essential principles on which the Fellowship was founded. No one could be happy in it who did not regard the Scriptures of the Old and New Testaments as divinely inspired and historically reliable. No one could be happy who shunned the Cross, who did not honestly desire to take the way that the Master went, of shame and suffering if need be, so that the people of India may not only hear of Him but see His life being lived in a

company of His disciples.   No one could be happy who did not
accept His standards, and seek first His kingdom.

Again, no one could be happy to whom a denominational
affiliation is of major importance.   Dohnavur is set in an area
where the churches were originally brought into being by
members of the Church Missionary Society, and are now part
of the Church of South India.   Amma herself was happy in
this environment, but as the work grew the Indian pastor in the
village church begged her to arrange separate services for her
children, since the church was overcrowded.   For some years
he and his successors came regularly to administer Communion,
but eventually one of them suggested that members of the
Fellowship should preside at the Lord's Table.   Moreover, by
this time the Fellowship included quite a number of men and
women who were not members of the Church of England.
There was no decision to break away from the Church of the
diocese, but a gradual loosening of the outward links with it.
The happiest relations exist, and help is given when requested.
The members of the Fellowship are free to accept invitations for
spiritual ministry anywhere in South India.   There is no
thought of establishing a new church, and converts won
through the hospital or the village work are encouraged to
join the church nearest to their homes.   Within the Fellowship
the rule concerning controversial matters is: " Let every man
be fully persuaded in his own mind."   Christians in Dohnavur
are members of Christ's Body, and desire fellowship with all
their fellow-members.   Relationship with other Christians is
on a firm basis, personally and spiritually, if not ecclesiastically.

Amma always distinguished between principles, which were
not open to alteration, and customs, which were subject to
revision.   Perhaps this is the place to refer to the strange
notion that she was a sort of dictator, who desired that even
after she had left it, the work should continue to follow, in
detail as well as in principle, the lines that she had laid down.
Actually, the counsel which she gave to those who might
succeed her in the leadership of the work was this:

> When decisions have to be made, don't look back and
> wonder what I would have done. Look up, and light will
> come to do what our Lord and Master would have you do.
> It may be that decisions which seem to change the
> character of the work will have to be made. But if the root

principles which have governed us from the beginning are held fast, there will be no real change. The river may flow in a new channel, but it will be the same river.

If you hold fast to the resolve that in all things Christ as Lord shall have the pre-eminence, if you keep His will, His glory, and His pleasure high above everything, and if you continue in His love, loving one another as He has loved you, then all will be well, eternally well.

Some reference must be made to the losses which the Fellowship has suffered from time to time. There were, of course, those who were unable to face the physical strain of living in a tropical climate, and who therefore left Dohnavur on medical grounds. Of the rest it seems hardly sufficient to say that they went out from Dohnavur because they were not of it, though there have been spiritual casualties here, as on other battlefields. In some cases, no doubt, a decision was reached to accept a candidate concerning whose background and spiritual fitness there was insufficient knowledge. When Amma was convinced of a need, and gave herself to prayer concerning it, it was no wonder that she should consider an offer from one who seemed fitted to meet that need, for she expected her prayers to be heard. Perhaps in the early days she took risks too readily. Certainly, as time went on, she reached no decision without consulting others. On the other hand, when it was known that Amma was inclined to accept a candidate, her judgment naturally weighed with others who had read the correspondence. Knowing that through all the years in India she had so constantly received direct guidance from God, they would be slow to differ from her. This, at least, is certain. Right up to the last four or five years of her life she was writing in the plainest terms to intending candidates, suggesting every possible reason to shake their sense of call, if it could be shaken! And on their arrival new workers were given such a welcome, and provided with such helps through the difficult early years, that failure could never be set down to lack of loving forethought on her part.

But Amma was cut to the quick when such failure occurred. Her first thought always was to blame herself. Could she not have understood the situation earlier? If she had been loving and humble enough, would it ever have developed? Like Samuel in the case of Saul, she sometimes " cried unto the

Lord all night " concerning one who was not fitting in happily. She continued to believe the best, even when there was clear evidence of disloyalty. Those who loved her dearly would say, " All Amma's geese are swans ", and they were thinking of themselves, and not of others, as the geese. It is no breach of confidence to state that there are at least a few members of the Fellowship rendering valuable service today, concerning whose stability Amma had serious misgivings. But by the grace of God, and in answer to her prayers, they came through the shocks and testings of the early years, and are now " steadfast, immovable, always abounding in the work of the Lord ".

With some, perhaps, the difficulty has been impatience with what appears to be the slow tempo of advance towards the ideal, an unreadiness to reserve judgment until knowledge of the language and the people and the background has given them a right to speak. It was easier for them to see that changes were desirable than to wait until the time was ripe for their introduction. But, thank God, severance from Dohnavur, whether the fault has been largely theirs or not, and whether it has come about by their own choice, or because others felt it necessary, need not be the end of useful service. There are those who may have said, " I mistook God's guidance; I ought never to have come here ", or concerning whom Amma may have said, " We mistook God's guidance; we ought never to have encouraged you to come here." Yet in other spheres, whether in India or elsewhere, they are still engaged in the same warfare, instruments useful to the same Master. And He can restore even the very few, whether Indian or European, in whom Satan gained a temporary advantage, whose names were never out of Amma's thoughts and prayers to the very end.

Their names are not mentioned in this book, nor indeed is it possible to refer by name to the far larger number who found in Dohnavur the one place to which God had been leading them, and in Amma the one leader whom they were utterly content to follow, because they knew her to be in such close touch with " the Unseen Leader, Christ ".

And shall I pray Thee change Thy will, my Father,
  Until it be according unto mine?
But no, Lord, no, that never shall be, rather
  I pray Thee blend my human will with Thine.

I pray Thee hush the hurrying, eager longing,
  I pray Thee soothe the pangs of keen desire.
See in my quiet places wishes thronging,
  Forbid them, Lord, purge, though it be with fire.

And work in me to will and do Thy pleasure,
  Let all within me, peaceful, reconciled,
Tarry content my Wellbelovèd's leisure,
  At last, at last, even as a weanèd child.

CHAPTER XXX

"THERE SHALL BE A PERFORMANCE"

1926 was a critical year for Dohnavur. There were three prayer requests which Amma had been holding up continually before the Lord. First, there was the obvious need of a leader for the boys' work. Secondly, as the need of a hospital became clearer, she saw that, unless it were to be limited to women patients, a man was required who could give help in the building of the hospital and co-ordinate all this side of the work. Thirdly, since Amma was in her fifty-ninth year, she was constantly thinking of the future leadership of the whole work. Disappointment had been all the greater because along each of these lines it had seemed that prayer was being answered.

Then, as we have seen, the visit of Godfrey Webb-Peploe en route to China had awakened a desire which, in loyalty to China, she sought to stifle. If he had been free, he might have been the answer to the first prayer, and possibly to the third. He was not free, but for his sake a very warm welcome was offered to his mother and his elder brother, Dr Murray Webb-Peploe, who arrived in Dohnavur on January 30th, 1926. They also were en route to China, where the doctor was expecting to serve with Dr Gordon Thompson at the C.M.S. Hospital in Hangchow. His relationship to the C.M.S. was unusual, for it had been agreed that if for any reason Dr Thompson should leave Hangchow, Dr Webb-Peploe would be free to reconsider the whole arrangement.

The two brothers were grandsons of the Webb-Peploe whom Amma had known as a speaker at Keswick. Graciousness may surely be inherited, even if grace is not. At any rate, the beauty of the Lord our God rested on the lives of these two men. They were different in temperament: Murray the more eager, full of initiative, the " gay troubadour of God " that he desired to be, and Godfrey quieter, steady as a rock, perhaps more conservative but no less intense. Both were aflame with the love of Christ, both were walking humbly with God.

Of the three doctors who arrived in 1924, Dr May Powell was the only one now in Dohnavur, and she, of course, was busy with Tamil study, and was therefore refraining from much in the way of surgical work. With Murray's arrival, even though he was only a visitor, the little operating theatre was immediately prepared for action, and with Dr Powell as anæsthetist, adenoids and tonsils and some other organs were removed, and Murray began to lay the foundations of a reputation which continues to this day. Apart from the medical work, which included a fortnight or more with Dr Howard Somervell at Neyyoor—when Amma rejoiced that through her visitor she was able to repay a very little of the debt that she owed to Neyyoor—Murray accompanied Amma to Caruniapuram, to Madura, to Three Pavilions and Joppa, and to a number of towns and villages near at hand. "We had glorious raids on the kingdom of darkness together," writes Amma. No one could know both Amma and Murray Webb-Peploe without being sure that they would prove to be kindred spirits. The earlier generation of Amma's children remember how she would suddenly appear and call them to go out preaching with her. Everything else had to be set aside, and they were gone in a few minutes. It was a kind of activity, and a kind of attitude, that appealed to Murray. The journeys in the Ford were sometimes exciting, but who minded? There was plenty of laughter as well as plenty of solid work done.

The best hours of all [says the *Dohnavur Letter* for May, 1926] were those we spent round the table after dinner during the last ten days or so, for something happened in those last ten days, and we were all most wonderfully knitted together in Him. After dinner when the things are cleared off the table, and only the flowers and lamps are left, we generally hearten ourselves after the long hot day with song (" My lips will be fain when I sing unto Thee, and so will be my heart which Thou hast redeemed ", is a true word), and lately we have taken to reading for a little while together too, and Dr Webb-Peploe sometimes gave us the food on which he had been feeding, straight from his little well-worn Greek Testament, and somehow it was always the food that was convenient for us. It was God's own blessed manna to us all.

God bless that dear Mother and her two sons who have

been more to Dohnavur than we can say. To the most loving One Who sent them our thanks rise now, for He knoweth whereof we are made and He is very kind to His poor dust.

Thus began a time of very severe strain for Amma. There had come to her the clear apprehension that these two men were exactly fitted, with their gifts of mind and spirit, to meet the urgent need of Dohnavur, yet she shrank with shame, almost with alarm, from the thought that she was beginning to covet men whom their Lord had called to China.

Soon after Murray had left, she writes in her private diary:

" Surely I have quieted myself "—have I?—" as a weaned child "—am I? This sadness [the recent disappointment] does not pass, and it has left an aftermath of perplexity. . . . Then Murray—but so different this. Still my heart turns to him as Thy chosen leader for the hospital, and refuses to be forbidden. Lord, work Thy work in me. I cannot quiet myself. O do Thou quiet me. Let me not even wish for him—and yet my heart sees in him all that I ever asked of Thee. I see in him and in Godfrey my very heart's desire. Control my prayers. Let me not covet my neighbour's goods—nor his menservants. Murray and Godfrey are China's menservants. Lord, help and forgive.

On September 23rd, after long waiting upon God for direction, she paid the first advance for the land which is now the boys' compound. No leader for the work was then in sight, but she wrote in the margin of *Daily Light* ," Help will come. Our God hath not forsaken us."

The diary of the very next day speaks of

a time of very great need. . . . It is as if the evil one were seeking to undermine what he failed to overthrow by open assault, even our perfect unity. He is distressing the dearest and truest of our Indian Fellowship, as well as some of us. O Lord, deliver.

But a week later she writes:

One of those about whom I was specially thinking has been relieved. The cruel and the evil one has had to withdraw. The chief anxiety is not relieved yet, but—O blessed be Thy love, my Lord!—yesterday a cable came from Murray asking if his mother and Godfrey can come.

For some months there had been anxiety concerning God-frey's health, and at least a suspicion of tubercular trouble. The doctors ordered rest, and the minds of the Webb-Peploes turned to Dohnavur as a place where it could be obtained— far enough from China and yet not too far if his health were re-established.

On the night of October 8th Amma was at Joppa. The house was not yet built, so the party slept on the sand dunes " in a cool wind under the stars ". .Amma was

> wakened towards midnight by a dream of great happiness— Murray and Godfrey with us at Dohnavur. Dreams have no conscience, and I was untroubled by a sense of China's loss, or by fear of selfishness. It was a moment of quite pure joy, so vivid that it woke me. I feared, pushed it away, and asked to be kept from deceptions.

The entry for October 23rd is: " The Mother and Godfrey here. Now, Lord, hold my heart."

> *November* 19*th.* On the morning of the 16th I was wakened by this clear word: " You have never asked Me to give Murray and Godfrey for the future leaders of the work." I said nothing, for I was troubled. I had thought it would be wrong to ask. Then He said, " Why have you not asked Me for them? " But I answered, " O my Lord, Thou knowest why I held my heart back from asking." And He said, " Ask Me now."
> On Sunday, November 21st, again came that strange urging to rise and kneel and pray for M. and G. for the future leadership. I had hurt my knee but could not resist, so rose and prayed. *Godfrey is my Benediction.* [It was one of her favourite names for him.]

Meanwhile the Lord had been speaking to Godfrey. He remembered his exercise of heart during the visit of the previous year. Even in China the Lord had spoken to him several times, and later, when dates were compared, they proved to be occasions when there was acute need in Dohnavur. On November 14th he wrote to the C.S.S.M., resigning from the work in China, but of course he did not feel free to speak of this until the letter was acknowledged.

> On December 11th, while driving [writes Amma], I was with God about Dohnavur, and said, " Lord, if Thou givest Godfrey and Murray to us "—but He said, " Why do you

say *if*? Did I not tell you to ask for them? Why do you not say *when*?" So I waited a minute and then said "when".

She felt she ought to mention the matter to Mrs Webb-Peploe, " knowing how easily I might mistake, and fearing presumptuous sin, and yet unable to resist the sense of God in the matter "

December 14th was " a burdened day ". Amma talked with Alec Arnot about the need of the boys, and he referred to Godfrey, though she had not mentioned him. " He has no thought of staying," he said. " He's getting strong for China."

> At dinner [says the diary] Godfrey said (and his mother agreed) about future plans, " Don't count on me for anything." I felt much afraid then. . . . A troubled night, for His Word had seemed so clear and sure, and if I had mistaken it, in how many other ways might I not be mistaking Him?

Was it all a delusion?

And then early on the morning of December 15th came a little note from Godfrey offering to the Dohnavur Fellowship:

> I don't feel one little bit fit to join you all, or to be an elder brother to the boys, but I pray God may make me to walk worthy of His high calling—for of the fact that He has called I have no shadow of a doubt.

> I read that note many times over [writes Amma]. Then for half an hour I was where time does not count, and there are no words. There is such a thing as being silent in joy. . . . The children call him my " great birthday present ", and the 16th was a day of very special happiness.

For more than twenty-two years Godfrey brought untold happiness to Dohnavur. Gradually his health was re-established and, to Amma's deep content, he showed unusual aptitude for Tamil and won his way into the hearts of the people.

But what of Murray? In Psalm 18, verse 6, David tells us how he called upon the Lord in his distress. The Lord heard his voice, and verse 7 follows immediately with the astonishing statement, " Then the earth shook and trembled." The prayer of the hunted fugitive who, as he says to Saul, felt himself to be as insignificant as a dead dog or a flea, sets

tremendous forces in motion. Nothing is too much for God
to do in answer to the cry of His servant.

Now He Whose never-failing providence orders all things in
heaven and on earth was no doubt over-ruling events in China
in 1927 for far-reaching purposes, into which we cannot enter
here. But none the less it is true to say that as Amma prayed
the civil war in China increased in intensity. The Nationalist
armies began their famous drive to the Yangtze, and Hangchow, where Murray Webb-Peploe was at work, was in the line
of their advance.

Here is the record in the diary:

> *Sunday, February* 20. Again that urge to pray for Murray,
> for clear leading there, the word that assures, and for myself,
> for quietness in waiting, no impatience of desire. Heard
> that Hangchow was now only ten miles from the Southern
> Army.

On Monday came the news that Hangchow had fallen, and
Amma prayed with Arulai, from whom she never had any
secrets, concerning Murray. On the same day the Fellowship
met and " after talking over the minimum number needed for
the efficient carrying on of the work and for extension ", they
asked for fourteen new workers of God's choice.

Together with other missionaries, Murray reached Shanghai
in safety, and after waiting some weeks to discover whether a
return to Hangchow would be feasible, he decided to apply for
six months' leave, and made straight for Dohnavur, arriving on
May 31st.

> *May* 31. He is here—the same dear Murray. My
> Father, how can I thank Thee enough? Startled but
> steadied in joy, by *Daily Light* morning and evening.

She refers especially to the words of Luke 1. 45: " Blessed is
she that believed: for *there shall be a performance* of those things
which were told her from the Lord." " Made vital again
today," is her marginal comment. " Do as Thou hast spoken,
November 16, 1926."

In July Murray heard that he might be needed at Hangchow
in September. In the Forest in August Amma held on to the
word of Luke 1. 45, but it was a difficult time.

> I was just shattered with the pain of it all. . . . Then
> gentle words fell, " Why these tears? Why this tension of

desire? Why not rest on My word to thee?" But the
thousand tangles, Lord. There was no China and no
Gordon Thompson when Moses was given his Joshua.
Moses was not selfish. Am I selfish? How can we of the
D.F. gain if it means loss to any other? How can we wish
to gain? . . . Very broken prayer by the stone outside my
room. At last peace came, and again the words, " Open
your windows towards the sunrising."

Once or twice during those " burning days " (as she calls
them) she " let down the barriers ", so that Murray could not
but know what her hopes were. He had written to Dr
Thompson, whose own movements were very uncertain, and
suggested an extension of leave. But at the same time he was
" plunging deep into our mud " i.e. helping in most brotherly
fashion to bear spiritual burdens. Of one who had been a
source of anxiety for years Amma writes, " God gave to
Murray the key of X——'s heart." Yet every evidence of the
grace of God in him only increased her desire for the fulfilment
of His promise to her, and when on several occasions she over-
heard him saying in conversation with others, " Of course I'm
only a visitor ", the words cut her to the heart.

December 15th was remembered as the first anniversary of
Godfrey's becoming *sonthum* (a very favourite word with
Amma, meaning something like " our own " but not easily
translatable).

> For this last year I thank Thee, for comradeship that never
> once has failed, for the glorious days to come, I thank Thee.
> Because love is eternal I thank Thee. Because he is so true
> and dear and loyal to the core, because of all he has to give
> to these boys whom Thou hast given us, and to us all, from
> the ground of my heart I thank Thee, my Father.

The tension of spirit made her more than usually sensitive.
Once or twice it seemed as if some little expression of love was
refused by a member of the Fellowship to whom it was offered,
and she writes in the diary:

> Things to remember quietly when one's little pot of oint-
> ment seems to have been broken in vain. Of Thine own
> have we given Thee, for love is of God. The love, then, was
> His, and to Him first of all it was offered—to the human dear
> one not first but second. No pot of ointment was ever
> broken at His feet without giving Him some little quick sense
> of pleasure. So it was not all in vain. Then if it seemed

to miss what we meant it to do for the one we love down here, it may be only for the moment. The remembrance may return and be very sweet, like a fragrance.

The more loving the heart is, the more it looks forward to giving a pleasure to one it loves, the keener therefore the pang of disappointment when it fails, and the fiercer the inrush of depression. The heart is grieved and cannot rise to be glad. At such times it does help to know that love cannot really be as water spilt on the ground. For it is of God. The fragrance of the ointment will yet fill the house. The one to whom we wanted to bring comfort will in the end find that which we brought. But the sweet and immediate comfort is—" Of Thine own have we given Thee ". Dear Lord, did it comfort Thee?

April 13. At prayers Murray read from Luke 11, especially verse 8, " because of his shamelessness ". I have often been ashamed in asking for so great a gift. . . . Only, Lord, let it be so clear that nothing can ever shake it, a *certainty* from Thee alone that will carry him through any storm of devils, any assault of man, any disappointment in those he loves and serves, through anything, everything, on to the end.

If Amma was strengthened to pass through those long months of tension, perhaps the reader can bear to read of them. As 1928 crept by, and this background of ceaseless waiting upon God had to be added to all her normal tasks without neglect of any, it is no wonder that she was very tired. But strong assurance came from God's Word over and over again, and at last a half page of note-paper is pasted into the diary, empty except for these golden words: " July 13th, 1928. *May I stay here? Murray.*"

This, then, was the performance of those things which had been told to Amma from the Lord, and the petition for that date in the diary is as follows:

Lord, he is Thy corn of wheat. How dear he must be to Thee. Thou knowest we have nothing to offer him but a patch of bare ground into which he may fall and die. When it feels very dry and bare, dear Lord, give him, even if it be only for a moment, to look through the blue veil and see what *is*—fruit unto life eternal.

Lord, make of this our pleasant field
　A garden cool and shadowy,
A spring shut up, a fountain sealed
　For Thee, Lord Jesus, only Thee.

And fill it full of singing birds
　On every bough of every tree,
And give the music and the words
　That will, Lord Jesus, pleasure Thee.

And, as from far untrodden snow
　Of Lebanon the streams run free,
Dear Lord, command our streams to flow
　That thirsty men may drink of Thee.

CHAPTER XXXI

PLACE OF HEAVENLY HEALING

BEFORE the Fellowship had its own clock-tower, with a quiet room from which the whole compound can be seen and, of course, the mountains to the west—and in which the Lord reveals Himself continually to those who seek Him there—Amma frequently climbed the tower of the village church when she longed for a wider view. On the evening of January 30th, 1921, as she has recorded in *Gold Cord*,* she went there with a few others to see the sunset.

> It was a glorious evening. We stood in silence drinking in the beauty, and then as we looked down on the scattered villages and towns, and thought of the people there and of their need of skilled and loving succour, an urgent prayer was given. We asked for a Place of Healing for the people, and for a doctor to lead our boys and girls out into this loving service.

In the following year, moved with compassion (as always) for the many around her who were sick and had none to help them, and having read of healing Missions in North India, where it appeared that glory was given to the Lord Himself as the Healer, and there was no suggestion that He might not also use medicine or surgery for the relief of suffering, Amma began to wonder whether she herself ought not to ask for the gift of healing. There is an entry in her diary on May 4th: "Asked for cleansed hands. Asked for the gift—I fear to write it even now, but I did ask, was constrained to ask. Told no one."

The very next day one of the servants came to her in much pain, and said, "Lay your hands on me, Amma!" "I told her there was no power in my hands—Jesus was the Healer. But she took my hands and gently directed them to the place where the pain was, and waited on her knees." She was followed by a gardener, also in pain, and after the laying on of hands both were relieved, and did their full day's work.

* *Gold Cord*, p. 278.

Shortly afterwards one of the *Accals* who was suffering from a damaged finger was marvellously healed.

Naturally it was not long before these things were noised abroad. One morning the Hindu sub-magistrate from Nanguneri happened to call at prayer time, and stood watching through a window.

At prayers that morning a baby boy had been brought that he might return thanks for his healing, and a little girl stood up to thank the Lord for hers. The feel of the room was very joyful indeed, and it impressed the sub-magistrate immensely. "I did not know that anywhere the Lord Jesus Christ was doing these things now," was his last remark. He had heard of the healings and had attributed them to auto-suggestion, but when he heard of the babies he was dumb.

Sometimes, as in the case of one of the *Accals*, Manoharum, who was taken to Neyyoor for an operation, Amma recognized that it was the Lord's wish to heal otherwise. Sometimes healing was not given. And always the healing of the spirit was regarded as far more important than the healing of the body—though for a time it seemed that " the one has greatly helped forward the other ".

Then, almost suddenly, the healings ceased. It was partly that in that year, 1922, Amma's whole mind was more and more concentrated on the two dacoits, Jambulingam and Kasi, but in addition she began to be fearful of too much limelight for Dohnavur, and of too many people bringing their sick for healing, and looking to her personally as a wonder-worker. Looking back, she always felt that the obloquy and shame that came upon her through Jambulingam's affairs was in a sense God's corrective to the danger of popularity.

On July 12th there is a further note in *Daily Light*: " Asked for the gift of healing for the sake of others ", and she adds the words: " Answer, ' No '." It was not that she ever ceased to look directly to the Lord for healing, or that she did not see His Hand guiding the loving hands of doctors and nurses in the years that followed; but the main work of Dohnavur would have been side-tracked if she had allowed the countryside to look to her as a worker of miracles.

But the prayer of January 30th, 1921, was not forgotten, and it was partially answered through the coming of Dr May

Powell in 1924. But the other two doctors who arrived in that
same year had already left when on January 30th, 1926—
Amma loved to notice these dates because she believed God
noticed them—Murray Webb-Peploe came to Dohnavur en
route for China.   In April he was gone, and who knew that
he would ever return?   Funds earmarked for the hospital
began to trickle in, but no large gifts at all till August, 1927,
when Amma was welcomed as she climbed up to the Forest
House by happy children crying, " £100 for the hospital! "
and Murray, who was then (as he said) a " visitor ", was asked
to give thanks.   Then in January, 1928, Amma felt clear that
it was right to consider the purchase of land for a hospital.
On January 20th came a letter from a friend, and Amma read
it to the whole Fellowship.   It suggested that the word
" dipped " in Joshua 3. 15 means " plunged ".   " We too ",
said the writer, " have so often to make a plunge, not just the
slow, cautious step but the plunge in faith, and then things
happen."   It was God's word to Amma, but she waited
because she felt that in so vital a matter the whole Fellowship
must be united.   Here are the entries in the log-book for the
latter part of January :

Sunday, 22.   Much prayer about Joshua 3. 15.
Wednesday, 25.   Prayer with some of D.F. about Joshua
   3. 15.
Thursday, 26.   Ditto.

Unity was given on January 30th, but strangely enough it
was not till later that Amma linked this happening with the
prayer of seven years earlier.   Almost immediately came the
confirmation of a gift large enough to cover the cost of the
land.
   When Murray became *sonthum* it was possible to begin
making definite plans.   " Did Moses enjoy his pattern of the
tabernacle ", writes Amma, " more than we are enjoying
ours of the hospital, I wonder?   Line by line it is being given."
They revelled in the story of a Hindu in Travancore who met
someone from Dohnavur, and said, " I hear you are to have a
hospital in Dohnavur; you will make it a Paradise."   That
was suggested in the name Parama Suha Salai, or Place of
Heavenly Healing—a name which they all felt had been
" given ", like the pattern.   The Indian gentry of the neigh-

bourhood were deeply interested in the establishment of a hospital, and their leader was asked what he thought of the proposed name. He was inclined to question its fitness. " Those words imply spiritual vision, and therefore that Other-world health which follows upon spiritual vision. But is it not rather upon the good medicine to be given that we should direct the thoughts of our patients? " " Why," said Amma, " you have exactly described what we most of all desire." " In that case," he said, " Parama Suha Salai is the one perfect name."

Medically, or surgically rather, the theatre is the heart of a hospital, but from the Fellowship point of view the Prayer Room is the real heart, and you can't have two hearts, architecturally. But look at the pattern given on the Mount. In the centre is the theatre ; above it is a room with a tank and the pumps, for water will have to be pumped by hand to get it sterile for the theatre. *And above that is the Prayer Room.* It will look across to the House of Prayer, and by a signal of bells it will be very easy to communicate, so that prayer at important times can be united.

As the plans were worked out, Dr Webb-Peploe began to realize that the cost must be very heavy. " Is it going to be too expensive? " he asked Amma one day in June, 1929. She hesitated to answer, but next morning she was directed to the word in *Daily Light* for June 4th, " The house that is to be builded for the Lord must be exceeding magnifical." This word, she says, " lifted the matter of cost to the heavenlies— where the air is clear ". By " magnifical ", she explains, she meant " perfect for its purpose of glorifying the God of love, so that men and women will be drawn to Him. He is also the God of beauty, and it follows that ugliness jars. He has no pleasure in it—nor in dirt."

They calculated that a place after this pattern, simple, clean and beautiful, but with no extravagances anywhere, would cost £10,000, a sum so huge that Amma asked every member of the Fellowship to pray over it for some weeks. Then they met on August 15th for an unhurried time of prayer, and the entry in the log-book is significant: " Asked for, and received, according to I John 5. 14, 15 £10,000 for the Parama Suha Salai "—to which all signed their names.

The story of the first gift of £1,000 for the hospital, which

arrived on the day before Amma's sixty-second birthday,
December 15th, 1929, is told in both *Gold Cord* and *Windows.**
Windows tells also the story of a second £1,000, some years
later, which Amma regarded as the sign for the completion oɩ
the work, even as the first £1,000 had been the sign that so
encouraged them at its inception.† But most of the money
came in small gifts, and the children themselves contributed in
tiny ways. For instance, the margosa tree yields berries from
which oil is extracted. It takes time and patience to collect
the berries and skin them and bring them to an *Accal* for sale.
A kerosene tin full of berries brought in only half a rupee, but
the children knew that Amma rejoiced over their willingness
to help, and, indeed, they do all such tasks heartily, as to the
Lord, and not unto men.

More and more, as the plans slowly came to fruition, Amma
saw in the Place of Heavenly Healing one important answer to
the question which was always prominent in her thinking,
"What is to be the future of the children?" Could not a
large number of them be trained to be nurses and technicians,
so that the whole staff of the hospital would be made up of
Dohnavur's own boys and girls, "trained to serve, evangelists,
lovers of souls"? She saw the hospital "served by Franciscans
(so to speak), who serve for our Lord's sake only, with a freedom
and a gaiety of spirit that makes service one great song."
"Our chief evangelistic field", she writes later, "is surely the
Parama Suha Salai, with all its contacts. . . . I take it that
God has definitely shown us it is His pleasure to use the
Parama Suha Salai as the main stream from Lebanon which
He intends should flow from this garden." For through it
"the Lord Himself was bringing to our doors the very
people of the villages and towns that we longed so much to
reach."

But the building of the new hospital was spread over many
years, and the medicals who shared in supervising it were
doing full-time work in the crowded Door of Health, while
the more spacious Place of Heavenly Healing was in course of
erection. Early in 1931 Amma began to feel that Dr Webb-
Peploe ought to take a brief furlough, even though the work
was not complete. She found that Dr May Powell was of the

* *Gold Cord*, Chapter XLVII. *Windows*, p. 12.
† *Windows*, Chapter XXXI.

same mind, and told Murray. In Amma's private notebook
she tells how the matter ended :

> He prayed . . . " Of one mind in an house." He
> leaves us in June. " How can I render thanks enough to
> God for you, for all the joy you make me feel in the presence
> of our God ? "

" He is always, as it were, with his back against a wall, fighting for life against principalities and powers, men and sin. So it must always be with a man who is not an opportunist, but aims at an ideal. *His life must be one long fight, which will not end till he dies or till he gives up his ideal and falls back into despairing acquiescence in the existing order.* But for Paul only one thing was possible. He could not rest; he could not abandon his ideal; he must fight on to the end."

From SIR WILLIAM RAMSAY, Paul the Traveller.

If, in the paths of the world,
Stones might have wounded thy feet,
Toil or dejection have tried
Thy spirit, of that we saw
Nothing—to us thou wast still
Cheerful, and helpful, and firm!
Therefore to thee it was given
Many to save with thyself;
And, at the end of thy day,
O faithful shepherd! to come,
Bringing thy sheep in thy hand.

MATTHEW ARNOLD, Rugby Chapel.

CHAPTER XXXII

"ONE LONG FIGHT"

ALL through the years from 1901 to 1931 the Warfare of the Service had been continuing, and Amma was very tired, but she was greatly concerned that no one should know it. Once she found comfort from the story of Jacob in Genesis 48. He was " tired out by years, half blind, but not tired out of loving ".

> Sometimes people come to us when we feel as though for the time being we have got to the end of everything, but when Joseph came that day, Israel strengthened himself (verse 2). It is possible, in that moment of tired-out weariness, to look up, to strengthen oneself in God, and so to be ready to meet what has come. The natural life breaks here, but we are not called to live the natural life. Lord, help me to meet every demand in this spirit—on the instant to strengthen myself in Thee, not showing tiredness to others, to pour out love all the time, to catch the directing word of the Lord, however softly spoken—never to think I am too tired to listen, too tired for that spiritual girding up of the loins that used to be part of my very life.

The diary tells of another time, near the end of this period, when she felt too exhausted to go to the Communion service, and wandered round the compound thinking of relieving some-one else who was caring for the small children. She found one of the *Accals* who was not intending to go, and eventually persuaded her to come with her. During this service she could hardly kneel, and since she was at the back of the House of Prayer, she lay down on the floor, thankful to be unobserved.

> Presently I began to see the first Supper as John tells of it. " Now there was leaning on Jesus' bosom one of His disciples whom Jesus loved." I said to Him, " Lord, I am too tired to kneel—if only I could lean " (i.e. lean back as John did, be as close as John was), and surely it was His Voice I heard, " *You may.*"

Thus she was comforted.

> " To pour out love all the time, to catch the directing word

of the Lord, however softly spoken "—this is what she desired
to do, and all her Family would say in chorus, " This is exactly
what she did." See her, for instance, in 1923, soon after
Jambulingam's death, going to Sermadevi railway station to
meet Irene Streeter, Home Secretary for Dohnavur and
Amma's great friend. But sitting on the platform between two
policemen was a poor woman, in the extremity of wretched-
ness.* And immediately Irene Streeter is forgotten, and
Amma is sitting holding the woman's hands in hers, hearing
her story of *himsa* and of the month's imprisonment which lay
ahead of her, because she had once given food to Jambulingam.
Not until her sobs had ceased, and Amma had seen her into
the train, promising to take messages to her family, was it
possible to welcome the long-expected guest and explain why
she had taken no notice of her arrival. Her loving compassion not only comforted the woman but drew her to the
Saviour, Whom she has been serving joyfully ever since.

Or see her in Madura in 1928 meeting, " by chance ", the
one man in a population of 180,000 who could show her the
way to the house where boys were being trained for the drama,
arriving just when their trainer was opening a parcel of books
from Dohnavur; desiring to give him the word, " What is a
man profited, if he shall gain the whole world and lose his own
soul? ", yet for the moment quite unable to remember where it
was to be found; looking therefore to God for direction, and
then opening her Bible on the very verse, Matthew 16. 26, to
the awed amazement of the man. Pouring out love, catching
the directing word of the Lord—that was Amma.

She entered upon the year 1931 with her mind clear concerning His plan for the future leadership of the work. On
January 17th, when Murray happened to be away and Godfrey
was ill, she gathered all who could come in God's Garden, and
found that they were of one mind with her. Did it not appear
that God was preparing Murray and Godfrey to be leaders on
the men's side, and May Powell on the women's side? † I
think Amma would have been ready then and there to sing her
" Nunc dimittis " as she rejoiced in God's provision, and in

---

* The whole story is told in *Widow of the Jewels*.

† It must have been on an earlier occasion—also in God's Garden—
that Arulai was designated as prospective leader on the women's side.
Probably Amma had already become uncertain about her physical fitness
for the responsibility.

the oneness that He had given to the whole Family concerning it. She quotes Darby's translation of Philippians 2. 2: "That you may think the same thing, having the same love, joined in soul, thinking one thing ", and then adds: " Loops of blue, clasps of gold—' that the loops may take hold of one another, and it should be one tabernacle according to the fashion thereof which was shewed thee in the Mount '." How could any of them guess that two of these leaders chosen, as she says, to be " Servants of all ", would have been removed before she herself went Home?

Another Fellowship meeting which had concrete results was that held on August 6th, the monthly Day of Prayer. The word which had come to Amma was from II Chronicles 26. 5 : " Zechariah, who had understanding in the visions of God." But she felt that the afternoon meeting had accomplished little, and so without previous arrangement a special gathering was held in her room in the evening. It was a time of access. There was prayer especially for the Great Undone, that the Fellowship might lengthen its cords, remembering " 100,000 Muslims within half a day's car ride " and many more Hindus; that at the same time the stakes might be strengthened. This would mean at least two more doctors, a dispenser and a teacher. And whether for the lengthening of cords or the strengthening of stakes, " we asked that none should come save those who were of the order of Epaphroditus ". As to finance, expenses for July for the Family of over five hundred amounted to Rs. 4,000 more than the gifts received. " Funds short," says the log-book, " the very time to look for an advance. . . . Great joy tonight in the sense of moving on together."

The beginnings of this advance were the establishment of small bands of *Sitties* and *Accals* (shock-troops, as it were) for dispensary work in the Muslim town of Eruvadi (called Song of the Plough in *Gold Cord*), and the Hindu town of Kalakadu, or Joyous City.* Amma was thrilled by the " field dispatches " which came from the *Sitties,* telling of the dirt and stones thrown not only into the yard but into the newly whitewashed rooms at Eruvadi. Crowds swarmed in day after day, and the men were definitely hostile. But faith and courage were given to hold on, and the tide seemed to turn

* *Gold Cord,* pp. 336–6, 345–6.

when the mother of a man who had called a meeting in the local mosque to make plans for evicting the Christians, went to the Sisters for the treatment of a painful carbuncle. Their loving ministrations made him a friend instead of an enemy.

In the middle of September a foothold was secured in Kalakadu. A house which had stood empty for three years because it was haunted was offered and joyfully accepted. Amma loved to visit every place where any of her Family might be stationed, and to make personal arrangements for their comfort and well-being. On October 9th she writes in the log-book: " To Kalakadu to see about bathing shed, etc." On the 14th and again on the 21st she was at Eruvadi and Caruniapuram.

In the early morning of the 24th Amma was at prayer. She had been asking for guidance about money, and then, after a long time of quiet, she prayed this one prayer: " Do with me as Thou wilt. Do *anything*, Lord, that will fit me to serve Thee and help my beloveds." In the late afternoon she went over to Kalakadu in the car, in order to assure herself that all was in order. The key of the house was not immediately forthcoming, and when it arrived it was already twilight. Coolies had dug a pit where no pit was supposed to be, and Amma failed to see it. She slipped and fell. Although no one knew it, that was the end, for Amma, of the Warfare of the Service.

PART III

THE KEEPING OF THE CHARGE

wherein Amma learned to know Christ, in the power of His resurrection, and in the fellowship of His sufferings.

Two glad services are ours,
Both the Master loves to bless.
First we serve with all our powers—
Then with all our feebleness.

Nothing else the soul uplifts
Save to serve Him night and day,
Serve Him when He gives His gifts—
Serve Him when He takes away.

C. A. Fox.

" And a light shined in the cell ",
And there was not any wall,
And there was no dark at all,
Only Thou, Immanuel.

Light of Love shined in the cell,
Turned to gold the iron bars,
Opened windows to the stars,
Peace stood there as sentinel.

Dearest Lord, how can it be
That Thou art so kind to me?
Love is shining in my cell,
Jesus, my Immanuel.

CHAPTER XXXIII

THE ROOM OF PEACE

Truly no one knew that Amma had passed from the Warfare of the Service to the Keeping of the Charge. The injury caused by the fall was serious enough—the leg broken just above the ankle, the ankle dislocated—but surely she would be well and active again after a few weeks' rest. Was not the Family still in urgent need of her? Was it not clearly for the glory of God's Name that she should make a speedy recovery? The people of Kalakadu who crowded round the house while help was being rushed from Dohnavur attributed the fall without hesitation to the malignant demon which haunted the house. In Eruvadi, the Muslims were confident that the accident was the curse of Allah upon one who had dared to challenge the might of Islam. Ronald Procter drove Amma forty-six miles to Neyyoor, and Dr Howard Somervell was there to set the limb. When she returned to Dohnavur on November 3rd she herself wrote the entry in the log-book: "Home. Goodness and Mercy."

It was true that the pain continued when it might have been expected to diminish, and the sleepless nights were very wearing. But prayer was made, special prayer throughout the Family on November 20th, and on January 3rd, after a meeting of the Council of Eight (the senior *Accals* such as Arulai and Purripu), it was decided that arrangements should be made for a chain of uninterrupted prayer throughout Monday, January 4th, from 6 a.m. to 9 p.m. On Wednesday Amma had a good night, and seemed so much better that the log-book records, "Children tremendously cheered." On her birthday a few of the *Accals* had been allowed to see her for a quarter of a minute each, but Arulai had led the special meeting that evening, though it was Amma's message that she gave. On Christmas Eve carols were sung outside her room, and she appeared on the veranda. After that she began to go out occasionally in the car. When Dr Somervell visited Dohnavur on February 16th he was satisfied with the progress made and told her that she would walk—in time.

But the Warfare of the Service was over. For nearly twenty years she was an invalid who rarely left her room. Acute neuritis disabled one arm. Later she suffered from arthritis in her back. Possibly there had been a jarring of the spine at the time of the accident. There were other physical symptoms, including chronic infections which flared up whenever she exerted herself too much. But probably even the combination of all these painful things would not have disabled her as they did if she had not been suffering from the accumulated effects of overstrain. She had spent thirty-six years in India without a break. She had never spared herself in the unceasing conflict with the powers of darkness. She had travailed for the souls of her children. The long periods of tension described in earlier chapters had taken their toll of nervous energy. Occasionally she would admit it. " Sometimes I think the kind of tiredness that comes after such years as those that lie behind, could never be rested anywhere but There." So she writes to a D.F. on furlough in July, 1931. But she hastens to add, " It is only your blessed letter that pulls such admissions out of me. I'm not really tired at all—not as others are without ever showing it." The Warfare of the Service had been more exacting than she knew.

So she passed to the Keeping of the Charge. What this actually meant for the Levites is left largely to our imagination, except that they continued to " minister with their brethren in the tabernacle of the congregation ". What it meant to Amma these chapters will show in some measure. Only let it be made clear at once that it did not involve " honourable retirement ". There were, of course, times of more acute suffering when interviews, letter-writing, even praying, became impossible; but until the very latest years she emerged from these periods into activities which would have made heavy demands on the mental powers of much younger and healthier people.

For instance, when Murray Webb-Peploe was in Australia in the years 1933–5, or when Godfrey was on furlough in 1938, she wrote scores of letters to them, so that they might be kept in touch with all the inner history of things in their absence; and even when they were in Dohnavur she wrote to them constantly letters of loving appreciation, of comment on the day-to-day happenings, and of advice concerning individuals and situations. The Perfect Nurse (Mary Mills) and Neela, whom she called her " right-hand ", wrote thousands of letters in English and Tamil in order to spare her. But there are in the possession of members of the Family vast numbers of letters, or notes, or scraps of notes, which she wrote to them on their birthdays or Coming Days or whenever she heard that they were especially needing counsel or comfort. Because she was confined to her room, she would often use her meal-times for writing—or at least the time saved through being alone. These letters are treasured by the recipients, and many of them have been read over and over again.

She wrote thirteen new books after October, 1931, besides preparing for the press many editions of older books. She was constantly writing verses which were given to the Family, set to music, and sung at the daily prayer meetings and in the House of Prayer. There was a tremendous increase in the number of Christian people throughout the world who were deeply moved by the challenge of her books. I think it is true to say that God used her pen for more widespread and deeper spiritual blessing during the post-accident period than in all the preceding years.

As to interviews, it is difficult to give a true impression. Often there would be a stream of visitors all day long, and she would plan to see groups of children at regular intervals. Except during the days of more acute suffering, she saw the Fellowship leaders every day. Sometimes the number and the length of visits had to be " rationed ", though it was by no means easy to persuade Amma that certain people need not see her, or need not stay more than a very few minutes. If she were at all fit—and sometimes when she was not fit—she had long talks with any member of the Family who was causing anxiety. Indeed, when there were disappointments through the failure of some who had seemed to run well, or when there was spiritual defeat of any kind, she was always inclined to reproach herself for not having kept in personal touch as she might have done.

Naturally, there was eager competition for the privilege of a talk with Amma. Those who had been accustomed to see her as she " flew " round the compound found it almost impossible to become accustomed to the new situation. A word or a look from Amma had been sufficient to encourage the faint-hearted and to support the weak. When access to her was denied, some began to murmur, half in jest but half seriously, that the only sure way to obtain a talk with Amma was to behave really badly. The pain had to be acute and prolonged before she would be willing not to see anyone whom the tempter had made his special target.

At first she was content that Godfrey Webb-Peploe should write the *Dohnavur Letter*. Some issues contained a brief message from her, and gradually it became the custom—a custom established in face of Amma's reluctance or open displeasure—for the Perfect Nurse to contribute a few sentences about Amma herself. Scores of readers probably turned to this bulletin before reading anything else.

The *Dohnavur Letters* were well written, but the friends of the Fellowship—and most of them felt that they were Amma's friends—longed for something from herself, partly, no doubt, as an evidence that their prayers for her recovery were being answered. She on her part longed to tell them what God was doing, and *Dust of Gold*, first issued in 1933, was the result. The name is taken from Job 28. 6: " The stones of it are the place of sapphires: and it hath dust of gold." She was fond of quoting C. A. Fox's words, " No jewel mines for Christ like heathendom ", and she explained in the first issue that she thought of the regular *Dohnavur Letters* as showing the sapphires of which Job speaks, while " this letter may perhaps bring you a handful of our dust of gold." If Godfrey dealt with the main items of news, she was free to touch on the tiny things that a more sober and less imaginative person might overlook. Moreover, *Dust of Gold* could be written at intervals when freedom from pain allowed her to concentrate a little more easily. So for two years the D.L. and *Dust of Gold* brought joy and inspiration and fuel for prayer to the friends of Dohnavur, who would have been quite content for the arrangement to continue. But here and there they began to overlap. Godfrey was exceedingly busy, and it was clear that Amma could produce an occasional letter without overstrain; so finally *Dust of Gold* superseded the D.L., and until 1948 she continued to write the major part of it.

Thus the chief difference between the Warfare of the Service and the Keeping of the Charge was not that Amma ceased to be active, but that activities were confined, for the most part, to one room. There were golden hours when the car took her to the House of Prayer for part of a service, or for the weddings of Murray Webb-Peploe and Hugh Hopkins, or to the Place of Heavenly Healing, where she saw with her own eyes the fulfilment of the dreams of many years, typified by the flowering of the trees (especially those which are popularly termed " flame of the forest ") which she had planted there. For several years—though the journey became increasingly difficult —she was carried up to the Forest in September, and perhaps the fact that it was considered unwise for her to attempt the journey in 1936 was evidence, both to her and to the Family, that the full recovery for which they had all longed and prayed might never be granted.

But for the most part she was like Paul, who " dwelt two whole years in his own hired house, and received all that came in unto him ", except that the time was nearly twenty years, and the climate of Dohnavur is much more exacting than that of Rome. Once she was vividly reminded of the Missie Ammal who was compared to a hare for swiftness of movement when she had a visit from Blessing, an early member of the Starry Cluster, whom she had not seen for twenty-eight years.

Blessing [writes Amma] has her funny old way of shaking down her hair and doing it up while she talks. She showed us the " me " of forty years ago, not walking nor even running but *flying*, with many a glance at a wristlet watch " lest we waste moments "! (I had no idea I had that absurd habit, but I saw it now, and the two or three of us who were her audience shook with laughter as we watched the pantomime.) A shake of her head and down came her hair, a quick twist of a skinny old hand like a bird's claw, and up it went. " And frequently, yes, frequently, you said to me, ' Art thou an elephant to walk so very slowly? ' " Then down came the wisp of hair again.

Friends all round the world have tried to picture the room where she lived so long. She described it in an early *Dust of Gold*. " It was not built to be a personal room at all, but a general home-room, with a wide veranda so that many girls could sleep here with me." Those were the days when she and her children lived very much together. After 1931 her conscience unkindly suggested that she ought not " to use so

roomy a room in this personal way ". But she was persuaded
to recognize that " it would give trouble to others " if she went
to a smaller room, so she stayed. " Trouble " is an under-
statement. The whole Family would have been so horrified
that the change would have provoked a revolution. Over the
door outside was written in sepia on light brown teakwood,
" The Room of Peace ". Inside was " In heavenly places in
Christ Jesus ". This, she says, was " the word that so often
helped me to ' sit ' elsewhere when this room was the busy
hub of our little universe." It helped her to lie there when
movement was impossible, for it is no more true to state that
John was " in the Spirit " as well as " in Patmos ", or that
Paul was " in Christ " as well as " in Rome ", than to speak of
Amma as simultaneously " in " that one room, and " in
heavenly places " free from every limitation. What the
Perfect Nurse wrote in the early days of her imprisonment for
Christ's sake was always true:

> All through these months her room has been a place of
> peace, of joy and of song. These words were born there,
> and I give them to you for sharing, who have shared so
> much:

> > What a God Who out of shade
> > Nest for singing bird hath made.
> > Lord, my Might and Melody,
> > I will sing to Thee.

From Australia came Acts 12. 7 (R.V.) by cable: *And a
light shined in the cell.* The words were the theme of a lovely
little song (which faces this chapter), and Mabel Wade set
them to music. Truly there was light in the cell, and it shone
to the farthest corners of the earth.

But to return to Amma's description of the room:

> A teakwood partition divides the room into two, a great
> convenience in long illness, and as you come in through the
> blue curtains near the door you see on the right hand teak-
> wood panelling and on the left the bookcases to which the
> household come when they want biography, missionary and
> otherwise, and books of other kinds too; for all through my
> life friends have sent me books. They are my great luxury,
> my mental change of air.
> Facing you as you come in are three big windows looking
> out on greenness where a pair of blue kingfishers continually
> fish for minnows in large vessels set under the trees.

As time went on a small aviary was built close to the veranda, and birds of various sizes and colours delighted both Amma and the children who came to visit her.

Two or three pictures were a continual inspiration. She writes in January, 1939:

> Nothing seems more impossible just now than another *Dust of Gold* letter, but on the book-rest close by me is a picture of the Matterhorn—that trumpet-call to endeavour—and open beside it is my little New Testament at II Corinthians 9. 8 with its glorious " God is able " underlined in blue. So I begin.

Facing her as she lay in bed was an oil painting of Nanga Parbat by Dr Howard Somervell. He called it his " Christmas card " for 1938, though it measures four feet by one. Amma longed to search the compound for " a place worthy of it, a place where its great voice might speak undisturbed by lesser voices ". But no suitable place was found (Amma wondered a little whether the Perfect Nurse had tried hard enough), and so " this glorious thing faces all who come to see me ".

> By night [she goes on], with a lantern turned low on the desk below, the picture changes in the strangest way. I never get to the end of its mysterious beauty, and the snowy mountains have become my Delectable Mountains, whence one may see the Gate of the Celestial City. Gone from me is the thought of woods, vineyards, fruits of all sorts, flowers also, with springs and fountains, as in Bunyan's lovely story. I see instead, steep ascents, precipices, a shining summit. When I was at Neyyoor after that fall in 1931 I could not sleep. Nothing gave me sleep. But I could read hour after hour (I can't do that now, which is one reason why the picture is such a boon), and I read all through those nights. Once, in the small hours of the morning, someone came for the doctor. I heard him being called, heard the heavy, rather slogging footsteps of a tired man passing along the veranda and down the steps, and heard him return an hour or so later. And I thought, " He is climbing higher now than ever he climbed on Everest or anywhere else on the Himalayas."
>
> God bless all His mountaineers—so many of them from whom we have letters are tied to bed, or if most blessedly on their two feet, doing all manner of common work, work that doesn't look like climbing. If only their hearts are set on ascents, they are somewhere on those heights.

This, then, was the room which continued to be the centre of the whole compound as long as Amma was there. From the first the routine work of leadership was done by Godfrey or Murray, May Powell or Arulai. They consulted her whenever it was possible to do so, and she on her part rejoiced that the grace of God was upon them, and that the Family knew it. But the Fellowship still had a leader, and the Family a mother.

Lord of all our times and seasons,
    Not of vain caprice
Suns revolve.   Command Thy coolness,
    Dews of peace.

When each duty crowds the other
    Through the sultry days,
Plant the little flower of patience
    By our ways.

When the slothful flesh would murmur,
    Ease would cast her spell,
Set our face as flint till twilight's
    Vesper bell.

On Thy brow we see a thorn-crown,
    Blood-drops in Thy track,
O forbid that we should ever
    Turn us back.

CHAPTER XXXIV

"THE WAGES OF GOING ON"

THE last twenty years of Amma's life do not lend themselves to historical treatment. There is much more incident in the Warfare of the Service than in the Keeping of the Charge. It is not that the story of the Dohnavur Fellowship was uneventful, but that the emphasis in a biography of Amma must be less and less upon outward events, or upon the growth of the work, and must concentrate increasingly on her own inner life, upon the relation between the lover and her Beloved, upon her transformation into His image. Many of the things which happened during these two decades were important, but we shall record them in bare outline, concentrating rather upon the things which happened *to her*, and how they fell out to the furtherance of the Gospel.

Murray Webb-Peploe returned from a short furlough four months after the accident, and was busy in medical work and in planning for the completion of the Place of Heavenly Healing, but he had time, too, for the "spiritual surgery" for which God had trained him. It was still Amma's hope that when medical reinforcements arrived he could be set free from routine work of every kind, whether medical or otherwise, and concentrate on the "Heavenly Health" of all the Family, as well as of those outside it. Meanwhile it is clear from Amma's letters that Godfrey was growing all the time in spiritual stature, and in favour with God and man. Perhaps it was no wonder that the health of both brothers seemed to be constantly under attack. Murray was so seriously ill that in 1933 it was necessary for him to go to Australia for convalescence. His marriage to Oda van Boetzelaer, the first Dutch member of the Fellowship, took place just before he left Dohnavur. It was an immense relief to Amma when they and their twin boys returned in June, 1935. Godfrey's health was frequently uncertain, and, as if she did not suffer enough, Amma was always wishing that his headaches, his fevers and other ailments could be transferred to her sensitive frame.

One anxiety of these days was the misunderstanding which arose in England and in America concerning Dohnavur's relation to the Oxford Groups.   It was quite true that certain members of the Fellowship had travelled with Group teams, and had been deeply impressed by the lives of some who had responded to the challenge of the " Four Absolutes ".   The teaching concerning direct guidance as a result of listening to God, and concerning His demand for complete surrender, was in close agreement with all that Dohnavur stood for.   Indeed, it might be said that Group standards were Dohnavur standards.   Thus Amma found it difficult at first to understand the dismay of many of her friends when they were misled into believing that Dohnavur was in some way connected with the Groups.   Naturally, the D.F.s who had had early association with the Groups were men who had a solid foundation of knowledge of the Scriptures, and an unswerving confidence in their inspiration.   One of them wrote privately to leaders of the Groups pointing out the danger of confusing mere psychological release with a spiritual reception of the living Christ, the necessity of the new birth before a man could expect to " listen " and receive direction for the day, and the peril of flippancy in " sharing " sin.   Finally, in order to reassure any friends of Dohnavur who were seriously puzzled, a statement was prepared, signed by Amma and the two Webb-Peploes, which made the position clear to all who honestly desired to understand it.   To quote an extract from this statement: " You who have read the *Dohnavur Letter* and the Dohnavur books know where we stand, and for what we stand.   Today we in the D.F. all stand together where we have always stood, in a deeper unity as our numbers grow, and a firmer faith that these are the eternal principles of God's inspired Word."   The language of the statement expresses clearly the theological position of evangelical Christians everywhere, but with a fervour born of love for Christ and for souls which one would expect from the three signatories.

Amongst the overweights of joy were the conversion of a Muslim and his wife in Eruvadi, and their baptism in Red Lake;   the baptism of Mimosa's husband;   the return after many days of two women, very dear to Amma, who had been absent for fourteen and twelve years respectively;   and a Mission conducted by R. T. Archibald and Quintin Carr, who reaped what others had sown. Sowers and reapers rejoiced together as boys and girls of all ages responded to the message. The careful preparatory planning, which ensured that all could attend the meetings intended for them, pleased Amma all the more because she knew all that was involved, and because she herself had no hand in it.

One of the griefs of 1933 was a postcard headed " Noteece " from a young man to whom Amma had been greatly attached. His name appears in *Raj*, and for some years after his baptism he had lived at Dohnavur. Amma arranged his marriage with one of her own children. But he proved unstable, and for a long period he tested Amma's patience. At first she utterly refused to doubt his sincerity, and she bore with him long after others had ceased to trust him. " Many a day of prayer and fasting, many a night of vigil, many a refusal to accept defeat, filled those years." And now this " Noteece ": " I, X, son of X, came from the Hindu Way to the Christian Way in 1923, and having received baptism have until now been a Christian. Now, having no belief in the aforesaid Christian religion, I, leaving and forsaking it, return to the Hindu religion. This I make known to you by means of this Noteece."

The analogy of the Levites and their service breaks down if we press it too far. Amma was not *hors de combat*. For her there could be no discharge from the war. Battle news could not be kept from her, even though her room was " The Room of Peace ". She watched eagerly for bulletins from the various outposts. The struggle to rescue children in danger, and to counter the adversary's unceasing attacks upon children already rescued, did not end when Amma's physical activities were circumscribed. At the risk of appearing inconsistent, therefore, it must be stated that while she kept the charge she was always a soldier, and " soldiers are not shelved ".*

Though Amma made hundreds of new friends through her books, and many of them were drawn very close in love, she suffered keenly as nearly all the earliest and closest friends of the Fellowship were removed, and she often wondered why she herself lived on.

> They are all gone into a world of Light,
> While I alone sit lingering here.

* *Rose from Brier*, pp. 33–5.

Irene Streeter was killed in an air accident in 1937. Amma never ceased to praise God for her loving service as Home Secretary from 1913 to 1933. There was a day in 1921 (September 9th) when the Lord met with her, silenced her doubts, and satisfied her heart. She cabled to Amma, " Satisfied. Hallelujah. Irene." When she awoke in His likeness on September 10th, 1937, would she not have sent the same message if it had been possible to transmit it?

Ten years later a still older friend passed on. Amma had known Mary Hatch since the Manchester days, and she and her friend Ella Crossley had visited Dohnavur when the work of rescuing children in danger was just beginning. Such friends cannot be replaced, though their departure reminds us of the all-sufficiency of the Friend of friends. Amma quotes a sentence from Mary Hatch's notes, and it fits Amma so well that I think Mary Hatch must have had her in mind as she copied the words: " There is nothing so kindling as to see the soul of man or woman follow right over the edge of the usual into the untracked land, for love of Him, for sheer love of Him."

There was continual competition between Amma and those upon whom the functions of leadership mainly devolved in the matter of sparing one another. Sometimes they joined forces with the Perfect Nurse and Neela in acting as buffers between Amma and the world outside; on the other hand, she was most ingenious in arranging to interview difficult people in order to ease the strain for others. But matters affecting members of the Fellowship, their entrance into it and, still more, their continuance in it, could never be kept from her. For reasons which have been partly explained in Chapter XXIX there were sorrowful departures from Dohnavur as well as joyful arrivals. There was a period, for instance, which she called *Adria* (" driven up and down in Adria ", Acts 27. 27) when the Fellowship suffered serious losses, and the fact that all the older workers were agreed about their necessity did not make the severances less painful. Then, as so often happens, the facts were twisted when they came to the ears of sympathetic friends, and the ensuing correspondence failed to clear up the misunderstanding. How she longed to discover " a certain creek with a shore ", but the battering continued until it seemed that " all hope . . . was taken away ". It was then that in a private note-book she coupled Acts 27. 20 * with Romans 15. 13: " That ye may abound in hope ". " X has spent three hours with Murray," she writes, " who is tired out with this weary *Adria*," and then, a line or two below, " Romans 15. 13 is still true."

But both her private letters and *Dust of Gold* are full of grateful references to the many members of the Fellowship who became *sonthum* on the day of their arrival, or even before they sailed for India at all, who went through the mill (as Walker used to call it) of the first year, and continued to face the exacting conditions of life in a community, a life which demands all that a man has, and yet offers such rewards that those who have a taste for them can never feel that they are making any sacrifice.

Even in *Adria* Amma proved again the love and loyalty of the D.F. To some who were in the Forest she wrote:

> It is a long time since I wrote to you, but there have been weeks of stress and I know you understood. . . . I thank God, as I look back and then forward, that so many of you are young. O how I love you all. I cannot write separate notes, but I think of you each separately, and dwell upon each one in thought and love and thanksgiving. I know that you have thought much of Godfrey through these very painful days. From March 11 till yesterday there was no respite in the pain for some of us; though, thank God, not quite all that time was heavy on Godfrey. But he had a great deal that was very hard to do, and he was most wonderfully carried through. Yesterday it did my heart good to see his face so lightened. " It seems all victory now ", he said.

By comparison—does it seem strange to say it?—the anxieties of the Second World War were easy to bear. As in the years 1914-18, in spite of rising costs (e.g. the price of a bag of flour increased nine times between September, 1939, and the spring of 1943) every need was met, and there was a balance to begin essential building when materials were obtainable. Dohnavur was kept in peace in 1942 when a Japanese landing was seriously expected. Certain measures were taken, and then they rested in the promises of God. With her acute sensitiveness to suffering, Amma agonized with Poland and

* " When neither sun nor stars in many days appeared, and no small tempest lay on us, all hope that we should be saved was then taken away."

every other country that was overrun.   Three D.F.s served in
the Forces, and a fair number of Amma's sons joined the
Indian Army and Navy.

When a suggestion was made that some of the D.F.s who
remained might enrol in the Civic Guard, she was enthused
with the idea of a Spiritual Civic Guard, which would do
propaganda work in the villages.   So she wrote to Murray:

" The people that do know their God shall be strong and
do exploits."   I was thinking of you as I opened my Bible
on those words.   Can you even begin to imagine what it
means to me that while I lie here like a slug on a cabbage
leaf (or in certain moments feel like a bird breaking its
wings against the bars—but those are bad moments and
don't last) you are strong and doing exploits?   This Spiritual
Civic Guard . . . you are the one to lead it.   You have
the glorious double message to give—the certainty of the
triumph of righteousness, whatever the sacrifice be, and the
fact that all this turmoil is perhaps the last herald of the
Coming of the King. . . . I mustn't get too hot over
Spiritual Civics—it's just the heritage of my Scottish-
Northern Irish blood.

The more she thought of the suffering of the world, the more
she longed that Dohnavur might bring a little comfort to our
Lord.

I am asking that through these days when so much that
must grieve the Love of God is going on [she wrote to Frances
Beath], we in our little Dohnavur may continually offer the
comfort of Love to our Lord.   I want Him to find here the
cooling of His weariness [" I will cool your weariness " is
the literal translation of the Tamil in Matthew 11. 28].
He has passed beyond the reach of what we mean by weariness, and yet He is as He always was.   The grief and suffering
of the world touch Him, even There.   So I want Him to
find comfort here.

But even the barest outline of the story of those years cannot
omit a reference to those events which touched Amma more
closely than any others—the removal of three of those on whom
she had confidently counted for the future leadership of the
work.

God of the Heights, austere, inspiring,
  Thy word hath come to me,
O let no selfish aims, conspiring,
  Distract my soul from Thee.
Loosen me from Things of Time;
Strengthen me for steadfast climb.

The temporal would bind my spirit;
  Father, be Thou my stay.
Show me what flesh cannot inherit,
  Stored for another day.
Be transparent, Things of Time.
Looking through you, I would climb.

Now by Thy grace my spirit chooseth
  Treasure that shall abide.
The great Unseen, I know, endureth,
  My footsteps shall not slide.
Not for me the Things of Time;
God of mountains, I will climb.

CHAPTER XXXV

"CLIMBING UNAWARES"

I HAVE not been able to discover when it was that the metaphor of climbing as a picture of the Christian life so gripped Amma, but it was in her thoughts all through the years of the Keeping of the Charge. In the very early years of her association with Walker, at a time when he was tempted to wonder whether he was merely marking time, both in his ministry and in his own soul, she had comforted him with C. A. Fox's words:

> Like the staircase in ancient houses,
>   Long, winding, and strangely dim,
> It is faith that is needed for climbing,
>   Faith, rather than length of limb.
>
> But there's light at the different landings,
>   And rest in the upper room,
> And a larger range of vision,
>   And glorious thoughts to come.
>
> How much of our life resembles
>   Time lost in going upstairs;
> What days and weeks seem wasted,
>   *But we're climbing unawares.*

The words—or the thought behind them—could be applied to herself from 1931 onwards. She never ceased to climb, though often she feared that she was losing ground. In November, 1935, she happened upon a line in Henry Vaughan's poems which both cheered and challenged her: " O let me climbe when I lye down ". Then the spiritual climb could continue when physical movement was impossible?

> Lord, am I climbing? [she writes] O Lord, forgive. Thou didst deliver David from the strivings of the people, canst Thou not deliver me from the strivings of my longings to be well and with my Family again? But a thousand, thousand thanks to Thee for their longsuffering love, for everything, and for every one.

A much later poet, Stephen Phillips, wrote words which Amma copied and " read many times after October 24, 1931 " :

> Make me Thy athlete even in my bed,
> Thy girded runner though the course be sped.

Extracts from some of her " prison letters " and from the private notes of these years (never intended for any other eyes, and therefore showing with utter candour the cost of staying the course) confirm the testimony of all who cared for her, that the Room of Peace was " a joyful place ", and that the athlete on her bed ran with patience the race that was set before her, with her eyes towards Him Who said as He neared the end of His race, " I have finished the work that Thou gavest me to do."

In 1933 she was beginning to realize that the Lord might be saying " No " to her prayers for recovery rather than " Yes " or " Wait ". The Perfect Nurse hoped that she might be content with this answer.

> There are more vital things which she only can do, than plodding about the compound doing what other folk ought to be able to do.   And those vital things can be done in her own room, and far better than if her body was just worn out with an output of energy that she can scarcely spare.

Yet sometimes she wondered if the Fellowship and the Family generally were not missing something that she only could supply.

> John * comes to me every day at 10.30—such a joy [she writes to Murray in 1934], and I see the others as often as possible and am kept in touch with all.   But even so, I do pray to be out of bonds at least so as to be able to be at meals and about the house.   I think many trials of various kinds could be avoided if only the Family could be a bit more " mothered ".   It isn't a question of age exactly (there are dear older ones ready to help) but of mothering . . . I *have* cast the burden, and all through these two years I have believed—and yet every now and then things are told me that indicate a strain of soul that need not be—a strain I could in some measure prevent just by being there.   There are things that I long to intercept, and perhaps could do so.   After all, it's a mere matter of " buffering ", spiritual " buffering ".

* John Risk, a naval officer who joined the Fellowship in 1928, and speedily became second in command to Godfrey on the boys' side.

" Mothering " and " buffering "—truly no one could do either as Amma could.

Of course her children missed her continually, especially on great days such as Easter Sunday. One of them writes in 1934:

> We missed our darling Amma, as she used to come with us and share our joys in singing round God's Garden, and then we used to take her along to the organ wherever it was and ask her to play, " Low in the grave He lay ". We loved her playing it, for she played the music in a way that stirred us and made us sing joyfully. [The mill girls in Belfast and the children in Broughton always said the same.] . . . Between the two services the whole Family (as many as could come) stood in the passage and in the Prayer Room, and sang to Amma, " Low in the grave He lay ", as joyfully as we could. We heard afterwards that Amma's eyes were filled with tears of love and joy.

Neela writes in May of the same year:

> It has been a hot week, and Amma often had such pain in her right arm that she was unable to write much. But every day the Lord Jesus sent His little surprises. Often when she was tired and in pain she received lovely things— either a new book, or the Lord Jesus gives her a new song, or He sends in some beautiful cards or some comforting letters.

On July 14th, 1934, one of the doctors ventured to suggest that her Glory Day might come in " about five years—perhaps only three more ", and Amma wrote on the 15th:

> I wonder if ever before you made anyone so happy with just a few words. You would not have said such a blissful thing lightly. I know He might even now ask for longer than that five years, but that there is even a natural hope of that little while being enough, is purest golden joy. Last night I lay awake too happy to sleep . . . and I walked up and down just talking with Him about it and thanking Him —and afterwards slept splendidly. You have taken away my one fear, and lighted a lamp that will light every hour from now till then. Only pray that He will " take from me all slothfulness that I may fill up the crevices of my time ", and truly finish all He wants me to do. I don't want to leave loose ends about . . . O to think of you all *not* burdened even with the love-burden of me, to think of Mary free for the thousand better things she can do—to think of

your Amma set free to serve you all with eternal vigour, to serve Him in holiness, perhaps in five years—can you wonder that you have made me happy? Now nothing matters—anything, any way of living—I mind nothing, for you have taken away that smothering fear that by all this cushioning, every chink by which anything *could* get in that would end me was being closed up, and so the one thing to do is to use these last precious opportunities to the utmost of the utmost.

Well, the five years lengthened out to sixteen and a half. Sometimes, half humorously but with a trace of seriousness, she would question the code whereby doctors and nurses use every possible means to keep the spark of life alight, or, to change the metaphor—and these are her own words—" you dear doctor people have something to answer for sometimes, I think, when you shut that shining door, or at least don't give it even the gentlest push open ".

All those who were privileged to nurse her speak of her sense of humour. " It pervaded everything," says one of them, " except when she was in severe pain. She gave appropriate names to her bad leg and arm, etc., and she would make up nonsense verses on the spot." But Amma was always like that. She writes of a subject that was perhaps nearer to her heart than any other—the danger of " unlove ", and then immediately goes on: " How it hurts the heart to be out of love. I couldn't bear to be out of love with a hedgehog—if there was any way of getting into it again."

Acceptance of her helplessness never became easy.

> The greatest difficulty [she writes] is to readjust, to see others daily worn down by the Warfare of the Service, and to be oneself sheltered from all the hardest things. . . . Bring me out of this fog of the spirit. . . . Quicken Thou me. And till this prayer is fully answered, let no shadow of mine shadow any who come to this room. No, never, Lord.

That prayer was heard. There must have been few indeed who did not see the Lord when they entered the Room of Peace. She, on her part, rejoiced in the visits of members of the Family because she saw Christ in them.

> It is not only human love, it is something different that quickens the joy. I do truly see Him Whom we love best, in each one as he or she comes into the room, and I do

" hear in each tone His well-beloved voice." The half hours you can spare out of your full days are filled with much more than earthly sweetness because of that.

November 9th, 1937, was her first Coming Day when it proved impossible for her to see anyone, but she treasured a note from Murray, " Peace be on every minute of your day, and love immeasurable from us all ", and she gave God thanks " for May's and Godfrey's beautiful thought that instead of coming to my room, all should spend a little while in the House of Prayer for me."

A few disconnected notes show how she learned more and more to lean on her Beloved as she climbed.

> *January* 25, 1936. This morning a thought came. Tara and I had been speaking of the excitement and joy of the children who have just gone up to the Forest, and I was longing to see their pleasure as they see it for the first time— such a foolish feeling—when suddenly I remembered that I shall see them when for the first time they look at the loveliness There. I shall be There to show them everything.
>
> *November* 14, 1937. Dedication of the new land. Art thou content—content not to be there? Yes, Lord, yes. And once more I thank Thee for those who are doing every- thing so perfectly now. But, Lord Jesus, wilt Thou not hasten my perfecting?
>
> *October* 27, 1938. Is it imagination, Lord, or Thine own word to me, that I shall come to Thee in sleep—no rending goodbyes—no distress to anyone? " I shall take thee in thy sleep "—is it Thy Voice speaking, Lord? However it be, I ask that it may be the easiest way for my beloveds.
>
> *November* 2, 1938. " If so be that we suffer with Him ". Lord Jesus, Thou hast made my prison so beautiful and my bonds so light that I greatly fear I do not " suffer with " Thee. . . . Do not let me miss the deepest thing Thou hast to give—the fellowship of Thy sufferings.

Once she had a vivid dream that she was healed. She walked three miles rejoicing in her strength, and then, when she began to tire a little, she saw a taxi pass. It stopped, but she hesitated, not sure if she had enough money for the fare. But the man said, " Don't spoil my joy ", and so he drove her home. She told him how she had been healed by the touch of the Lord. " I had such a happy time with him." But she awoke, and it was a dream.

September 13, 1947. Woke at 2 a.m. with a daft head. Could do nothing but hold the Fellowship, its present problems, its finance, and its future in the Presence of the Lord. Then at 6 a.m. came this, " I have never failed you, I will never fail those who come after you, I will never fail them nor forsake them." O Lord, in listening to Thy Voice there is peace. " For Thou, Lord, hast never failed them that seek Thee."

There is no real incongruity in the sequence of the disjointed phrases written on January 22nd, 1948:

Sleepless from midnight till about 4 a.m. Woke feeling like ashes—as dull, as grey, in spirit —and all one ache in body. But

> To God thanks be
> For cups of tea
> And A.P.C.*

And above all for His Presence in the bush. O Lord my God, Thou art my Flame of fire.

Her letters are full of wise advice, yet it is offered with such restraint that no one could charge her with attempting to dominate.

It's a curious fact of life that we learn most by our mistakes. I could have told you a good deal about the running of ——, but it wouldn't have done much for you. Each generation has to learn for itself, and one can help most by just loving you all, and looking on in love, and looking up in love.

She wonders if

we are wasting much of our treasure, and keeping from our younger ones especially much that they should have, just because of the blessed Ruts of life. Don't mistake me, Ruts have a valuable purpose to serve, but they can tend to dominate thought. . . . God can do miracles again if only we don't lose ourselves in the machinery, useful and good though it be.

In 1946 it was necessary to move Amma from the Room of Peace, because the bungalow, 117 years old, required extensive repairs, but there were advantages in the change. Her temporary home was a small room, but there were no steps, and she could be wheeled out under the trees.

* A patent medicine—compound of aspirin, phenacetin, and caffeine.

It was heaven to see the pattern of branch and leaf against
the sky after ten years and four months without once being
out from under a man-made roof.

And then an inspiration came to some of the D.F.s who,
indeed, were continually devising new plans to ease Amma's
imprisonment. While the bungalow was being repaired, they
built a terrace leading directly out of Amma's room into the
garden outside. It was flippantly termed " Wigan pier ",
and the secret was well kept. They were well repaid by her
joy in seeing it, and by the use she made of it. It ended in
what she called her Green Nook. " The terrace path is so
contrived that twenty-five children or grown-ups can easily be
with me." It was a time when the pain was a little easier,
and she sat there for two hours or more in the evening.

I am seeing the older boys in turn, and of course others.
It is so quiet and private there, and so airy. . . . I can
walk out on the terrace in the morning too for a few minutes.
. . . It is joy I can't express to be under His roof again.

But difficult days recurred.

Last Wednesday evening D—— helped me to come in
from my Green Nook. I was very halting, and this had
troubled me a little. It felt so feeble, somehow, so unlike
what I want to be.

But she was comforted by the word concerning Jacob in
Genesis 32. 31 : " He halted upon his thigh."

Once she felt that she had shown impatience when Murray
was talking to her, and she wrote as soon as he had left her :

I am very sorry. I asked to be kept from ever giving way.
Pain is nothing, nothing is anything except this not being
able to lift burdens. It seems to be the one thing that bowls
me over. All is clear now—I had time before Godfrey
came to receive strength. So forget, only ask for whatsoever He sees will do most for this beloved Family.

On another occasion the twins were unwell.

Last night how I longed that my being awake might mean
they slept. I lay and looked at the darling little faces till
3 a.m., and then slept. In the morning I heard they had
slept *till* 3 *a.m.* !

There was a special source of strength to which she rarely
referred.

You may hear of a bad night, and of a very difficult thing that has to be done today—something that will call for spiritual energy, for the human will be useless. I want you to know that if this has to be so, all is well. For many years I have almost every morning " remembered His death "—a morsel of bread, a few drops of water (He still turns water into wine)—and something happens. I can't say more, only I am conscious of life received. . . . I have marked this letter " private ", as to talk of it, even to write of it, is rather like pulling the petals off a flower.

Was it not a true sacrament? I think she received by faith the " benefits " of the Lord's Supper as they are set down in the Prayer-book Catechism. " What are the benefits whereof we are partakers thereby? The strengthening and refreshing of our souls by the Body and Blood of Christ, as our bodies are by the Bread and Wine."

On June 12th, 1948, there is a note which goes deep:

Not relief from pain, not relief from the weariness that follows, not anything of that sort at all, is my chief need. Thou, O Lord God, art my need—Thy courage, Thy patience, Thy fortitude. And very much I need a quickened gratitude for the countless helps given every day.

June 22, 1948. " The thing of a day in his day " (marginal reading of I Kings 8. 59). X——a bit overpressed. I also, as one thing after another came before I had " obtained access ". See verse 56: " There hath not failed one word of all His good promise." If we take time to let this soak in, there is rest in the midst of pressure.

It had been a time of wearying pain and of difficult interviews. On the following day, June 23rd, she slipped and fell in the Room of Peace. Her right hip was badly damaged, and her right forearm broken. Surely her time of release had come? Had she not nearly reached the summit towards which she had been climbing so long and with such determination? No, the gates of the City seemed to be swinging open, and then they closed again. God knew that her Family needed her a little longer.

There is a path which no fowl knoweth,
  Nor vulture's eye hath seen;
A path beside a viewless river
  Whose banks are always green,
For it is the way of prayer,
Holy Spirit, lead us there.

O lead us on—weigh not our merits,
  For we have none to weigh.
But, Saviour, pardon our offences,
  Lead even us today
Further in the way of prayer,
Holy Spirit, lead us there.

CHAPTER XXXVI

" THE WAY OF PRAYER "

ALL through her life, since, at the age of three, she prayed for blue eyes, Amma had been a learner in the school of prayer. As she grew in understanding of its power in her own life, so she coveted the prayers of others for the Family, and longed that every member of it should know the way to the Throne of Grace, and that the Fellowship in particular should be knit together by prayer, should meet all the assaults of Satan by prayer, and by prayer discover along what lines every advance should be made.

When I sailed in 1893 [she wrote to Godfrey] I remember being told by one of the leaders of those days that she had never known anyone go forth who was so much prayed for. I know that the two reasons for that wealth of prayer were, first, the beloved ones who let me go and who were so loved, and, second, my own tremendous need. Now I seem to see a third reason for such loving-kindness. The Lord knew about all of you and the Family—for He Himself knew what He would do—and so He gathered up that mighty prayer-wave all those years ago, not for me only but for all our Family. Nothing but that love and that prayer accounts for what has happened since.

Did the Levites who kept the charge spend much of their time in intercession? In *Rose from Brier* * she refers to the common notion that a sick bed offers natural soil for the precious flower of prayerfulness. " I have not found myself ", she says bluntly, " that illness makes prayer easier. . . . A bed can be a place of dulness of spirit as well as of body, and prayer is, after all, work—the most strenuous work in all the world." But prayer did " soar on high " from the Room of Peace during those twenty years, and it did " move the Hand that moves the world, to bring salvation down ".

Sometimes it was a very simple word which the Holy Ghost illuminated for her as He taught her to pray.

* *Rose from Brier*, pp. 55–8.

Last night [she wrote to Godfrey in 1941], after trying to pray, and failing rather badly, I turned to a small copy of Isaiah that lay by me, and those words about the gates of Zion caught my eye. " Thy gates shall be opened continually; they shall not be shut day or night." Like the lovely words in Revelation about the gates of pearl which are not to be shut at all, I suppose they are figures of the true. The gates of access into the Father's presence are open continually. There is no need to push—perhaps " trying to pray " is sometimes a sort of pushing. This was how it came to me—*If the gates are open there is nothing to do but go in.* It sounds too simple to tell, but it helped me very much.

The private note-books record many answers to prayer. Here is one of which she wrote later,* but there is a special vividness about the private record made at the time:

February 27, 1935. Yesterday a very low day. Read Samuel Rutherford's prayer about being granted house room again to hold a candle to this dark world. Longed to be able to do so. Then came a note from P——. In the envelope was a cheque for £200 to do *Rose from Brier* and *Ploughed Under* into Braille. Into Braille—to hold a candle to someone perhaps in that dark world. O Lord, Thou art wonderful. It is not only what Thou dost but the way Thou doest it. And now, return unto thy rest, O my soul, for the Lord hath dealt bountifully with thee.

Many of the answers concerned meetings in the House of Prayer, which she could no longer attend. Once at the beginning of an important meeting she had an overwhelming sense of satanic attack, and she prayed " that somehow God would allow her to be, as it were, a lightning conductor to draw off the wrath of the enemy." At that very moment a man, dishevelled and completely unclothed, rushed into the Room of Peace, flung his head down in Amma's lap and crouched there, talking wildly. If he had gone into the House of Prayer (as he probably intended), the shock to the children might easily have ruined the meeting. Amma was able to soothe him until Murray and Godfrey appeared with a sheet, in which they wrapped him, and led him away. It proved to be a former *sunnyasi* (Indian religious mendicant), called Lover of Jesus, whom Amma had been

* *Windows*, p. 170.

teaching for some time. Afterwards he told how he had been
drugged by some who were determined to cripple his testimony
for Christ. The following morning he was clothed and in his
right mind, and Amma prayed a rather surprising prayer—
" that the evil one might be signally defeated by his baptism
next day ". And so it was. Dr May Powell felt that his mind
was sufficiently clear to know what the step involved.

But he was like a sick man, in that the fuss of going to the
water, and the crowd, would have been too much for him.
Also there wasn't any water, it has all dried up now [i.e. the
water of the Red Lake, the scene of most of the Dohnavur
baptisms]. So he was baptized then and there in my room,
according to the prayer given in the night. And we had a
most glorious sense of a foe vanquished and retreating,
beaten off the ground just when he thought that he had scored
a victory.

Such a lovely word came while you were taking the
meeting [she wrote to Godfrey on a later occasion]. I was
holding you in the Presence more than actually praying, and
then it came, " In Thy Presence is fulness of joy "—and part
of the fulness is what He is doing in the House of Prayer
tonight, and will do, on and on, because of this meeting.

The longing to be in the Prayer Room or the House of Prayer
was sometimes very acute. On the night of a Fellowship
Meeting in 1936 she writes:

My Lord and my Beloved, I thank Thee for holding off the
sharpness of the pain and longing this evening. I can even
hear them singing without crushing back the tears. This is
the first time it has been so. It is Thy love, Lord Jesus.

Her prayers for the meetings were often answered, not only
in a general sense but in detail. On the afternoon of her
birthday, December 16th, 1935, she had been praying for the
special meeting to be held that evening as usual, but she had
been discouraged because she " so seldom lost the sense of
hindrances such as mosquitoes ".

To pray alone, without the uplifting wings of music and
the warm fellow-feeling of others like-minded is, I find, a
very stripping thing. Nothing but bare prayer is left you,
prayer stripped to the bone; and you learn, sometimes with
dismay, how little you know of real prayer. At least that is
how it often is with me. It was so that afternoon and evening. And I was more than a little troubled. Have I had

access at all, I wondered? I did wish I could have done more to help; the thought of that interrupted prayer lay like a cloud on me. Then came the Thanksgiving and I was indeed in the House of Prayer in spirit, but in the pause after the Glory, Glory, Hallelujah, I longed with a great longing to be there in body too, to give the children that strong word: " I know Whom I have believed ". I knew that, according to his usual careful custom, Godfrey had prepared beforehand for those few minutes. But God—time is nothing with God, and I looked up quickly and asked that Godfrey might read just that one verse in the pause after the Hallelujah.

Next morning he came to tell me about things. I need hardly end the little story. You know the end. *He had read that verse* (II Timothy 1. 12) *and just that one verse, in the pause after the Hallelujah.*

Was it not like our Father to let this be after that afternoon of such poor prayer? It was like His love *not* to say, " Why didn't you think of it before? You settled everything you wanted done with Godfrey yesterday, you could easily have mentioned it then ", but instead of that, to give me this renewed assurance (though indeed I did not need it) that all was more than well. In our dear Godfrey we have one whose ear is open unto Him, and this tender kindness told me that even to me His ear is open. That was the wonder of it—even to me.

She was always deeply concerned about the daily Fellowship prayer meeting. To her that meeting was " the innermost heart of its being ", for it was primarily a Fellowship with God, and only secondarily a company of men and women in fellowship with one another. Writing to Godfrey some months before the accident, she mentions a certain need:

Have we prayed enough as a Family about the need? I often name it at the prayer meeting, but it is rarely taken up by any of you whom it most deeply concerns. I have noticed that God sometimes waits until as a Fellowship we wait on Him about something. When we do that, things happen. Sometimes at the meeting there is a drag. Is our Father trying to show us that if He is to work wonders for us we *must* be in earnest about it, we *must* stir ourselves to lay hold of Him? There are words in the Bible that make one wonder whether we do really as a company go very far in prayer. I want to go much further.

And in a later letter:

If prayer matters then it ought not to be counted continually second in our scheme of life. . . . All the time the
devil is fighting our half-hour's prayer, he never tires of
fighting it. Sometimes there is a dulness which is a cloud of
hell, sometimes a fiery assault.

She speaks of some who did not come, " or came too pre-
occupied and tired to help in an output of spiritual energy".

Her true humility suggested to her mind that perhaps she
was the hindrance.

I would so gladly stay out if you, or one of you, could
draw all together better. I am often distressed because I
have to pray again and again. It is a kind of tiredness, I
think. We droop, instead of stirring ourselves to lay hold
upon our God. It used to be a life and death business with us.

No—she was certainly not the hindrance. But a few months
later came the accident, and thereafter she could not be
present. She missed the meetings sorely. Someone would
write on a slip of paper for her the subjects for praise and prayer
each day, then she would follow the meeting, and judge of its
progress, by the songs which punctuated it—for the prayer
room was close at hand.

The songs, of course, were usually of her own composition.
She loved the story of the singers whom Jehoshaphat appointed
to go out before the army, to praise the beauty of holiness, and
to say, " Praise the Lord; for His mercy endureth for ever "
(II Chronicles 20. 21, 22). It was when they began to sing
and to praise that the Lord set ambushments against the
enemies of His people.

I wonder if you feel as I do [she wrote to John Risk] about
the heavenliness of song. I believe truly that Satan cannot
endure it, and so slips out of the room—more or less!—when
there is true song. It leads to a sort of sweetness too, " My
lips will be fain when I sing unto Thee; and so will my soul
whom Thou hast delivered " (Psalm 71. 21 P.B.V.). Prayer
rises more easily, more spontaneously, after one has let those
wings, words and music, carry one out of oneself into that
upper air.

But she could be severely practical in reminding D.F.s of
the things that hinder united prayer. Once she noted down
" three facts that if remembered save time and energy in a
prayer meeting ":

1. We don't need to explain to our Father things that are known to Him.

2. We don't need to press Him, as if we had to deal with an unwilling God.

3. We don't need to suggest to Him what to do, for He Himself knows what to do.

" Lord, all my desires are before Thee." " Do Thou for me, O God the Lord."

Concerning the same need which called forth the " three facts " she wrote:

> This early morning as I looked up about our special prayer for X—— a light fell on the words, " We know *that we have* the petitions that we desired of Him." We pray from the ground of that certainty; not towards certainty but from it. (Is that why we have the words, " In everything by prayer and supplication *with thanksgiving* "? We give thanks before we see).
>
> Then the thought came, " What is it that we *have* in this sense already received? Surely just this: that the glory of the Lord will be manifested (for is not this what we desired of Him?), and that the very best will be done from His eternal point of view, for the work committed to us.

Once in the Forest in October, 1933, a prayer meeting was held in her room.

> Yesterday [she wrote to Godfrey] we had the prayer meeting in my room, and the one thing we prayed about was Prayer. I know we have all, for some time back, felt the need of something more in our prayer life. I have, person-ally, and I know others have, and there are the many in our Family who come to prayer meetings because it is the custom to do so, but who are not urged by a great desire. It is the lack of prayer-hunger that often makes a big united meeting difficult. The one thing we seem to need most is a revived prayer life in our own souls—then the wave will flow out to the others. So we prayed on those lines, and God was with us. I think we shall go on, waiting on Him together for a few minutes every day till we go down [from the Forest]. If we prepare the wood, the fire will fall and kindle it. It was wonderful to be in the prayer meeting after the two long years, and so good to feel the living throb of the other five. The hour passed like five minutes.

The time always seemed to pass quickly when Amma was leading a meeting. She wrote to one of the leaders in 1942:

I have been thinking this—don't get too heavy in talk and prayer. Earnestness does not necessarily mean heaviness. It is the *joy* of the Lord that is strength.

And here is a word to Murray in 1943:

This day in 1929—shall I ever forget it? I kept the whole Family for two hours in the House of Prayer while you did your first big spectacular operation. So much depended (in those early days) on that operation that lessons went to the wind, and the two hours full of prayer and song went like two minutes, and then your messenger came, and the excited, delighted children saw the result in a big basin! Bless God for those days—and these!

On the eighth anniversary of the accident she wrote to the whole Fellowship, thanking them for their prayers for her, but urging that some, at least, of their prayer energy be devoted to more important needs.

For eight years many of you have daily prayed for me, not the ordinary costless prayer—" God bless her ", but something far more vital, and to each one I want to say, " From the first day thy prayers were heard ". I can never, never thank you enough for those prayers. From the depths of my heart I thank you.

There were often times of special prayer. I do not forget this, and the most wonderful love that caused this to be. I can never understand such love.

I thought then that the bars would be broken. Every day I thought, " It will be tomorrow." The answer has come otherwise. You know what it has been. What you do not know is that there have often been times when the little song about the iron bars turning to gold has seemed very far from true; such hours come even now. At such times no words can tell you what your prayers mean to me.

But, my dear D.F.s, listen. Apart from our own war, the world is so full of the tremendous and prayer-compelling, that I do not want you to spend one minute on me. I don't want to be demanding either in the matter of seeing you whom I love so much, and hearing of all that is my very life, or in any other way. One can easily slip into a dreadful kind of selfishness. I don't want to do that. I want to learn to pour out each several cupful of natural longing as well as natural love before the Lord. Almost every day gives a chance to do that.

I believe there are a few things more to do before I touch John 17. 4. If you, in your dear love, do still at times feel moved to pray, ask that I may fully finish the appointed things and then not hang about, using up the strength of others, but pass on to serve you in strength and vigour again.

It was a perfectly sincere request, and the Lord, Who knows our frame, would not charge her with inconsistency because, after another eight years, she wrote in her private note-book:

> For years patiently the prayer meeting went on praying for me. It does not seem to do so now. I was feeling the need of prayer very much, but to ask for it would be selfish. So I had settled that I would not do so, when this word came: " I have prayed for thee ". My dear, dear Lord.

She was mistaken in thinking that the Family had ceased to pray. Often there was special prayer—for relief from pain, for sleep, or for some other urgent need. On one such occasion she writes:

> I have heard of the prayer. Thank you all so very much. One can " run " into the strong tower in all waking moments, but in sleep nobody can " run ". Your prayers have put up a shield. Two sheltered nights have renewed my strength. It feels too good to be true, but isn't!

Right on to the end her thoughts were far more with others than with herself. In the closing lines of Archbishop Trench's noble sonnet on prayer:

> Why, therefore, should we do ourselves this wrong,
> Or others—that we are not always strong,
> That we are ever overborne with care,
> That we should ever weak and heartless be,
> Anxious or troubled, when with us is prayer,
> And joy and strength and courage are with Thee?

she has heavily underlined the words " *Or others* ". If we fail to pray, there is loss to ourselves, but it was the loss to others that Amma feared most.

Twice in later years she writes to Murray concerning attacks on the unity of *Annachies* in the Fellowship.

> The devil is subtle and he goes for the true and sensitive in spirit in a most cruel way. But I fall back on my rock-word, " Greater is He ". X—— will tell you how I feel you should meet this attempt of the devil by prayer together. Powerful prayer is possible only where there is agreement in the New Testament sense. Once when one of our dearest *Sitties* was on the edge of what would have separated, just because of this earnestness to follow fully, two or three of us prayed and the spell was broken. There are more of you

now, and I shall be with you in spirit. What matters more, I believe Christ will be the Ground of your beseeching. The need may soon be urgent to know how certain dividing things are to be met, and there is need, too, for a peaceable (not a fretful) spirit to be given; for fretfulness has a deadly way of spreading. One of my first inward questions when a new worker comes is: Will he, will she, take things by the right handle or the wrong? Some by nature do one, some the other—thank God!

Prayer was answered. Here is the second letter:

This evening after dinner we prayed as perhaps never before about X——. If only the spiritual miracle be wrought, then, whatever happens, all will be peace. There will be no hurt to the heart, even if there should not prove to be strength enough for all India means. We are all clear about having this time of prayer, and I know you are holding the whole matter in the Presence. Conybeare and Howson's note on II Corinthians 2. 11 is never far from me: "They would all be overreached by Satan if he robbed them of a brother." If this happens for which we ask, then, come what may, nothing can "rob us of a brother".

Amma's message to the Fellowship meeting held on February 5th, 1948, is a fitting close to this chapter, for no one but Amma could have written it.

After October 24th, 1931, when life changed for me, what I missed most was the daily united prayer meeting.

Once in those over sixteen years I had the joy of being in the Fellowship meeting. We were in the Forest then (1933), and the meeting was in my room. This was the time when the words,

> Come ill, come well, the cross, the crown,
>   The rainbow or the thunder—
> I fling my soul and body down
>   For God to plough them under

gripped Hugh Evan Hopkins, and he went down the Forest path next day saying those words over and over to himself. He will never forget that meeting, nor shall I. After that, the nearest I ever had to the joy of united prayer was when I could follow the course of a prayer meeting by means of the choruses.

Through those years I began to learn, as Bishop Moule said about a greater thing, the lesson set to the weaned child, "how to do without".

Then suddenly a loving D.F. who knew nothing of this— no one knew anything of it—suggested that the first fifteen minutes of the Council prayer meeting should be in my room. That quarter of an hour was like one long drink of cold water on a hot day. First came the thought, " I am glad that the others have this almost every day." Then as I drank deeper and rejoiced in the vital tone of the prayers (so different from my own), a new sense of confidence was created within me, and has ever since possessed me. How can we fear when love delighteth ever to meet our need? The greatest need of all, men and women of prayer, is being met. Will He not with them also freely give us all things? Surely the Presence of the Lord was in the room that day, for that which was done then has not lost force, rather it has increased.

Often since then in the night, when every fear is magnified in some strange way, I went back in thought to that meeting of January 17th, felt again that surge of prayer about me, felt again that Presence, and again took courage. Let the foe be mighty, the threatenings against our little Fellowship be tremendous, the way through the difficulties ahead be quite unknown, what does anything matter if God " unseen as air " be on the field? *But God, but God*—the words rang through me like the notes of a trumpet.

And a new desire has been born in me. It is that none of you may miss the peculiar blessing there is *in united prayer*. Two little sticks burning together can make a glow, thank God; but how much more warm the glow of forty or fifty if each be on fire? The loving, living present Lord preserve your meetings from ever becoming stale, tepid, ineffective. May they always be as those blessed fifteen minutes were to me, kindling and creative, spirit and life.

> How can we fear?
>   For love delighteth ever
> To meet our need—
>   And great it is indeed;
> For we go forth,
>   To meet a foe who never
> Before mere man doth cower.
>   But God, our Tower,
> Is our defence, He is our Power.
>
> Our fingers He
>   Doth teach the art of fighting.
> His bugle call
>   Hath summoned soldiers all
> To rise and go;
>   In faith and love uniting,
> This war is His affair,
>   Unseen as air,
> Upon the field, He will be there.

Take this book in Thy wounded Hand,
  Jesus, Lord of Calvary;
Let it go forth at Thy command,
  Use it as it pleaseth Thee.

Dust of earth, but Thy dust, Lord,
  Blade of grass, in Thy Hand a sword—
Nothing, nothing, unless it be
  Purged and quickened, O Lord, by Thee.

(When the first printed copy of a Dohnavur book is received, it is
placed in the Prayer Room, and these or similar words are sung by
the Fellowship as they ask God's blessing upon it.)

CHAPTER XXXVII

AMMA AS AUTHOR

HALF an hour spent in examining a list of thirty-five books, larger and smaller, that Amma published between *From Sunrise Land* in 1895 and *This One Thing* in 1950, is a heartening experience. It is rare to discover a book of which less than ten thousand copies have been printed. There are nine books in the " 15,000 and over " category. *Things as They Are* and *Mimosa* soar far higher, but who would have thought that more than twenty thousand people would care to read *If* and *Gold by Moonlight*? Is it not clear that amongst His children all over the world there are more than one might have imagined who want something deeper and more searching than most missionary books supply?

For Amma's books are not " popular " in the ordinary sense of the word. When in 1947 she saw them thus described in a Christian publication, she wrote in her private note-book: " Popular? Lord, is that what these books written out of the heat of battle are? Popular? O Lord, burn the paper to ashes if that be true." And in a *Dust of Gold* much earlier she had written:

> Pray that every book, booklet, letter, that goes out from this Fellowship may have blood and iron in it. Pray that we may never degenerate to the merely interesting, the pretty.

Before her name was widely known she had sometimes found it difficult to discover a publisher who would venture to print the truth. The letters eventually published in *Things as They Are* were rejected as too pessimistic for a Christian public whose complacency was fed by stories of success and advance. Even the story of Suhinie in *From the Forest* was returned by a missionary editor who wrote: " You must not pump cold water unawares upon a gracious public full of nerves." It would not be good for children to read of little Suhinie " in the grip of a huge man who was twisting her wrists ", and even for adults the story should be " modified ".

It never occurred to Amma to ask herself what would suit
the public taste. She asked for " fire-words " (see page 102)
knowing well what the cost would be to herself.

> Thou shalt have words
> But at this cost, that thou must first be burnt . . .
> Not otherwise, and by no lighter touch,
> Are fire-words wrought.

When a much younger author consulted her about a biography
which she was preparing to write, she replied, " Generally
speaking, I think the rule should be—the truth whatever people
think. It is truth in a book that helps." She questioned the
use of the words " artistic touch". " So often in missionary
books it is just that ' artistic touch ' that kills one's faith in
the utter truth of what is written." *

> There is a false suavity about most that is written from
> this land now. We are so afraid to offend, so afraid of stark
> truth, that we write delicately, not honestly. Our smooth-
> ness glides over souls. It does not spur them to action, even
> though they be Christians to whom the thought of the glory
> of the Lord being given to another ought to be unendurable.

To Amma it was unendurable, and she wrote in the belief
that there must be other lovers of the Lord who cared as she
did. The outcry in missionary circles, even in India, which
followed the publication of *Things as They Are* amazed but did
not dismay her, and the fact that the book was reprinted twelve
times justified her conviction that there were people who
wanted to know the truth, however unpalatable it might be,
however contrary to the popular conception of what missionary
work was, or ought to be.

There is no doubt that *Things as They Are* did " spur to
action " many thousands of Christian people. They began to
pray as they had never prayed before, to take the challenge
of heathenism seriously, to recognize that Bunyan was wrong in
writing of Giant Pagan having been " dead many a day ".
Things as They Are ranks with such classics as the two-volume

---

* Incidentally both Amma and the Perfect Nurse greatly appreciated
the privilege of offering advice and criticism concerning this manuscript,
which was sent to them chapter by chapter during 1948. The letters bear
evidence of the clearness of Amma's mental perception and the youthful-
ness of her heart when she was already eighty years of age, and had been
suffering acute pain intermittently, but often over long periods, ever since
1931.

Life of Hudson Taylor in this respect, that through reading it scores of men and women have found themselves unable to evade God's call, and are to be found serving Him today in the high places of the field.

In 1947 it was suggested that *Things as They Are* should be reprinted for the thirteenth time.*

> There is very little to revise [writes Amma]. I had not looked at the book, much less re-read it, for forty years or more. To read it was like reading a new book—a new story, and a scorching one. Again and again I had to stop. I couldn't bear it at all, I think, if I could not shut my eyes and see the House of Prayer full of redeemed children, the nurseries full of babies—and *such* babies!—the Place of Heavenly Healing and all its lovely activities, the Converts' Home too, and so many there and elsewhere saved and protected from the wrongs and sorrows of which the book tells.

It is worthy of note that in later years Amma not infrequently re-read her own books, and her personal copies are marked with her own underlinings. Clearly she was comforted with the comfort which she had ministered to others. The little book *His Thoughts said . . . His Father said*, which appeared in 1941, was " made up of ever so many people's thoughts, talking aloud as it were. . . . Some are very private thoughts "— and very searching. " This morning ", Amma wrote to Godfrey in 1947, " I was reading *His Thoughts Said*. Constantly I find that the things His Father said open out, and I see what I did not see before in those words." This need occasion no surprise if we recall that Amma always believed that her books were " given ". She made no foolish claim to inspiration in the technical sense, but she was quite sure that it was God Himself Who said to her from time to time, " What thou seest write in a book ".

Obviously there were reasons other than those already mentioned for the ready sales of some of the books. For instance, what lover of children could resist the pictures in *Lotus Buds*? Who would not be thrilled by the unexpectedness of a whole series of photographs at the end of *Kohila*? Often in her forewords she would make grateful reference to " our

---

* The reprint was delayed but is now definitely in preparation. Some books can be allowed to die, for they have served their purpose, but *Things as They Are* is not one of them.

friends Messrs Vandyck " who produced the pictures. She had very happy relations with S.P.C.K., who from 1928 onwards have published most of her books. The attractiveness of their format is due partly to the publishers, but partly also to Amma herself, who had very clearly defined ideas of what she desired. In 1934 she wrote to Dr Lowther Clarke, who was at that time Secretary of S.P.C.K., concerning *Ploughed Under*:

> You say, the more work I can do on it by thinking how I want it to look, the better you will be pleased. That's the sort of publisher I enjoy. After all, a book is a child, it's impossible not to know how one wants its hair curled. Well, first I want the book thin. I don't like podgy books. . . . Don't let my little lover come out fat.

Then follow detailed instructions concerning paper, print, cover, stuff (i.e. the type of cloth used for binding), pictures, end-papers, etc. Then as to price:

> Here as usual we are a nuisance. But think: we are both (you and I) out to do heavenly business. The earthly part of it is only a detail. The people for whom this book is written are not rich. . . . *Please* don't groan, but just do it.

And she signs herself, " Yours troublesomely ".

Another factor which lifted all her writing above the ordinary was the limpid quality of her style, the grace and the charm of it. If a writer is the bearer of a Divine message, we are constrained to read what he produces, even though its literary expression is flat or uncouth. But even one who knows little of the art of writing cannot but be uplifted by the cadences of Isaiah 40, or touched by the simple beauty of Luke 15. Amma could write, and she appreciated good writing. When, in the closing years, the Perfect Nurse tried to provide her with fairly light reading which might distract her tired mind and make the pain a little easier to bear, she knew that it was useless to offer her anything poorly or shoddily written. She herself wrote quickly when inspiration came, but every sentence, almost every word, was carefully weighed, and a good deal of the manuscript re-written, before it left Dohnavur for London.

When Godfrey was preparing his book, *Brothers of the Lotus Buds*, she wrote to him:

You will find if you leave it for a while that oddments for its betterment will come, a loose end to be knitted in, or a not very clear sentence elucidated (but you probably have none!). These are trifles, but all help to make for perfection. I feel like offering a slab of chocolate to anyone who will tell me of a superfluous word, i.e. a word that has no work to do. Words should be like colours, each one a dot of colour supplying a need, not one over.

But it was not a style with a universal appeal. There were those who found it difficult to follow the flights of her fancy, and preferred something more pedestrian. Every imaginative device that she employed, either consciously or unconsciously, added force and point to the message that she intended to convey. Amma could not be prosy, even when she was writing prose, but it has to be admitted that the very quality which lifted and inspired so many made her seem obscure to others.

At least there was no careless writing. She loved to quote John Wilkins' lines:

> Who never negligently yet
> Fashioned an April violet.

If God never makes an imperfect petal, she felt, " it makes the tiniest points of grammar seem worth noticing ". " Dowdiness ", she said, " is not acceptable to the Lord of beauty, but the first appeal of a spiritual work must be spiritual, and therefore eternal." In writing of such a work, therefore, one cannot " think of making one's books a ' success ' ", for that would be to enter another sphere, the sphere of time.

Of the thirteen books written after the accident of 1931, seven were not " missionary " in the ordinary sense, whereas the twenty-two written before that date—with the exception of two slim volumes of verse—were all in the category of missionary biography or had a direct bearing on the Dohnavur work. There is not one without a vital spiritual message, but surely it is clear that, as Amma entered more fully into the fellowship of Christ's sufferings, He gave her words which could not have been written apart from that experience. The first of them, *Rose from Brier*, is still bringing comfort and cheer to sufferers everywhere. She had discovered, as she explains in the introduction, that " tracts for the sick " were often unhelpful " because they were obviously written by the well to the ill, to do them good." But things written from the ill to the ill " did something that nothing except the words of our eternal Lord could ever do." And thus, apart from their wide circulation, *Rose from Brier* and *Gold by Moonlight* evoked more letters of appreciation than almost any others of Amma's books.

Rose from Brier was originally written in the form of letters to the Dohnavur Invalids' League, with whom Amma felt herself linked very intimately after 1931. Under Amma's new name, " Companions in the Patience ", this group is still closely in touch with Dohnavur. The " Companions " are lovers of the Lord who, in so far as their infirmities permit, give themselves to the vital but sadly neglected ministry of intercession for the things that concern His kingdom.

After a time it was suggested that another book in the *Nor Scrip* series, continuing the record of God's provision given in *Tables in the Wilderness* and *Meal in a Barrel*, was required. For a time Amma hesitated. Had she the strength for a task that required, as she pointed out to Godfrey, " so much looking up of records "? " It is far more tiring than the writing of a straightforward story like *Mimosa*."

But at length *Windows* began to take shape. In her private note-book for July, 1936, she writes:

> For the first time since last October power came to work at *Windows*. Suddenly on the morning of the 24th (after a poor night) I felt I was to do it, and could do it. Worked without stopping that day and the next—about thirteen hours each day—and on the 26th the same except for two breaks. Cannot account for it on any natural ground, as nothing is different. Lord and Master of my life, Owner of my every minute, I thank Thee.

Windows and its successor, *Though the Mountains Shake*,* were much more substantial volumes than *Nor Scrip*. They did indeed make mention of God's loving-kindness in the matter of financial provision, but they covered much ground besides. They helped to bring the record of *Gold Cord*, which describes the origin and growth of the Fellowship and of the whole work until the end of 1931, up to date. For instance, *Though the Mountains Shake* contains a poignantly beautiful account of Arulai's illness and death, completing the story already told in

---

* Her last major work—since *This One Thing*, though containing much new material, is essentially a revision of the earlier *Walker of Tinnevelly*.

Ploughed Under. Indeed, there is many an excursion into other realms than finance, and if the texture of the books is less closely knit, the reader is not inclined to be critical, for the colouring is finer and more beautiful than ever.

Amma was truly and sincerely astonished to find that there were so many people who read her books, and prayed that strength to write would still be granted to her. " It can only be because you are praying ", she wrote to the Fellowship, and that was an explanation that satisfied her. It was always a joy when her own children found help from the books. " I am gladder than I can tell you ", she wrote to one of them in 1940, " to know that *If* helped you. I would rather help one of my own Family than anyone else in all the world."

For some years after the accident help for the Family was provided by *Daily Manna.* Each day Amma wrote of some word or some thought that had come to her in her daily reading, and ten to twenty lines of typescript were copied and circulated. The manna was always fresh. Here, for instance, is the food provided for December 9th and 10th, 1933. It was thus that even in weakness, as a faithful and wise steward over her household, she gave them their portion of meat in due season.

December 9, 1933. This morning with the unexpectedness of a revelation, a question flashed through my mind: Have we any prayer like " Use me, O Lord " in the Bible? We have it in hymns. I expect we have often prayed to be used, and prayed for others too, that they may be used. But as I looked through my Bible after this strange question I could not find any such prayer anywhere.

The word in II Timothy 2. 21 simply says that if it be clean the vessel will be ready for the Master to use. And in Isaiah 6 the " send me " was in answer to the question " Who will go? "

It is at least interesting and suggestive to find every other verb occurring in prayer—teach me, lead me, bless me, and so on—and not this verb which we would naturally expect. Is it that there is no need for it? If the vessel be clean and ready to hand, the Master will use it. It is not necessary that it should ask Him to do so. The Captain will use the soldier if he be prepared for use; words of beseeching on the soldier's part are not required.

December 10, 1933. *Pens.* II Timothy 2. 21. " Very usable." Yesterday's note leads to this: the one thing that matters is that we should be very usable (Young gives " very

usable " as the meaning of " meet ", in II Timothy 2. 21,
and that seems to mean " clean, and to hand ").

I have three pens, one for ordinary writing, one a little
finer, and one for fine work like corrections. Preethie
Sittie keeps these pens clean and filled, and they live in a vase
of wood shaped like a flower which Philippe *Annachie* gave
me. This vase is always near me. The pens are always
ready for use, " very usable ". There is no need for any of
the three to ask to be used. They are clean, at hand, never
occupied about their own business, but always free for mine.
So they are used because they are " very usable ".

The pens are cleansed and filled once a week. Our pens
need to be cleansed and filled continually, but we know the
arrangements God has made for that. So there is no need
to be unusable because of not being clean and filled. Even
so, just as a fountain pen is all the better for being sometimes
left under water, so our souls do often need to be bathed
afresh in the Love of God—that Love that penetrates with
cleansing power to the innermost part of us. And we are
given one day in seven for something of this sort. Let us
remind ourselves of the best way to use the day. First,
preparation for the House of Prayer, full use of the minute's
silence, a true worship together (not just a formal drifting
through, or passive following the leader) ; and throughout
the day, however the outward part of us may be occupied,
a quiet steeping of the spirit in the deep, deep Love of God.

As far as records go, the total number of languages into
which one or other of Amma's books was translated is fifteen.
Of these seven are European languages, and eight Asiatic,
including Tamil and four other Indian tongues. *Mimosa*
easily heads the list, for it has appeared in ten languages.
That is not surprising. I have in my hand a letter from a
Swedish lady whose mother read *Mimosa* to her children in
1928. " We are deeply affected ", she writes, " by this story
of faith, and I have related it many times at meetings. Now I
am happy to have four children, and I have read most of your
book to them." Her boys were greatly interested and full of
questions. " Mother, do you think she is still living? And her
sons, Music, Kinglet, and the others, are they also Christians? "
At last they would not be content until their mother had
written to Dohnavur for further information. This Swedish
family was not alone in its desire to welcome Mimosa and her
children into the circle of personal friends. Barbara Osman
tells how in the Nilgiris she met an Indian Bible-woman who

loved the Tamil version of *Mimosa*. " Later, she and a sister and a young niece came to visit us, and I realized that they thought of Mimosa and her family almost as their own. Their joy was great when I showed them a photograph of Kinglet (Rajappan)."

It was a special joy to Amma that twelve of her books were transcribed in Braille for the National Library for the Blind in England, and eight for the Braille Circulating Library in the United States. Some of the books have been transcribed for other circulators also.

The imaginative gift, which shows itself in everything that she wrote, naturally appears most clearly in her verses. Many of them were written only for the Family, but *Made in the Pans* and *Toward Jerusalem* were volumes of short poems, and two longer poems, *Pools* and *The Valley of Vision*, were published together in 1938.* It is not usual for a book of verses to run into several editions, unless they are of exceptional quality, yet that is what happened with *Toward Jerusalem*. There are Christian verse-writers who produce with painfully glib facility a great number of short " poems " suitable for Christmas card greetings. Amma's songs—they are usually called so in Dohnavur since most of them are set to music, and are actually sung at the daily prayer meetings, as well as in the House of Prayer—are in a very different category. As poems, it is true, they are of unequal merit, but many of them are of great beauty, and if a good poem is one which expresses ideas with greater force and pungency than if they were expressed in prose, then there are many good poems in *Toward Jerusalem*. Long ago a little volume called *Wings* appeared. It was virtually a collection of the songs, words and music, which had been printed on the cover of the *Dohnavur Letter* or *Dust of Gold*. Amma always spoke of music as providing "wings" for her words. In a sense this book is her legacy to the Lord's lovers all over the world, and I do not say that through it she who is dead will yet speak, but rather that through it He Who is alive for evermore will speak in comfort and challenge to His disciples.

* *The Valley of Vision* had appeared separately in 1917.

But all through life I see a Cross,
Where sons of God yield up their breath:
There is no gain except by loss,
There is no life except by death,
And no full vision but by Faith,
Nor glory but by bearing shame,
Nor Justice but by taking blame;
And that Eternal Passion saith,
" Be emptied of glory and right and name."

From *Olrig Grange*, by WALTER C. SMITH.

(A very favourite quotation with Amma.)

CHAPTER XXXVIII

"THE CROSS IS THE ATTRACTION"

"I HAD a dream last night," wrote Amma in 1934. "I dreamed that we had an elderly female called Matilda Dempster who had somehow become a D.F., and wasn't in the least D.F., and I couldn't weld her in. I woke in a perfect stew of distress, and could not pacify myself till I read through the list of names in my Bible and found Matilda wasn't there!"

The dream shows how greatly she dreaded the possibility of unsuitable recruits for the D.F. Indeed, her concern was based on experience and not merely on dreams. "I have had many a hard day", she wrote to Murray, "because of those who either wanted to join us and could not be joined, or (as you know) those who did join and had to be un-joined." It was no wonder that she gave serious heed to the advice of an old missionary, "Guard your gate".

One obvious step was to discourage doubtful people from offering. Yet she hoped to help them, so that there might be spiritual gain from their touch with Dohnavur, even if they never joined the Fellowship.

I am feeling sad about X—— [she wrote]. Could you have special prayer for him? Our letter will be a sad blow. His mother used to write to me when he was a small boy. Irene and Olive were in touch. When he was a boy of seventeen his whole heart was set on coming to us.

All are agreed that he wasn't the D.F. sort, so there is no question about the rightness of " No ", but I'm all one ache for him. He does not seem to have a doubt or fear, so it will be pretty hard. Let us pray for preparation at the other end. . . . I wish we could find some way of gently detaching such from us before a long-prayed-over and longed-for offer emerges. We have other offers of the same kind pending. . . . I should be grateful for prayer about these who love us and yet whom we can't have. A sad letter from Y——'s sister [Y—— had offered and been rejected] tells us that she is drifting and wretched.

Ever since Irene Streeter's retirement Olive Gibson had been

bearing the burden at the home end.*   Amma found it safe
to rely on her judgment, and therefore she was constantly
urging her to avoid overstrain.   She wrote in 1939:

> How we are cast on our God.   Never, I suppose, was so
> large a community with so small a root in England—just
> a single tap-root.   Go gently.   Don't do as I know I did,
> for truly I had to do it.   Don't work each day till you are
> unable to do one minute more.   *Don't*.   Leave a margin.
> It doesn't matter that I did it, for there are all these ready to
> take over, and the old should leave the young to it.   The
> part of the old is to love them through the difficulties that
> are bound to come, and lend a hand when needed.   So I
> am more than content, but you are still in midstream, and
> there is no one as yet preparing to be *buthil* [substitute], so
> conserve strength.

Perhaps it was a counsel of perfection.   It may have been a
little easier for Olive Gibson to " go gently " than it had been
for Amma, but this is a precept which those who offer it rarely
reinforce by their own example.

But when she told intending candidates that Dohnavur
desired only those to whom the Cross was the attraction, she
was speaking of what she knew, for it had always been the
attraction to her.   To one who had been accepted she wrote:

> Above all my prayer for you is that you may be a good
> soldier, ready for anything, any suffering, any misunder-
> standing, any blame, *anything* for Jesus' sake.   The life of a
> missionary can be as easy and as pleasant as any life at home.
> Crossing the sea does not make any woman a missionary
> in spirit, nor does it turn soft iron into steel.   Spend much
> time at Calvary before you come.   Look at that love, look
> and look till you can say to Him, " Yes, Lord, *anything* ". . . .
> I long to have you out tomorrow and to pour the language
> into you, and send you out to fight the powers of evil with
> the Powers of Love.   Don't fear—the mud-throwing will
> not be over when you come.   You will get thoroughly
> splashed.   I'm so glad you don't mind the prospect.

And of another she wrote:

> If her soul leaps to hardship for the sake of the Crucified
> all will be well.   It is those who for His sake *choose* to follow
> Him in this way who make the valiant warriors.

* " The home end " means England in this context.   But it cannot be
too strongly emphasized that to members of the Fellowship Dohnavur is
home, as it was to Amma.

" Don't let us lower the standard "—this was the theme of many letters.

We shall begin to perish if we do. That is, the deepest in us will do so. We shall get bigger, but gradually we shall slip into soft iron, not tempered steel. What a mix-up of simile, but I leave it. God keep us true to the heavenly vision.

She longed that the vision should be shared by the relatives of D.F.s, and especially their parents.

I delighted in your action and decision, and when I heard of your parents' response—their soldierly response—I just sang for joy. . . . The soldierly choices of the soul—it is those that are assaulted, and with one voice most Christian parents and friends join in the assault. . . . I can see no reason for the creation of our D.F. if we are to be satisfied with the usual.

Amma's frequent references to Sainte Chantal, Mère Angélique of Port Royal, Père Didon, and other Roman Catholic writers, must not be misconstrued. She hated the iniquities of the Roman system, she constantly read stories from *Foxe's Book of Martyrs* to the older girls, and she was not in the very least tempted to accept Roman Catholic doctrine. But since she could discern wheat from chaff and believed that members of the Fellowship were sufficiently mature to do the same, she did not hesitate to recommend as of great value for intending missionaries *The Spiritual Letters of Père Didon* as well as the second volume of the Life of Hudson Taylor. She could never have worked with the former as she could with the latter, but she read eagerly the writings of men and women who were ardent lovers of the Lord, and mourned that " the joy of sacrificial living " seemed to be found more often " amongst those whom we cannot follow in doctrine ".

We [i.e. we Protestants] have had some who have gone back to the early ideal, and lived it out. But they have had to press through the solid weight of modern Christianity, a sort of piled up decorousness, comfortableness, utter negation of *the Cross as lived*, shocked surprise at the bare thought of that. . . . My most longing prayer is that as a Fellowship we may go on there, and not become mere talkers or singers about it.

And she prayed for parents who would not " call their children back from going to the last extremity of the jewel mine. It is just there that the richest jewels lie ".

I am reading for my night book [she wrote in 1942] the story of Louise, daughter of Louis XV of France. It makes one utterly ashamed of the shallowness of desire to be in all ways "conformable unto His death". Not that I think the way that dear girl took was (for us) the right way, but that the intense earnestness which shrank from nothing if only self could be trodden under foot and the Lord magnified, is searching and rebuking too. She, a Princess of France, set her heart on joining the Carmelite Order of nuns, a very strict Order. She held to this desire for eighteen years in the frivolous, evil Court of those days. . . . It is the utter earnestness of purpose to be wholly on the altar of our Lord that speaks to me, the earnestness in " downing " the " I ". Don't you think that because we see a better way of doing this than hair shirts, and so on, we are apt to slide into not doing it at all?

The medieval Order of Servants to the Sick appealed to Amma. The novice gave himself to God " and to our lords, the sick, that all the days of my life I may serve them ". Since " our lords the sick " were, for the most part, poor, their Servants were to live without personal possessions.

How I used to long to follow this vow literally! I wanted to have no possessions except what I could carry in a big handkerchief! But that would have meant much less to give to others, books and all the treasures therein for example, and so I am reconciled to our way of life, but I think we have much to learn from the spirit of the old vow.

On New Year's Day, 1947, she quoted " this very old saying " in writing a word of greeting to the Fellowship. " Who goeth in the way that Christ had trod, is much more like to meet Him than he that travelleth byeways." To Amma it was funda-mental that a community desiring to tread " the way the Master went " *must* be knit together in unity " by love, golden love ". To a group of *Sitties* in the Forest she wrote suggesting that they look through the New Testament " with all the versions you can lay your hands on, and find out everything the Lord says about love and unity ".

You will find some amazing verses. . . . At dinner you could talk over the finds of the day. It would be a wonderful study, and very searching. . . . But be sure to end your talks with singing together some love song, some prayer for love, something kindling about His love. And then pray. Confess the failure. Let us humble ourselves very low. Let us ask Him to make us moss for His feet in this matter of vital intertwined love and unity that *nothing* can sever—no, not for an hour. I long and thirst to have our Fellowship utterly satisfying to Him. He must be so often disappointed. Let us not disappoint Him.

The way of the Cross was not intended only for D.F.s. Amma longed that members of the Family should all be trained into " inner readiness for all life's unexpected calls ".

I have been reading Hebrews [she wrote in 1942]. It's a wonderful book. " Here have we no continuing city, but we seek one to come." That held me this morning. Dohnavur, Naraikadu (the Grey Jungle)—how they hold the heart. But we must not become entangled. How are we to prepare our children for the Anywhere, Anywhen sort of life? J—— was telling me yesterday how far from that some are, on whom he wants to count. Let us hold it clearly before our *Carunias* [girls of the Family who are growing up]. It used to be taken for granted. All *Sitties*, all girls who were His in any vital sense, were ready to go anywhere, at a moment's notice. I am not sure that it is so now. The nestling down habit is strong. God save us from it. If only I could show the way instead of doing the opposite it would be easier to help.

It was not love which refused to ask the uttermost from the *Carunias*. She sometimes spoke of the command not to offer honey with sacrifices.

I linked it to the word in the Revised Version margin of Hebrews 12. 1, " the sin which is admired of many ". I think this sin is often the weak kind of sympathy which does not brace the one who receives it but sends her away saying, " How loving so-and-so is. *She* always understands me."

One who had known Ponnammal and Arulai could not question the capacity of Indian D.F.s for leadership. Amma was keenly aware of the danger of western forcefulness and impatience.

Our place is always behind the scenes, never in front. To the burning spirit and the forceful spirit anywhere is easier than the rear. We always want to be in the van.

To Godfrey on furlough in 1938 she wrote:

If you are asked about our willingness or otherwise to accept evangelists, isn't this the thing to stress? We accept *no others*, but we ask for those who believe as we do that India can be best reached by Indians, and who are ready to cooperate with us in leading them out into service.

Once there was a good deal of anxiety about a young man who seemed to be proving unfit to carry responsibility. A series of notes to Godfrey shows how Amma helped both Godfrey and the Indian brother, whom we shall call X——.

Sleep has been impossible for hours, but I have had something far better than sleep, and now, before I try again to sleep awhile, I am writing this to give you a comforting thought that has only just come. Peter was all wrong, quite blind about one matter—so blind that he " dissembled " (Galatians 2. 12, 13)—and yet he went on and did not lose his apostleship. I expect he came to see later what he simply could not see when he dissembled and led others to do the same.

So it will surely be with X——. We (like Paul) have withstood him, and your talk with him will do that again. But Peter continues to be Peter, thank God. It was good to hear that it was not he who changed the plan. But he is ultimately responsible—we can't evade that point. Still, he continues to be Peter—except in this one point dependable and useful. It helped me to think of this.

Six months later the difficulty had not been removed.

I am with you in this trial. I am reading Ephesians just now, that Epistle of the heavenlies, but five times we are taken back to the cost paid. There *must* be something like the shedding of blood if ever there is to be what chapter 5, verse 27, describes—" that He might present it to Himself a glorious church, not having spot or wrinkle or any such thing, but that it should be holy and without blemish." I put X—— instead of the " church " as I read. It is the travail that Christ may be formed in him, that you are going through now. I pray that he may recover, for this is spiritual sickness.

A few days later she writes again.

I have been thinking much of X——. Do you think it can be that he is puzzled over questions being raised now, when he is, as he thinks, right with God? If so the puzzle may be blocking his way, so that he just can't see. P.S. My note was written some hours ago. It is now about 5 a.m. and all through these hours the thought of X—— has been with me. Read enclosed [evidently a note to X——].

If of any use, give it. If not, destroy, or hold it back. Do as you feel best. You know me well enough to know that I will not (for I cannot) yield one inch. Yet I feel that human love may help. At least, there is a chance that, under God, it might. I have known X—— like this as a little boy. It is not a new thing. Dear Godfrey, on you these many burdens fall. It is not for yourself that you mind, but the thought of the boys is your burden. Commit that too. Peter's fall must have been a fearful shock to many, but—well, you know all.

Here is the letter of the next day.

Thank you from my heart for sharing those searching, solemn questions with me. They were like lighted candles to my soul last night, as I went through them one by one with Him. Perhaps if X—— comes He may turn them upon him, even as He turned them upon me last night. Love can *pierce*. I pray this searching, burning love may find him and pierce through the clay he has wrapped round himself. . . . If I feel X—— is truly right on other points, and *willing for light*, even though so blind on this point, will you be happy if I speak as I would to any other soul similarly entangled? I cannot forget his years of loyal service, though often marred by pride. I have been through deep places with him. I fear despair for him, and the dangerous decisions of despair. We have a wily foe to fight.

Then after her talk with X——:

Such a good time. Straight down to rock bottom again, and his prayer true and very contrite. Just before he went he said, " Pray that I may have love, true love, and *humility*", and he added, " I have never asked anyone to pray that for me before." " As when the melting fire burneth "—what can the fire of love not do?

There is a final note written the same day.

Thank God. O Godfrey, you could not have sent me anything more " happifying ". Love won at Calvary— love will win now. I shall be with you at 9.45. I shall all but see Him lay one Wounded Hand on you and the other on X——, and Himself draw you close together. This is of Him only. " I, even I, will sing unto the Lord."

It was with such patient love, and with such sensitive regard for Godfrey's position, that she restored one who had begun to slip. X—— is still following hard after Him Whose love took Him to Calvary.

O Father, help, lest our poor love refuse
For our beloved the life that they would choose,
And in our fear of loss for them, or pain,
    Forget eternal gain.

Show us the gain, the golden harvest There
For corn of wheat that they have buried here;
Lest human love defraud them, and betray,
    Teach us, O God, to pray.

Teach us to pray remembering Calvary,
For as the Master must the servant be;
We see their face set toward Jerusalem,
    Let us not hinder them.

Teach us to pray. O Thou Who didst not spare
Thy Well-Belovèd, lead us on in prayer,
Purge from the earthly, give us love Divine,
    Father, like Thine, like Thine.

CHAPTER XXXIX

WHEN Ponnammal was in hospital in Nagercoil in 1913, expecting an operation which might mean entrance into Life for her, but separation from the Family in Dohnavur, she wrote four letters—one for the older girls, one for the children, one for the *Sitties* and one for Amma. " I can see her now ", writes Amma, " sitting up in bed, eagerly and with pain—for it hurt to sit up—writing quickly." These letters were read after the funeral. " Love filled them, overflowed them; mine ended with these words: ' the kisses of eternal love '."

Was it these letters which suggested to Amma that she should write similarly to her children? In any case, from 1919 onwards she wrote hundreds of letters to individual members of the Family or to groups, in case any had been overlooked, and kept them all in a box which was not to be opened until she had left them. She did not keep a very careful list, and thus some received more than one letter. Meanwhile the Family had grown so large, and the time when she was well enough to write was so limited, that it became a physical impossibility to write to them all. But, like Ponnammal, she wrote " eagerly and with pain ", concerned that all whom she loved should have some message from her.

No words of mine could show so clearly the nature of the bond between Amma and her children, her intimate knowledge of them, and the yearning of her mother-heart that Christ might be formed in them. (Some of the letters are in a different category—written for special occasions, such as Amma's birthday.) The few which are quoted are typical of the rest, and no further comment is needed except that, since English was not their native tongue, she was careful to use language which they could readily understand. The order is chronological.

January 30, 1919. My own beloveds, how I love you all. This is just steeped in love.

It is meant chiefly for those for whom perhaps there will

347

be no separate notes. I may not be able to write to all. But I do want each one to feel loved and thought about. Not one will ever be forgotten—as the High Priest bore the names on his breastplate, so indeed do I bear your names. They are deep in my heart.

I often wonder if I shall be allowed to come back to you. I cannot imagine myself being myself and yet away from you. But that won't matter really, for you will have the only One Who matters, the only One Who cannot be done without, with you all the time. And in a very little while we shall be together again.

Listen to Him, my children. He speaks to you, He teaches you in a thousand ways every day. Through the love of those who love you and live to help you, He touches you, and He speaks to you. In the sunrise and the sunset, and in moonlight, through the loveliness of the things that He has made, through the thousand joys that He plans for every one of you, through the sorrows that come, too, in all these things, through all these things, He Who loved you unto death is speaking to you. Listen; do not be deaf and blind to Him, and as you keep quiet and listen, you will know deep down in your heart that you are loved. As the air is round about you, so is His love round about you now. It is enough. Trust that love to guide your lives. It will never, never fail.

Your Mother who loves you, every one, through all eternity writes this, knowing that it is true.

For December 16, 1934. The greatest comfort I have is in remembering Him Who loves you best. All our love flows from His heart of love. We are like little pools on the rocks at Joppa. You know how we have watched the great sea washing over them and flooding them till they overflow. That is what the love of God does for us. We have no love in ourselves, and our pools would soon be empty if it were not for that great, glorious, exhaustless sea of love.

Often, as I think of you all, my chief prayer is that your pools may be kept full to overflowing. Satan likes to make us content with much less than this. O my precious child, do not listen to him. God has chosen Dohnavur to be a place of love, like an overflowing pool of love—overflowing on others. Let us fear everything that would spoil that beautiful thought of God. My special prayer for you on my birthday morning will be the prayer written in Ephesians 3. 16–19. If you read it you will know what I shall be thinking of you, most likely before any of you are awake. If the sky is blue on that day, will you who are older take the little ones out to look at it, and ask them to say if they can tell how broad and long and deep and high it is, and when they say, No, then tell them how that blue is like the love of their dear heavenly Father. I should like this thought (which they will never forget) to be my birthday present to all our darling little children.

October 16, 1936. If you ever read this, it will be because I am out of your sight, but not out of your love, I know. And you will not be out of my love. . . . I want you to rest your heart upon the certainty of the eternal nature of love. Never say, " I loved Amma very much ". Always say, " I love ", as I shall do also. There is no end to love. . . . It will not be long before I see you again. Till then the lesson set to you is " how to do without ". You remember I quoted that in *Rose from Brier*,* because it has helped so many. Bishop Moule, who wrote it in a letter to me, has been for many years with his loved ones whom he learned " to do without ". He filled up the time (till His Lord called him to be with Himself and his beloved for ever), *not* in grieving and talking and thinking of past joys, but in loving service to others.

That is what I pray my precious child will do. So I will copy Jeremy Taylor's prayer for you, always remembering that obedience means forgetting self in service to others. " Lord, do Thou turn me all into love, and all my love into obedience, and let my obedience be without interruption! "

December 7, 1939. To my children who are comrades in the war. Once more I am writing to you while you, I hope, are sleeping, for, as the Song of Songs puts it, " My heart waketh ". I cannot rest because of the distress that comes to me as I think of a misunderstanding that need never have been between two of you who love the Lord Jesus and are wholly given to His service.

And this kind of distress comes too often. It is a heavy burden to me. It is costing your *Sitties* and *Annachies* far too much time and strength, time and strength that they should be free to give to younger ones.

Often these misunderstandings are about the merest trifles. You let them grow and grow till your whole day is shadowed. This delights the devil, but it terribly injures your own soul, and it sorely grieves the Spirit of Love. Also, and this is serious, while you are yielding to such feelings you are unconsciously sowing seeds of unlove and distrust in other hearts—in the children's hearts. These seeds will spring to life and grow up to your sorrow one day.

Why don't you keep the Law of the Family and go straight to the one who has (you think) done something wrong?

* *Rose from Brier*, p. 172.

You can't, do you say? You can. Love will find a way. If there be any difficulty you have your *Sitties* and *Annachies* who are ready to do anything to help towards your having an opportunity for the one thing that always puts things straight, a loving talk together in the Presence of your Lord.

I have never found this fail when there is truth on both sides.

Some of you remember how in old days if a Prayer Day meeting was lifeless and we could not get anywhere, I used to stop, and we scattered, and any who were not in love met somewhere, perhaps just for a minute under a tree, and then we met again, and *then* the Spirit led us into real prayer. We are too big a Family for that to be possible now, but it is as important now as ever that all should be clear, no one out of love with any other one, no one doubting anyone.

O my children, if only you would make up your minds never to doubt the love of another sister or brother in Christ, but *always* to think the best, to take the best for granted, and never admit an unkind thought in your heart, how happy, how heavenly life would be.

I could not endure it if for one minute I doubted any one of you. It would be like the sting of a wasp in my soul. Why do you endure it? Why do some of you even encourage that wasp to sting? I beseech you to have done with this. Refuse it. Hate it. It may seem a trifle, but it is of hell.

We are all human. We may forget things we should remember. A message may be undelivered. There may be some mistake or delay about food or some such trifle. Take it as a mistake, not as something intended. I remember once weeks of unhappiness because a certain curry was badly cooked—the cause could have been discovered in five minutes if only there had been loving frankness, and speaking *to* instead of speaking *of* the one who made that curry. Such things are absurd, but they are too sad for laughter, for they do harm. They wound love.

I remember how on the very first birthday meeting I ever took, I stopped, and feeling too broken to go on because of something which had happened to grieve love, I said, " If this were the last time I could speak to you I should say just these words, ' *Beloved, let us love !* ' " My children, our comrades in the War of the Lord, I say these words to you again, " *Beloved, let us love !* " . . . Do you remember that prayer of Moses? " Yet now, if Thou wilt forgive their sin——" There are times when I can only say something like that to God. I think of Calvary. I see that love, that pain ; I hear the words you know so well, the words of uttermost agony, " My God, my God, why hast Thou forsaken

Me? " And then I think of how we, redeemed at such a cost, can stop to think of some personal trifle and magnify it, and go on doing so till in very truth we are crucifying the Son of God afresh, and putting Him to open shame. And I am ashamed before Him. God forgive us. God forgive me. God forgive you. " And if not " —yes, I can and I do pray Moses' awful prayer, for what is anything to me if you, my children, are to be content to shame the Lord Who redeemed you? I see down the generations; your children will be as you are, the children you are bringing up, whether in your own homes or your Lord's nurseries, will be as you are. O God forbid that we should add to the unlove of India and of this sad and sinful world.

But with Thee is forgiveness, that Thou mayest be feared. Remember those last words. They are too often forgotten. Fear to sin against love. Fear to dishonour your Lord. Fear with a holy fear the least small beginning of this hellish sin. Beloved, let us love. We perish if we do not love. Let us *love*.

August 7, 1941. Sometimes I have been anxious about you because you have said, " If you leave us I can't bear to go on." That is all wrong, my darling. The more you love me the more steadfastly you will go on. You won't give way and fail. That would be utter defeat. I did not train you for anything so ignoble as defeat. " Be thou faithful unto death ", is His word to you today. Stand by your Fellowship and Family, and forget yourself in serving others. That is the way of joy.

There is much I long to write, but I cannot. If I can, I will add to this later. But if not, then He Whose you are and Whom you serve will Himself say all to you that I would say if I could. O my darling, my darling, by God's grace stand strong. Let *nothing* weaken you. Be one on whom all can count never, never to give way. Take the strong words of your Lord and live upon them. Many specially comforting words are in John 14 and 15. Read these chapters often. I do, they are continually opening to me. Remember St Paul's, " I can do all things through Christ which strengtheneth me." " All things " means *all things*.

Think what it will be to meet at the end of the day in joy, not in shame. O, if He comes, think what it will mean to meet in the air and be for ever together with the Lord and with each other. What does it matter if today be difficult? We have Tomorrow. And remember it will never be too difficult, and none of them that trust in Him shall be desolate.

For May 1, 1942. (Especially for the older *Carunias*.) This is a private little story. I did not mean to tell it, but

I hear that some of you have the same temptation, and so I let it go with the hope that the words which helped me may help you too.

One night lately I was greatly tempted because I felt so helpless. In the last war I could go about among you, and when once Government warned me that there might be danger to you, I felt like a mother-bear whose cubs are threatened. I felt *strong* to fight for you. Now there is no strength at all. Of course we have far, far stronger and better help in our dear *Annachies* and *Sitties* than anything that I could do, but somehow I wanted to be with you. And thoughts piled up as they do at night. I seemed to see every corner of this garden of ours, this dear garden. What if——? And the burden was heavy. And then it was as if a voice said almost aloud, " *Leave it to Me, child, leave it to Me.*"

Near by there were two white lilies which a *Carunia* had given me; they had opened after the last thunderstorm. Perhaps it was they which gave me the last line.

> Leave it to Me, child, leave it to Me,
> Dearer thy garden to Me than to thee;
> Lift up thy heart, child, lift up thine eyes,
> Nought can defeat Me, nought can surprise.

> Leave it to Me, child, leave it to Me,
> Trust in the Wall of Fire, look up and see
> Stars in their courses shine through the night.
> Both are alike to Me—darkness and light.

> Leave it to Me, child, leave it to Me.
> Let slip the burden too heavy for thee;
> That which I will, My Hand shall perform,
> Fair are the lilies that weather the storm.

April 22, 1943. If ever you read this it will be because I am not here. And yet I think in a way I shall be here, for I think Hebrews 12. 1 means that those who go before are like a cloud round about those who are running the race; just as you all stand round in a ring and watch the *Anandas* running the races—how well I remember when I stood together with you in the field and we watched and laughed when they ran well.

Perhaps it will be so. If so I shall lovingly watch every one of you, and I shall be praying for you with far greater power than I can now, and I shall be loving you with a purer, stronger love than I can now.

I want you to remember that you are each one precious to your Mother. Those who have failed—I pray for them that they may not waste their one life, but come *now* to Him Who can renew them in truth.   Those who have never, never disappointed me—I think of them and thank my God for them, and pray that they may never yield, and may never tire of loving and forgiving and hoping.   Those who are beginning the mountain climb—I pray that they may go on steadfastly, living for others, never for themselves.   So, my precious ones, I pray for you all, for each one of you as if there were no other.   Never feel lost in a crowd.   It is not so.   Each one of you is precious.

I must not write more now.   There is more in my heart that I want to say to you.   But the chief thing is, your Mother loves you and will love you for ever.   And this: look up far beyond your Mother, your *Sitties*, your *Accals*, look up to Him Who gave us this deathless love for you. Learn to go direct to Him and draw from Him all you need. He will never fail you, *never*.

Finally, here are a few disjointed extracts from letters which the recipients will treasure until they are reunited with their mother.

I wonder what your biggest temptation is.   Is it to be suddenly angry?   That was mine when I was a little girl. I used to feel something like a fire suddenly burning up in my heart.   If you feel like that, ask the Lord Jesus to pour His cool, kind, gentle love into your heart instead.   Never go on being angry with anyone; be Jesus' little peacemaker.

Isn't it nice to be tired and perhaps hurt (as you are now) in doing our Lord's business, not our own?   I am always so very grateful that I fell into that hole when I was about His business, not my own pleasure.

I remember once after writing a very solemn prayer-song, it was as if I heard the Lord saying, " Don't be surprised when the time comes to live this out.   Think it not strange, count it all joy."

October, 1945.   For nine happy years of nights you had care of your Amma, and I shall never forget.   So often when there was pain, and you got very little sleep, your love helped me.   You read to me and sang to me so sweetly, that sometimes sleep came while you were singing.   I wonder how many times you sang, " The sands of time are sinking "? Well, darling, the sands of time have not yet run out.   I have not yet reached the last clause of John 17. 4.   So ask for help for me still, strength and courage, and peace and joy, so that this room may be a Room of Peace to all.

I am the God of the stars,
They do not lose their way,
Not one do I mislay,
Their times are in My Hand,
They move at My command.

I am the God of the stars,
Today as yesterday,
The God of thee and thine,
Less thine they are than Mine;
And shall Mine go astray?

I am the God of the stars,
Lift up thine eyes and see
As far as mortal may
Into Eternity;
And stay thy heart on Me.

CHAPTER XL

ONE of the books which Amma wrote after the accident was *Ploughed Under*, the story of Arulai. It was written when Arulai was busily engaged in work of all kinds.

> She has shared in every part of the work from the beginning [wrote Amma a little later] and knows everything from the inside. The *Annachies*, English and Indian, as well as the *Sitties* and *Accals*, found in her something they have never tried to define but on which they knew that they could count. To me no word so perfectly describes her as the great word *loyal*. Her faithful heart has never swerved from the most flawless loyalty.

Her purpose in writing the book, she says, was to show " the way of the Lover of souls with the soul that He calls to Himself, His way as He prepares it to serve unhindered by the flesh, and His way as He answers prayer, according to a thought of His own that is larger and richer than ours ". What was His thought for Arulai? For many years Amma was sure that He was preparing her to be the future leader on the women's side of the work.

Intellectually and spiritually there was no question concerning her fitness. Her Tamil was good. She read widely in English. She feasted on her Greek Testament, and on the Septuagint version of the Old Testament. " She was one who could go anywhere, do anything," wrote Amma in *Though the Mountains Shake* * concerning the unexpected opportunities that came to her when she accompanied Amma to Travancore as a girl of fifteen. But it was always so. In later years there was no one whom Amma could trust more fully to explain the D.F. traditions, the Pattern of the Fellowship, to both *Sitties* and *Accals*. She was a good judge of character. Newly arrived *Sitties* probably did not know how eagerly their words were noted, and how closely their ways were scrutinized. " I believe they are wanting the highest," she wrote to Amma

---

* *Though the Mountains Shake*, p. 75 (American edition).

concerning one such little group. She and Amma together acted as Tamil examiners for them. She was anxious for them to get " Tamil-Tamil " rather than " English-Tamil ", i.e. to think in the Tamil idiom.

Sureness about her fitness for leadership was given, says Amma, when, in addition to the " straightness, love, humility and devotion " that had characterized her so long, she had learned something of the Lord's compassion. At the private meeting of *Sitties* and *Accals* in God's Garden when Amma suggested Arulai as future leader, their unanimity was not based merely on their enthusiastic respect for Amma's judgment, for each of them was assured that God had given them Arulai to be Servant of all.

But she had never been very robust. Amma had nursed her through two nearly fatal illnesses, and an old weakness began to show itself again. From 1935 onwards there was some anxiety about her health, but in 1938 she was fairly active again, taking meetings and having personal talks with many who came to her. She led a sort of preparation class of about thirty girls who hoped to become Sisters of the Common Life. It went by the name of II Timothy 1. 7 (" God hath not given to us the spirit of fear; but of power and love and self-discipline "). But at the beginning of 1939 " all the work which she had so joyfully begun to do again, had to be dropped ", and before long she was confined to bed.

Then began a time of grief as poignant as any that Amma had known, except that there was no bitterness in it. They exchanged notes, as long as she was able to write, but they never met. It was felt that the strain would be too great for both of them. " They feel it would make it harder for her if I went to her," writes Amma in the margin of *Daily Light* for March 29th. It was almost more than she could bear. She had never dreamed of separation before one or other of them was called Home. But comfort came, and as always her first instinct was to share it.

> I want you to have the comfort that was given to me a few nights ago [she wrote to Frances Beath]. It was a night when all seemed too impossible to face. I went into my little side room and turned off the light lest any should see through the blind, and then at last drew back the blind (the curtain over the small window) and I looked out.

I saw a few stars through the trees. That was all.

Then as I sat there, wave upon wave came over me. I thought of so many of our beloved D.F.s, tired and getting near the end of the day's work, and others not very strong. How could the Family go on? I thought of the forces against it, some openly ill-wishers, some secretly so, and the one who would have stood like a rock through any storm and strengthened the hands of all, perhaps going from us, almost certainly going from us. How could we go on? And if we could not, or did not, what then? So much seemed to hang on so few. The line seemed a very thinly held line that night. And the grief and everything was just too much —till I looked again, looked up again, saw the stars. " I am the God of the stars "—it was like a word spoken aloud in my ear. It was more than that.

At last I went out, this time to the bed you gave me, and I lay there and saw the stars more distinctly as there were fewer trees between, and again and again the word came, " I am the God of the stars ". The little thing enclosed * came later in the night. It only says a little of what those great words meant to me, but you will follow the thought.

Ask for me one thing if you hear that my child has passed on—ask that I may not weaken, but strengthen those on whom the heaviest burden falls. Ask for selflessness, power to help, console, lift the edges of the burdens if I can't lift the whole. Ask for love that forgets all but others.

She was anxious that the doctors, who understood what Arulai's illness meant to her, should know too that she trusted them completely. So she wrote to Dr Christian Rogan:

Be at rest about Arulai. She is perhaps the most precious thing I have on earth, and yet, as I think of all you and others have done to save her, I feel nothing more could have been done. I have no sad thoughts about that, no " If only——". This is her Baptism Day (1901) and every hour of the day is vivid. She has been the very joy of my heart, my utterly loyal child, and she is in His Hands Who loves her more than I do. . . . Don't be sad. It is the Trust of the Unexplained.

The entries in *Daily Light* margin are, as usual, transparently honest. On April 2nd, " Arulai sent me her lilies. Almost too difficult a day—but we have Tomorrow." In her copy of Conybeare and Howson's *Paul's Epistles* she has put " Arulai " for " I " in II Timothy 4, verses 6 to 8, and pronouns and

---

* The verses facing the beginning of this chapter.

verbs are changed accordingly.   Verse 9 (" Do thy diligence
to come shortly unto me ") had been Robert Wilson's message
to her in 1900.   Now on April 21, 1939, she writes:

> For years I could not trust myself to read these words
> which my dear one cabled to me.   I could not go to him, and
> one reason was Arulai.   Will it not be so one day with the
> words that come before and are tonight full of my Arulai
> and the rending of parting?

Daily, as the end drew near, she wrote little messages for
Frances Beath to give to Arulai—as long as she was conscious
and able to understand them.

> Next time you have a chance to speak to Arulai, tell her
> that after I see His Face *the first face I shall want to see will be
> hers*, and for ever and for ever we shall be together then. . . .
> Tell her that my longing to be with her is like the water
> from the well of Bethlehem, and I have poured it out before
> the Lord.   He has told me that He will gather it up and
> give it to me another day. . . .   I am trusting the Love that
> is greater than even a mother's to carry her Home.   She
> remembers how once I carried her over the thorny way
> through the wood at Pannaivilai—it is like that.   She is
> held close in the everlasting Arms—close to the heart of God.

May 24th, 1939, was Arulai's Celestial Birthday.   " He bare
them and carried them " is one of the verses for that morning
in *Daily Light*.   Amma read it at 6 a.m. and heard the Lord
saying to her, " I am holding her fast."   Then she read the
Psalms for the day, and when at 1.30 word came that Arulai
was with Christ she wrote in *Daily Light* margin: " ' And
carried them '—carried by the angels into the courts of the
Lord's house—with Christ in the land of the living." (Psalm
116, verses 9, 19).

Then (as Neela recalls):

> She called all Arulai's friends to her room and hugged
> them.   Tears were streaming down, but she told them they
> were tears of joy, and she helped and comforted all who loved
> her.

Murray was in the Forest, and she wrote to him that same
day:

> On March 15, 1899, Arulai heard for the first time that
> there was a Living God.   In today's Psalm (116) the words
> " the land of the living " came to me with great comfort.

I am staying my heart on them today. Tell all the Family when you gather them together, as I know you will, that Arulai never once looked back. Test after test came, and at the last the longest drawn out and hardest (that we could not be together) proved her to the uttermost. Her last note to me says, "What will Tomorrow be?" and her last message was "Alleluia". Tell the *Accals* and young girls that from the first it was upon Christ and His work, *not* the joys of being together or any earthly joy, that her heart was fixed. (So many are good and helpful if they can be with those they specially love—otherwise not.) What she was they know, only they don't know what it sometimes cost her to hold to that life. She was my first-born (in India) and I know. Tell them I want them to ponder that side of her life, steadfastly lived all through these forty years. O that some may follow in her train.

When one of Murray's twins heard of Arulai's Home-going he added a petition to his usual evening prayers, "And please will You give my love to Arulai *Accal*, if You have time?" The thought of our Lord giving a message to anyone who is already with Him is not based on any Divine revelation, but it is not forbidden, surely, to wonder whether He might do so. When Amma saw the first copy of her little book *If*, which Arulai had translated into Tamil, she wrote to Godfrey:

It is very solemn to hold her last bit of work in my hands. We had such plans to write together something about the Love of the Lord—a sort of Tamil *Loveliness of Christ*. That was not to be, but you have fulfilled her longing in doing this. I have been asking Him to tell her.

At that time there was no other Indian *Accal* who could take Arulai's place as the future leader on the women's side. There had been "a peculiar delight in looking forward to Indian leadership", but Arulai's death meant that this happy consummation must be delayed for a time, and meanwhile all were happy as they saw the grace of God in Dr May Powell, as well as in Murray and Godfrey Webb-Peploe.

No one who has read thus far, and has therefore noted Amma's conviction that she had received nothing less than supernatural guidance concerning the future leaders of the work, could fail to appreciate the poignancy of her disappointment when in February, 1947, it became necessary for Murray Webb-Peploe to return to England for family reasons. To her and to the whole Family it was a shattering blow, and Murray himself hoped against hope that it need not be. Yet it seemed that no arrangement could be made which would obviate the necessity.

Two days before Murray left (his wife and the twins were already in England), Amma wrote a letter to the whole Fellowship. She began with a quotation from " my warrior comrade, Mary Hatch ":

A voice spoke in my soul, "Dohnavur is built upon GOD." After that, what could I do but look up to our Lord and say, " Thou remainest ", saying it not as a sigh but as a triumph song? If we appear to have suffered a defeat and Satan says, " You see, you have had to fall back after all ", our reply is, " *Then we fall back upon God.*"

Amma's letter was addressed to " those to whom February 4 will bring pain of heart ".

In past days, when sorrow and loss were allowed to come to us, the first effect upon us was a firmer welding together, as in a new way we experienced the comforts of our God. I believe it will be so in this sorrow and loss.

For Murray *Annachie's* having to leave us, even for a time, is that. No one is irreplaceable, so some say. That is a shallow lie. Twenty years of knowledge of the East, all that is meant by fatherhood, cannot be passed on, as one might pass on a book or a garment. Apart from that, apart from what this parting means to the Parama Suha Salai, apart from everything personal, there is this: the sky is cloudy over India now. To Murray *Annachie* the entrance has been given to the hearts of men of all political colours. We are not asked to pretend that we lose nothing in parting from such a one. . . .

During this time of spiritual strain may He keep us from spiritual defeat. I pray that instead of that we may be led on into spiritual triumph. To help towards that, will you read words written long ago out of the midst of battle and suffering. II Corinthians 4. 8–11 and 16–18 are vital to us now. Notice the *while* of verse 18. It is only *while* we look not at the things which are seen but at the things which are not seen, that the things which are seen can work for us a far more exceeding and eternal weight of glory.

And let us use this whole matter as an occasion for proving afresh the certainty of the promises, the certainty of the Presence of our Lord Jesus Christ, the true Founder of this work, and its true Unseen Leader.

Forty-six years ago Walker Iyer told me that " forsake ",
in Hebrews 13. 5 is in the Greek a compound of three words—
" leave behind in ".   It conveys the idea of leaving comrades
exposed to peril in the conflict, or forsaking them in some
crisis of danger.   And Westcott translates the verse, " *I will
in no wise desert you or leave you alone in the field of contest, or in
a position of suffering.   I will in no wise let go—loose hold—my
sustaining grasp.* "

This promise cannot fail.   Come now, let us stand upon
it and rejoice in it.   Let us show to all who observe us that
those words are for ever true: Christ our Lord is with us.
He Who reigned from the Tree is our Leader.   The shout
of a King is among us.   Alleluia.

I see nothing in Amma's life more wonderful than her
courageous reaction to what she herself calls the " crashing disappointments " of the closing years.   Arulai was gone, who
was closest to her in love, and Murray, whom she regarded as
the spiritual father of the Family, and she herself was in her
eightieth year.   Yet, just as the first thought of the Family was,
" What will this mean to Amma? ", so her first thought was,
" How can I comfort the Family? " or, rather, " How can I
sound a trumpet call, that we may close our ranks and follow
Him Who goeth before? "

Well, at least there was Godfrey, whom Amma called her
Benediction.   She thought of the burden that he had borne
ever since her accident, " never shrinking, never giving way ".
" You know what I feel about being called leader," she had
written in 1937.   " I read that the Chief of a Border Tribe
died the other day, and he was 105.   They still called him
Chief, but he wasn't really.   And I'm not—it's you and Murray
and May who are bearing the burdens now."

She longed to lighten Godfrey's burden, and rejoiced that
John Risk could actually do so, to some extent—though he was
on furlough in 1947.   " It is always you, now, that the heaviest
things will come upon," she wrote once to Godfrey, " and I
can do nothing about it."   Then she opened her Bible at
Numbers 7, and the first word that caught her eye was in
verse 6, " Moses took the wagons and the oxen, and gave them
unto the Levites. . . . But unto the sons of Kohath he gave
none: *because the service of the sanctuary belonging unto them was that
they should bear upon their shoulders.* "   " So, dear son of Kohath ",
she concludes, " that's why you have no oxen and no wagon! "

But Murray's departure probably meant more to Godfrey than anyone could understand. They had been a team, each with his own strong, vital contribution to the spiritual life of the Family. Murray's initiative and Godfrey's steadiness were both of immense value, but it was a value which was more than doubled when they worked together. Now it was necessary for Godfrey to take over some of Murray's responsibilities, and the load was too heavy. Thus in April, 1948, Amma writes:

> Godfrey is under orders to rest for a while. Since Murray had to leave us, he has done much to hold the men's side of the hospital together. He has also had continual care for the Dohnavur village [a spiritual legacy from Walker!], and there has been all that Shepherd-work means for the Family.

In June came Amma's second accident. It was less possible to consult her, and the problems of the Family and, still more, of the Fellowship, were even more pressing than usual. The battle was fierce, and Godfrey fought on, but with increasing physical disability. Just before Christmas he became seriously unwell with thrombosis of the veins in his right leg. In January, 1949, there was some improvement, and plans were made for convalescence, perhaps in England. January 9th was the twenty-fourth anniversary of his first arrival in Dohnavur, and in a note to Amma he speaks of being twenty-four years old!

> I thank God for that day, and for all the twenty-four years of God's loving-kindness and long patience to one so wholly unworthy.

The Lord's Return was much in his thoughts.

> I am asking the Lord to use this illness to help me pray more. For me it is but " a day ", for you it is always, and yet not always, for joy cometh in the morning, and that morning may be very near when our Beloved One will come.

It was the last of his notes to Amma. Almost without warning he was taken seriously ill again on the evening of February 19th, and in a few minutes he was with Christ. The Perfect Nurse brought the news to Amma immediately. " What is it? " she asked. " What is wrong? "—for her face showed that something serious had happened. " There is

nothing wrong ", said Mary Mills. " God has trusted us with
a great trust. Godfrey is in heaven."

That was the keynote of Amma's message to the Family,
written that same evening. " Our God trusts us to trust
Him. . . . Let us not disappoint God. Let us rise to this
great trust."

Almost her first thought was to let John Risk know that she
expected him to take Godfrey's place. She gave him the word,
" As I was with Moses, so I will be with thee." " He had
been Godfrey's Joshua for many years ", she wrote, " and I
knew the whole Fellowship would be one in accepting him as
leader now."

The next day she wrote a further letter of encouragement to
the Family:

> Perhaps we shall never again have such a chance to glorify
> our God as we have now. Don't let us lose this chance to
> show His great enemy, and all the unseen watchers, that we
> do indeed trust our Father, and that nothing, not even this
> sore parting, can for one moment shake our confidence in
> Him.
>
> He has said, " All things work together for good ". This
> is one of the " all things ". He has said, " Be strong and of
> a good courage. Only be thou strong and very courageous ".
> Now is the time, by His mighty grace, to be strong and very
> courageous.
>
> Tears are not sin. Jesus wept. But to go on lamenting
> would be sin. It would be as though we doubted the love
> of our most tender Father. To wonder why this has been
> allowed to happen would be to dishonour Him. I found
> myself doing this very thing. " Oh, why am I left—I who
> am useless to you all—and he, who could do so much for
> you, taken? " Suddenly I knew that even to think such a
> thought for a moment, was sin. Thank God for the cleansing
> Blood. But do not let us grieve His love by wondering why.
> Faith *never* wonders why. Faith trusts. . . .
>
> My children, my heart goes out to you all. Let us help
> one another. Let us look up and see our *Annachie* rejoicing
> in the presence of his Lord, and with our own dear unseen
> family too, and be very glad with him.

Enoch had been one of Amma's names for him, though she
had said, half jestingly, that she hoped he would not be translated too soon. Truly he walked with God. " Though he
was so gentle and holy an Enoch ", she wrote a few months

later, " he was a rock of crystal, absolutely resolute when resoluteness was required. He was a tender father to our whole family of children and growing up men and women."

She could not write of Godfrey without mentioning Murray.

I cannot tell what these two brothers have been to this Fellowship and Family; and to very many, men and women, scattered about South India, their names are known and loved. I used to say to the Lord, " Lord, if Thou dost give these brothers to be leaders of the Fellowship, it does not matter what happens to me. Let me be broken if only they may be strong and fit." They have both gone, and I am left quite broken, but content, for I know that we are safe in the Hand of the mighty and loving One to Whom this Fellowship belongs.

She could not know it, but in her climb she had already entered the last defile before the summit.

THE LAST DEFILE

Make us Thy mountaineers;
We would not linger on the lower slope,
Fill us afresh with hope, O God of Hope,
That undefeated we may climb the hill
As seeing Him Who is invisible.

Let us die climbing. When this little while
Lies far behind us, and the last defile
Is all alight, and in that light we see
Our Leader and our Lord, what will it be?

CHAPTER XLI

THE LAST DEFILE

WHEN Amma fell in the Room of Peace on the evening of June 23rd, 1948, she entered the last defile of the spiritual climb, but it was nearly two years and eight months before she emerged at the Summit. Over and over again the Perfect Nurse, and others who cared for her with unfailing tenderness and devotion, thought that she was almost There, and were ready to rejoice in her joy, but then the mists slowly washed again over " the half-glimpsèd turrets " of the heavenly City. Movement of any sort was almost impossible, the pain which had been intermittent became almost continuous, and drugs gradually lost their power to relieve it.

Yet it would give a wrong impression to suggest that they were months of weary monotony or of complete inactivity. Towards the end of 1948, and in 1949, she still wrote occasional letters with her own hand and, as we have seen, she gave some time to the completion of *This One Thing*. To the friend who had submitted a manuscript to her for suggestion and criticism she wrote on December 31, 1948, a letter which throws light on other matters as well as her physical weakness:

> If you could see me almost flat, with the paper tilted against a blotter standing on one foot, so to speak, you would wonder that I had the temerity to write at all. . . . Year by year since 1935, when it seemed clear that recovery from the repercussions of the " accident " in 1931, was unlikely, I have asked that plans for the future, made clear to us early in 1931, might be implemented. We have splendid leaders in our beloved May Powell and Godfrey Webb-Peploe. I asked to be allowed to drop out and that they might be elected in the one " Kingdom Business " meeting held in the year. But up till now all I could say has been, as the Tamils put it, moonlight upon rock. And so now that I am still deep in everything and power to think has come again, there must be " thinks " together with one and another of this dear family. Just now we are facing the unkindest thing, and the most dangerous spiritually, that the devil could contrive for us, and much prayer and thought must be

spent upon it. I came out of the five months' exile, when pain held sway day and night, and Love held every burden from me, to meet an entirely unexpected situation. The Lord lead us through—the least slip would be used to His dishonour.

Perhaps some attempt should be made to explain the position concerning leadership responsibilities a little more fully. As long ago as 1928, more than three years before the first accident, Amma had written to Godfrey, " When I committed the D.F. matters to you last year they were off me altogether. I had prayed and pondered over them for hours before that day—after that I never gave them a thought. I think it is always like that when one wholly trusts." Thus there were at least some matters, probably of a more or less routine character, that had been handed over to Godfrey very soon after his arrival. Once when he wrote apologizing for seeming to " turn down " some decision of Amma's, she replied in the strongest terms, assuring him that she fully accepted what he had done, that, if there had been a muddle, it was her fault and not his, and that nothing could ever come between them.

Nothing ever did. Yet while both the Fellowship and the Family accepted the plan of January, 1931, whereby Murray and Godfrey and May Powell were to be the leaders of the future, and while, after October of the same year, these three were sometimes compelled by circumstances to act without previous consultation with Amma, yet most questions of importance were still brought to her, and neither the Fellowship nor the Family generally would have been content if it had not been so.

Was the arrangement a fair one, either to the Fellowship or to Amma? Taking the latter point first, it would seem that, if general agreement could have been reached on a point that touched the whole Family so nearly, it would certainly have been kinder to Amma to release her from the responsibility of leadership some years earlier. She would still have been the Mother of the Family, the human centre of its life, and perhaps when her health permitted she could have done more " mothering " if others were bearing the burden of leadership. She was utterly sincere in desiring this step to be taken. " Don't be afraid of leadership ", she wrote to Godfrey in 1947. " ' For that the leaders took the lead . . . bless ye the Lord '

(Judges 5. 2 R.V.).   Till you let me resign, which I hope you
are prepared to do next year, the responsibility of saying
definitely that such and such things can't be, is, I suppose,
mine.   But where the men are concerned I have always left
it to you as more seemly."

But would such an arrangement have been practicable?
It was not as if Amma could ever have moved elsewhere, even
to some place near by.   The very idea is inconceivable, and
any analogy with other organizations breaks down.   The
founder of a work may withdraw from it, and leave his successor
in charge.   But Amma was not merely the founder of the
Dohnavur work—she was the mother of a family.   Again, the
head of a Mission may leave it, and return home.   But
Dohnavur, and nowhere else, was " home " to Amma, and
no one ever dreamed of suggesting that she return to England.

From the point of view of the Fellowship, it is clear that
difficulties did arise, difficulties which were almost inherent in
the situation.   Sometimes, as we have said, Amma was too ill
even to hear that problems existed, let alone to advise concerning their solution.   Moreover, even when she was suffering
less intensely, there was a natural tendency to spare her.
" Who is offended, and I burn not? "   Knowing how she
" burned " when any member of the Family was " offended ",
the leaders sometimes hesitated to keep her fully informed, lest
the cost to her might be too great.   Occasionally, when they
reported to the Family that Amma had decided this or that,
there was a little questioning in the minds of some.   " Is that
really Amma's decision?   Can she know all the facts? "   It
was not so much that they doubted the veracity of the statements made, as that they wondered if she would have decided
differently if they could have put the case as they saw it.

On the other hand, if Godfrey had lived, and if he had been
willing to take Amma's place, the Family would have rallied
round him.   On the night of his death very few in the Compound could sleep.   No one was more beloved except Amma
herself.   The smaller girls would flock to his room to play
with him as readily as the boys.   " Before his translation he
had this testimony, that he pleased God."   He could honestly
have said of the Dohnavur Family what Paul said of the
church at Thessalonica : " It is within your knowledge that
we treated every one of you as a father treats his children,

encouraging you, comforting you, imploring you to lead a life worthy of the God Who now invites you to the glory of His Kingdom." *

Shortly before Godfrey's death Amma had been allowed to take a further step towards devolution of responsibility by appointing him as co-leader. But Godfrey was gone, and while John Risk could, and did, succeed him as co-leader, the time was not ripe for him or anyone else to succeed Amma, even though all agreed that the Hand of God was upon him and upon May Powell as leaders, with Amma increasingly in the background.

Thus, from the spiritual point of view, God had not indicated anyone, either Indian or European, who could even be considered as His choice for Amma's successor. Even on a lower plane, perhaps there could be no successor. Meanwhile from the administrative point of view it was a time when important changes were essential. If there was no easy, ready-made solution to the problem of leadership, no one person to whom the whole Family could look, might not God be indicating that the burden should be shared by a compact group, and, if so, might there not be one or two amongst the Indian members of the Fellowship whom He had been training for just such a time as this?

This book is not intended to be a history of the Dohnavur work, but it is important in a life of Amma to note that she heartily approved the formation of a Leadership Group,† consisting of John Risk and May Powell as leaders, and two or three others whose appointments might or might not be permanent. From the inception of this change of method in 1950 Mimosa's eldest son, Rajappan, was included in the Group, and at the moment of writing Ponnammal's daughter, Purripu, is also a member.

This is a transition period. The composition of the Group and its duties are open to revision in the light of—experience? Yes, but if the Pattern given to Amma is to be retained, then there must be a Shewing, a revelation of the will of the Unseen Leader, concerning any proposed changes.

---

* I. Thessalonians 2. 11, 12 (Knox's translation).

† As early as 1931, it will be remembered (p. 282), she had suggested that her responsibilities should devolve upon three members of the Fellowship, and all had agreed that God seemed to be preparing a small group, rather than one individual, for future leadership.

Opportunism is a characteristic of the enemy of souls, both in strategy and tactics. When Arulai, Murray, Godfrey and finally Amma were removed, the work would have been wrecked if the leaders had not maintained communication with their heavenly base. This book is being written at a time of fighting, when war bulletins are frequently presented to the Fellowship prayer meeting, but the Lord of hosts is " for a crown of glory, and a diadem of beauty " to His hard-pressed servants here, " for a spirit of judgment " to those who sit in judgment, " and for strength to them that turn the battle to the gate ".

Dust of Gold for March, 1949, records the beginnings of the most important single change in the training of the Family.

> We have begun to send some of our boys and girls to outside schools in order that they may get the school leaving certificate that is now necessary for almost any kind of training that has Government recognition. We hope in this way to gain Government-certificated teachers for our own schools so that we may, if possible, continue to run them in the way we believe the Lord has shown us.

The change was the outcome of Indian independence and the consequent development of a new system of education. It would be futile to discuss whether or not it would have been wise to make the change earlier, and particularly to ask what Amma would have done if she had been ten or twenty years younger, but certainly the Lord will honour the steadfastness of some of the older Indian workers who have sacrificed their hope of higher education outside in order to give themselves to the spiritual and mental nurture of the children of the Family.

In any case Amma, who preserved to the end the flexibility of mind which had always characterized her, was in full agreement with the new plans. It was she who gave the name of " Gideons " to the boys who attended the Middle School in Dohnavur village, preparatory to going further afield for High School education. She knew well that they would need the courage and faith of Gideon if they were not to lower their standards. The girls were called " Timothys "—a name which may sound less suitable, but Amma's word for them was: " Endure hardness, as a good soldier of Jesus Christ " (II Timothy 2. 3.)

As strength permitted she persevered in prayer, not only for the Family but for friends all round the world, especially in China, where Christians were facing the impact of a triumphant Communism. In April, 1949, she wrote to the Fellowship meeting:

This afternoon a new understanding was given to me of the tender patience of our Lord Jesus. He doesn't mind repeating things over and over again to us. We all know how helpful various positions in prayer can be. Sometimes to stand in silence before Him, our Lord and Master, brings a marvellous sense of His Presence. Sometimes to walk up and down listening to Him, and speaking with Him, helps most. (Where the terrace is now in my garden, I formerly had a path made, where I could walk with Him in the early mornings unregarded.) David sat before the Lord. I suppose from earliest ages people knelt. One does not know how much these things help, till one cannot stand, or sit, or walk, or kneel.

A few days ago I was feeling the difficulty of praying lying flat, and also hindered in other ways, when suddenly, for the first time, I seemed to see our Lord Jesus as He was for a few immeasurable minutes, not upright, but laid flat on His Cross.

I need not tell you the thoughts that came then.

But today as you were singing the sea prayer, " Lord Jesus, Intercessor ", the almost despairing feeling, of inability to pray, returned, just as if that memory of our Lord on His Cross had never come at all. And then, instead of a rebuke for forgetting what had been shown that day, *it was shown over again.*

I tell you this because some of you may find yourselves in hard ways. *Always your Lord has been before you.* Always He will come with a most heavenly understanding of what your heart most needs. And even if He has come in the same way before, He will not reproach you for forgetting. He will comfort you again, for He gives comfort as He gives wisdom, and upbraideth not. O truly, truly He is a dear Lord.

> Our love is like a little pool,
> Thy love is like the sea,
> O Beautiful, O Wonderful,
> How noble Love can be.

" And what shall I more say? " How can one give a true picture of this many-sided personality—of Amma lying on the ground after the first accident and, as she waited for help, urging the two *Sitties* who were with her to *praise* since it was she who had fallen and not May Parker, who was to occupy

that outpost for the Lord; of Amma lying helpless on the floor
of the Room of Peace after the second accident, telling Neela,
who rushed to her side, " Don't tell anyone—I shall be all
right in the morning "; of Amma who, if her nurses showed
any signs of impatience, told them that she was quite sure it
was her fault; of Amma, enquiring who was on the veranda,
and hearing that it was the sweeper woman, calling her in and
(to her amazement) thanking her—" How much you do for us
all. You are a King's daughter "—of Amma who was
reverenced by the whole countryside, whose coolies, as they
carried her chair up to the Forest, said quite seriously, " If you
decided to live in a cave in the mountains, we would come and
worship you "; of Amma, who influenced many I.C.S. men
and other non-missionaries, so that they never forgot the half
hour spent in her room? " She loved much ", and she is
greatly loved.

The hymn " In heavenly love abiding ", sent her by Bishop
Pakenham Walsh in September, 1949 (" I felt impelled to
copy it and send it to you who are living it out ") was kept
beside her during the last days, and she rejoiced especially in
the last verse:

> Green pastures are before me
>   Which yet I have not seen,
> Bright skies will soon be o'er me
>   Where the dark clouds have been.
> My hope I cannot measure,
>   My path to life is free,
> My Saviour has my treasure,
>   And He will walk with me.

Dr Nancy Robbins heard her, when in pain, voicing the fear
that had been in her mind even before 1931, that she might
linger on as a burden to others and to herself, having altogether
ceased to be a " soldier ". The doctor " happened " to come
upon four words in the Revised Version of Revelation 2. 9, 10:
" I know. . . . Fear not ". Amma had them printed on
wood and put up in her room with a light over them, so that
she could read them at night, and she dictated these verses a
few months before the end:

> *I know.* The words contain
> Unfathomable comfort for our pain.
> How they can hold such depths I do not know—
> I only know that it is so.

Fear not. The words have power
To give the Thing they name, for in an hour
Of utter weariness the soul, aware
Of One beside her bed
Is comforted.
O Lord most dear,
I thank Thee, and I worship—Thou art here.

To two friends whose photos were always beside her, who had been compelled to leave their field through overstrain, she wrote in August, 1950:

When I am in pain or too tired to find words, I look at a picture of the Matterhorn and the lake at its foot, and I let it pray for me for you.   Let the strength of the mountains be theirs, the purity of the snows, the beauty of the blue water, the steadfastness of the rocks, the loveliness of the flowers on the banks and, above all, the joy of the little stream that flows forth to bless others.

In December, 1950, the Perfect Nurse wrote: " Our Amma is going through a very difficult bit of the way.   She is definitely losing ground on this side, and the longing grows ever more for the day of Deliverance."   Her 83rd birthday came and went. Christmas passed, and the Meetings of Vision—evangelistic gatherings for men and women who gather by invitation, because some member of the Fellowship has been in touch with them, and hopes that they will respond to the Gospel.   But after the first week of January, 1951, she began to sleep much more, and when she reached the fifty-ninth anniversary of her call to the Mission field (on January 13th, 1892) it was clear that at last her feet had almost reached the Summit.

The Family were allowed to come quietly into the Room of Peace.   There was absolute stillness.   The pain had ceased, and the face which they loved best in all the world was calm and undisturbed.   Even the birds in the aviary seemed to fall silent during those days.   By turns, in fairly large groups, the Family stood and watched her, and a few who had known her longest were allowed to stay almost continuously beside her.

Before she sank into unconsciousness, it had seemed as if she were waiting for someone.   Was it one of those over whose going she had never ceased to grieve?   I think there was a great desire in the hearts of the children that she would waken and give them a last message, or tell them how the music was pealing from within the City Gates.   But her own prayer

had been that there would be " no rending goodbyes, no
distress to anyone ". " I shall take thee in thy sleep ", was
the word that she thought the Lord had spoken to her in
October, 1938. And so it was. Early in the morning of
January 18th the last step was taken, and she passed through
the Gates into the City. I do not suppose that she read *Daily
Light* for that evening, but many others did. " It is written,
Eye hath not seen, nor ear heard, neither hath entered into the
heart of man, the things which God hath prepared for them
that love Him ", and the selection ends with the comfortable
words of I Thessalonians 4. 13–17. When the Lord Himself
descends from heaven, Amma will rise, and all the members of
the Family who are " in Christ " will be caught up together
with her to meet Him in the air. She and they will be for
ever with the Lord.

By her wish the bells in the House of Prayer played the music
of one of her songs as soon as it was known that she was no
longer here, but There.

> One thing have I desired, my God, of Thee,
> That will I seek, Thine house be home to me.
>
> I would not breathe an alien, other air,
> I would be with Thee, O Thou fairest Fair.
>
> For I would see the beauty of my Lord,
> And hear Him speak, Who is my heart's Adored.
>
> O Love of loves, and can such wonder dwell
> In Thy great Name of names, Immanuel?
>
> Thou with Thy child, Thy child at home with Thee,
> O Lord my God, I love, I worship Thee.

" Now learn to live your songs ", was the word which the
Lord gave her half way through the Keeping of the Charge.
The aspiration of this song was now fulfilled—" Thou with Thy
child, Thy child at home with Thee ". She had sought to
lead her Family into the joy of worship. If she could send us
a message, would she not tell us that we are nearest heaven
when we respond to the invitation, " O come, let us adore
Him, Christ the Lord "?

Barbara Osman describes the day that followed, marked by
" beauty and order ".

She lay for a time in her room, and sweetness and peace shone from her face. By the time everyone had been in, and passed out, her bed was completely covered with the flowers her children had brought.

Later, at midday, she was carried to the Dohnavur church so that the people whom she loved, and who loved her, should see her face once more. Our boys and men lined up to make a bodyguard, and our older servants, with Per (of the book, *Raj, Brigand Chief*) were her bearers (that had been her own request). As the procession moved away the boys sang a Tamil hymn chosen by one of the elders. ("Let us sing that hymn about reaching heaven", he said to John, "for that was the song she taught us to sing, raising her hand and pointing—so!"—and up went his hand in a gesture that vividly recalled her.)

In the church the boys continued to sing as, for about an hour and a half, the people streamed in and out. Just as it was time for the service to begin, Bishop Selwyn (one of Amma's oldest friends in India) arrived with the Pastor, and he led the service, with others taking part.

Two men, one a resident in Dohnavur, the other the catechist from Village of Lovingkindness, spoke of Amma, giving glory to God for her and for the work He gave her to do. Each older one in the congregation received a text-card on which were printed verses telling of eternal life and of the way of salvation. These had been prepared several years before by Godfrey Webb-Peploe, when it seemed that Amma might not be with us much longer. (How little he thought that he would go ahead of her!) It was estimated that about twelve to fifteen hundred of these cards were distributed.

As the chimes in the tower rang out the tune of "Ten thousand times ten thousand", Amma was carried to the House of Prayer and our own service was held there an hour later. The House of Prayer was filled with our men and women, school boys and girls, together with representatives from the servants and work-people, and friends from the village. The "Widow of the Jewels" was there, finding it hard not to sob aloud. Neela, who has been with Amma all through these long years, was standing erect as we joined in singing, "Alleluia! The strife is o'er, the battle won".

John read some verses—Matthew 25. 21, II Timothy 4. 6–8, and Philippians 1. 19–21—then, after thanksgiving and prayer, we moved slowly to God's Garden, singing all the time. It was a very long stream of people, mostly clad in white, with children among them, waving ferns instead of palms as a sign of victory.

By the grave side Devabakti read I Corinthians 15. 50–58 in a gloriously clear and steady voice, though his eyes were full of tears. When Amma had been laid to rest, the boys led the way round the Garden, which we encircled, coming back to the huge old tamarind tree at the entrance, and pausing there for the end of the service.

It was Tara who led the unaccompanied singing, helped by a younger sister. Neither of them faltered. God's grace was seen in all those who are women now (some of them greyhaired)—Chellalu, Lola, and Leela, Preena, Suseela, Rukma, and too many more to mention.

At seven o'clock in the evening we gathered once more in the House of Prayer to sing of the Heavenly Country, where many of our family are now, safe at Home for ever.

These were the things that were seen, but no one saw the " horses and chariots, which were come down from above to accompany her to the City Gate. . . . So her children and friends returned to their place, for they that waited for [Amma] had carried her out of their sight." In her copy of *Pilgrim's Progress* Amma had marked these words concerning Christiana. The extract goes on, " At her departure her children wept. *But* Mr Great-heart and Mr Valiant played upon the well-tuned cymbal and harp for joy." Amma had characteristically underlined the word " But ".

There are no headstones to mark the graves in God's Garden. But Amma's grave is distinguished by a beautiful stone bird-bath erected beside it. If Amma knows about it, it is a memorial that she would approve, for the birds often reminded her of God's love. Her Family often sing her song:

> Lord of the brooding blue,
> Of pleasant summer skies,
> Lord of each little bird that through
> The clear air flies,
> 'Tis wonderful to me
> That I am loved by Thee.

It is they, her children, who will be her true memorial if the glow of God's great love shines through their whole being as it shone through hers.

" *He mounts me upon high places, that I may conquer by His song.*"
(Habakkuk 3. 19 LXX.)

We see not yet all things put under Thee,
And yet we see the glory that shall be,
We see Thee crownèd in Thy majesty,
    Alleluia, Alleluia.

We see the shadows gathering for flight,
Glory of dawn dispel the brooding night,
Triumphant march of the all-conquering light,
    Alleluia, Alleluia.

Therefore we conquer, therefore we are strong,
Though Thy feet tarry and the night be long,
For lifted up we conquer by Thy song,
    Alleluia, Alleluia.

CHAPTER XLII

I was reading the 60th chapter of Isaiah, which in my Bible is headed, " The light and glory of Zion ", and praying almost before I knew it that God would do for Dohnavur what He has promised to do for Zion. " His glory shall be seen upon thee " (verse 2). Is not that what Amma most desired? " Thou shalt call thy walls Salvation, and thy gates Praise " (verse 18). These are the Tamil words above the moon gate as one enters the Compound from Dohnavur village—or, rather, Salvation as you enter, and Praise as you leave. Well, Dohnavur is a place where " the Lord hath made known His salvation ", and where " the garment of praise " is regulation wear for the whole Family all the year round.

But when I read in the same verse, " Violence shall no more be heard in thy land, wasting nor destruction within thy borders ", and thought of little children who, in spite of legislative enactments, are still being sold to a life of shame, boys and girls in an environment so far from pure, so unlike that of Zion,* I knew that this is not a description of " things as they are " in this land, or, indeed, in any other part of a world that still awaits redemption from the curse of sin.

Yet I paused to pray over the latter part of verse 21. " The branch of My planting, the work of My Hands." Here, at least, is solid fact. All that blossoms and bears fruit here is of God's planting, and the work was established by no other Hands but His. This is always the " Ground of our beseeching ", that Dohnavur is the work of His Hands. And the last clause of the verse is a clear expression of His purpose. " Why did You begin this work at Dohnavur? " Some of the angel-guard whom He has appointed to protect it may well have asked Him the question; and His reply is very simple, " That I may be glorified."

I smiled as I read verse 22, the last verse of the chapter:

* A baby girl, rescued from danger, was brought to Dohnavur as this chapter was being written.

" A little one shall become a thousand ", for I had asked for a few figures concerning Dohnavur today, and knew that the Family now numbers nearly a thousand. The " little one " who fled from the temple precincts to the shelter of Amma's arms in 1901 has in fifty years become almost a thousand. This includes about a hundred and twenty older boys and girls who are in training as teachers or nurses, or studying in a number of Christian schools. There is a small number engaged in Christian work in other parts of India, and many more scattered in scores of places—young men who have joined the navy or found other work, girls who have married Indian Christians outside. They are not forgotten, and of course their inclusion would bring the figure very much higher. Or, supposing a census were taken on Christmas Day, as it was in the year that a Child was born in Bethlehem of Judaea, the thousand figure would be far overpassed, for there would be all the patients in the Place of Heavenly Healing and their relatives, all the servants, and converts and enquirers who are here for instruction.

Do you say, " What hath God wrought ! " ? All of us here in Dohnavur would echo that word, which (strangely enough) God put into the mouth of Balaam. They are still saying among the heathen around Dohnavur, " The Lord hath done great things for them ". It is true—a little one has become a thousand. But the words of the children's hymn rebuke any slightest sense of complacency :

> But *thousands and thousands* who wander and fall
> Never heard of that heavenly Home.

Thank God for a beginning made. Thank God for hundreds of little ones safe in the " heavenly Home ", and for the opportunity of feeding, sheltering, training, Christ's lambs under the direction of the Shepherd Who died for them, and will let no man pluck them out of His Hand.

But if Amma's heart was scorched after forty years by the re-reading of her own words in *Things as They Are*, if Amma was comforted in measure (but only in measure) as she thought of hundreds of children in the House of Prayer, and of the loving service of the Place of Heavenly Healing, I pray that God's " terrible and fiery Finger " may " shrivel the false-hood " or, if not falsehood, the complacency from Christians who, rejoicing in His working at Dohnavur, are tempted to forget the immensity of the unmet need, the danger of millions without God and without hope.

And if this book drives them to pray for the lost, and if in this connection it seems that the proportions in our Lord's parable are reversed—that only one sheep is in the fold, and ninety and nine are " out on the hills away "—I trust that they will also be made aware of the need of prayer for Dohnavur itself, along the lines of Amma's great desire that the miracle which could not happen in the natural world may be accomplished here, and that the " lambs " who have been rescued may be trained to become " under-shepherds ", who will seek the lost, and so, in part at least, provide the answer to the prayer for millions unreached.

" That I may be glorified ". Perhaps no one—not even Amma herself—has seen to its fullest extent the purpose which God had in view when He established the work at Dohnavur. What does He mean to do through these hundreds of boys and girls, and men and women? Those who train them must have " long patience ", never for a moment neglecting the seemingly humdrum tasks involved in " raising " a Family. Like Amma, they must " pour out love all the time ", yet be ready " to catch the directing word of the Lord, however softly spoken ", the word, perhaps, that will show with sudden clearness the objective for which the Family is being trained and disciplined, the share which it is to take in making known " the manifold wisdom of God, according to the eternal purpose which He purposed in Christ Jesus our Lord ".

Meanwhile there are many in Dohnavur who have turned over from the promises of Isaiah 60 to the prayers of Isaiah 64: " Oh that Thou wouldest rend the heavens and come down . . . as when the melting fire burneth ". That was a word constantly on Amma's lips. They are coming before the Lord with the humble confession of verse 6: " We are all as an unclean thing ". They are stirring up themselves to take hold of God (verse 7), and praying that the friends of Dohnavur throughout the world will thus bestir themselves too.

But they come also with the plea of verse 8: " We are all the work of Thy Hand ", for in spite of acknowledged failure they know without a shadow of a doubt that this is the work of His Hands. " Through your prayer "—you who read this book—

" and through the supply of the Spirit of Jesus Christ ", they believe that He will be glorified, and so, literally at the end of nearly every service and meeting, and in spirit throughout every hour of every day, they join in the angelic doxology: " Amen. Blessing and glory and wisdom and thanksgiving and honour and power and might be unto our God for ever and ever."

LIST OF AMY CARMICHAEL'S PUBLISHED WORKS

Available titles published by **SPCK** are listed on page 392

INDEX OF AMMA'S VERSES

INDEX

THE DOHNAVUR FELLOWSHIP

The work in Dohnavur still continues, and as in Amy Carmichael's day the Fellowship is a company of people, mostly Indian but with a few from overseas, whose common loyalty is to our Lord and Saviour Jesus Christ. Although we come from various denominations we are all evangelical. We do not belong officially to any of the organized churches but in fellowship with others of God's children we seek to make His love and salvation known to all whom we can reach from Dohnavur and the other places where we work.

The dedication of girls to the temples is now illegal, but we still provide a home for children who might otherwise fall into the hands of people who would exploit them in some way.

Girls of all ages from babies to teenagers still form a large part of the family in Dohnavur. But for some years we have not been admitting boys and those still in the care of the Fellowship have their home at Cheranmahadevi about fifteen miles from Dohnavur. The need to care for them all continues until they are securely launched elsewhere or have become our fellow workers. Our aim is still to bring them up to know and love our Lord Jesus and to follow His example as those who desire not to be served but to serve others.

The hospital treats patients from the surrounding countryside. They are from varied religious background, Hindu, Muslim, Christian. They include rich and poor, highly educated and illiterate. Through this medical work the Lord continues to bring to us the people we long to reach, those whose need is for spiritual as well as physical healing.

In matters of finance we follow the pattern shown from the beginning of the work. Amy Carmichael rejoiced in her Heavenly Father's faithfulness in supplying each need—we praise Him that His faithfulness continues the same today.

The Dohnavur Fellowship

Dohnavur
Tirunelveli District
Tamil Nadu 627 102
India

33 Church Road
Wimbledon
London SW19 5DQ

DOHNAVUR BOOKS
by Amy Carmichael
Published by SPCK

STORIES OF INDIAN WOMEN
Mimosa (*paper*)

DEVOTIONAL BOOKS
His Thoughts Said . . . His Father Said . . . (*paper*)
Edges of His Ways (*paper*)
If (*paper*)
God's Missionary (*paper*)
Gold by Moonlight (*paper*)
Candles in the Dark (*paper*)

VERSE
Toward Jerusalem (*paper*)

BIOGRAPHY
Amy Carmichael of Dohnavur *by Frank Houghton*